BENEATH THE PALE
BLUE BURQA

ONE WOMAN'S JOURNEY THROUGH TALIBAN STRONGHOLDS

(In Islamic Calligraphy this is the symbol for Allah)

BENEATH THE PALE
BLUE BURQA

ONE WOMAN'S JOURNEY THROUGH TALIBAN STRONGHOLDS

By Kay Danes

BIG SKY PUBLISHING
www.bigskypublishing.com.au

First published in 2010
Second edition 2015

National Library of Australia Cataloguing-in-Publication entry
Author: Danes, Kay.
Title: Beneath the pale blue burqa : one woman's journey through Taliban strongholds / Kay Danes.
ISBN: 9780980658286 (pbk.)
Subjects: Danes, Kay.
Humanitarian assistance--Afghanistan.
Taliban--Afghanistan.
Women philanthropists--Afghanistan--Biography.
Afghanistan--Social conditions--21st century.
Dewey Number: 958.1047

Big Sky Publishing Pty Ltd
PO Box 303
Newport, NSW, 2106
Australia
Phone: (61 2) 9918 2168
Fax: (61 2) 9918 2396
Email: info@bigskypublishing.com.au
Web: www.bigskypublishing.com.au

Cover and layout design by Think Productions
Typesetting by Think Productions
Printed in China by Asia Pacific Offset Ltd

Contents

Acknowledgements

Writing this book was challenging but never a lonely task. Friends from all over the world encouraged me but to list them all would be impossible. There are a few I must however acknowledge; my husband Kerry, a sincere individual, a faithful friend, a man of great honour and integrity and one who has unwavering loyalty to his country and to the Australian Defence Force. He is a soldier's soldier, a remarkable human being and an inspiration behind everything I do. Our children Jessica, Sahra and Nathan whom I hope will be proud of my efforts to assist people devastated by war. To my parents Ernest and Noela who instilled in me a desire to good wherever possible. My sister Karen and my brother Rick whom I hope will both enjoy this latest travel adventure of their *little sis*.

My intrepid travelling companions and fellow Rotarians — Diana Tacey, John Dell, Judy Hutcherson and Chris Dickinson. It was an honour to risk both life and limb with such incredible, like-minded adventurers. I hope we get to do it again sometime — Insha'Allah (God Willing). Tony Fox who for many years has been a source of inspiration and encouragement. Martin Hodgson who is the most selfless and tireless humanitarian I know. Stephen Kenny, an amazing lawyer and human being. Leann Hoelscher, Jeff Roberts and Murray Kidd who are always there for me. My writing mentor Lowell Tarling, who provided extensive and invaluable editorial input and creatively inspired me throughout the marathon of writing. Thanks to Denny Neave and Sharon Evans for direct assistance in publishing this book and to the entire team at Big Sky Publishing. It has been a pleasure working with such a professional team of people.

Sincere thanks to His Excellency Dr. Amanulla Jayhoon — Ambassador for the Islamic Republic of Afghanistan to Australia and his Personal

Assistant Miss Chamalee Prathiraja for your kind words of encouragement, invaluable assistance and support in endorsing and launching this book. Thank you to Andrew Laming — Member of Parliament (Australia) for the wonderful acknowledgment you gave in writing the foreword for this book and your generous support over many years. My highest regards to all the Defence Force members throughout the world who work tirelessly to provide a secure, global environment for all mankind. Particular thanks to LTGEN (Rtd) Peter Leahy, AC and LTGEN (Rtd) Ken Gillespie, AC, DSC, CSM for your personal support and friendship to Kerry and I over many years. My earnest thoughts and prayers are with the families who have lost loved ones and to those who have been injured amidst the carnage of war, both physically and emotionally. At times the price of freedom can seem too high a price to pay but for those who pay it, you are forever in our hearts. I also wish to acknowledge the valiant efforts of John and Danielle Bale, who founded 'Soldier On' and their team of volunteers throughout the nation — to enhance recovery, inspire communities and empower Australia's wounded, giving those who have served our country the dignity they deserve and the chance to do and be whatever they choose.

My deepest admiration and respect to my young Afghan brother known only to my readers as Muslim. I am humbled to know someone of your integrity. I am inspired by your courage and fortitude to overcome the many challenges that you and your family, and indeed the people of Afghanistan, face on a daily basis. May your journey always be safe and your family protected. Finally, my heartfelt gratitude to the people of Afghanistan for showing me *what is destined will reach you, even if it be underneath two mountains. And what is not destined will not reach you even if it be between your two lips!* (An Arabic proverb) This journey has taught me so much about life and myself. May peace come quickly to your most beautiful homeland - *Fi Amen'Allah (Go in the protection of Allah)*

Foreword

By
Ambassador for the Islamic Republic of Afghanistan to Australia

Beneath the Pale Blue Burqa strikes back at the shocking, disturbing and graphic image of the young Afghan woman in the middle of Ghazi stadium, executed by the Taliban Regime; however, no-one knows her sin and no-one heard her last wish. Though she was given the name Zarmina, even I am not sure it is her real name. Since then the Taliban has been removed from power and the Ghazi stadium is no more a place for execution, but the journey to restore the rights and respect for Afghan women is sadly still a long way off. There are thousands of women like Zarmina who remain captive to their destiny. They are caught in the legacy of three decades of violence which has inflicted severe pain, hardship and suffering to every citizen of this once peaceful country, particularly the women.

Women have suffered as mothers watching their sons or daughters killed in cold blood in front of them. They have suffered as wives when their husbands were taken away by the warlords, and sisters have suffered when their brothers did not return from the front. My own mother-in-law suffers in this way still. Her husband was taken by the Communist regime in 1977. She continues to wait for news of him all these years later. She has no grave to visit. All she has is the memory that he was taken away and that he has not returned. This is a tragic but familiar story in Afghanistan. As familiar as the young women like Zarmina, who were killed in cold blood. All of our lives have been touched by hardships and sorrow but we have learned not to give up. Atrocities come and go and world leaders promise that we will never allow human beings to ever suffer again in such ways. But the world seems to have a short memory at times. The world forgets women like Zarmina, women like my mother-in-law and the thousands who perished in the tragedy of 9/11. Women are left without husbands, and mothers without sons. We owe it to them to never forget and we must not be afraid to remember.

Kay Danes and her husband and many others in the world are trying to ensure an enduring peaceful environment in Afghanistan. They realise the importance of helping us provide an investment in the future of our future generations. They are helping so that Afghanistan will not roll back to the dark age of the Taliban. Childhood and youth are a treasure to any nation since the destiny of the country depends on them. The new generation can in time be the powerful pillars of society, and possibly the salvation of humanity.

As it is emphasised by Kay, it is high time we realise that young people in Afghanistan need to believe in a moral code, strong values, knowledge, health and wisdom. Thus government, leaders and parents have a moral duty to provide the education, nutrition, love, and a promising future for children and youth so that they might look forward to a happy, meaningful and rewarding life.

Kay, despite DFAT's travel advisories that frightens people to take the adventure of going to a war zone, accepts the risk to fly to Afghanistan and walk the streets of Kabul, Jalalabad and Herat to find the facts about the plight of the Afghan women and children. Afghanistan, despite being *dangerous* is, as Kay says, an amazing place. Very few people get an opportunity to do what she did. She did not go to *ski*; but skiing in Afghanistan is fantastic, the slopes are dangerous. She took to the roads, walked the streets, visited schools and prisons and produced a beautifully written, interesting, informative and insightful book — *Beneath the Pale Blue Burqa*. She did not use the painful and tragic existence of the Afghan women as *snapshot photography* of a passerby. She shared their tragedy and has lived that tragedy earlier when she was captive in a prison in Laos.

This book is a journey of a brave woman in a war zone and her experiences are heartfelt. When you read the first page you will be tempted as I was to finish the entire book. You will see my country through the eyes of one foreign woman who now has the dust of Afghanistan in her veins. Thank you for being brave enough to visit my country, Kay, and to share your journey with us. Yours is an important contribution that will enable others a rare glimpse of places they may never visit and of people they may never meet. So true is the saying that if you light a lamp for somebody, it will also brighten your path. Clearly you have shown through your writing that the Land of the Afghan is still a beautiful, promising country enriched with wonderfully fascinating people, despite all of its current shortcomings.

His Excellency Dr Amanullah Jayhoon
Ambassador for the Islamic Republic of Afghanistan to Australia

What is destined will reach you, even if it be underneath two mountains. What is not destined, will not reach you, even if it be between your two lips!

– An Arabic proverb

Prologue

By
Federal Member of Parliament (Australia)

Afghanistan demands superlatives – the 'coldest', the 'hardest', the 'poorest' and the 'worst'. It is a land of withering nights and punishing days. Dust which turns to mud, to concrete and back to dust again. This place has wrought boundless suffering upon foreigners who dared to interfere. For occupiers and liberators alike, survival hinges on weaponry and armaments, brittle truces and hard-won trust. An ageless Farsi proverb reminds us that blood cannot be washed out with blood. Yet this same land has barely known peace in generations.

From the first moment a Westerner drops between snow-capped ranges and into Kabul's airport, there is an overwhelming sense of isolation. So much of what happens in this country takes place behind a scorched veil of secrecy in places where most foreigners fear to tread. Language, culture and gender conspire to conceal the true face of Afghanistan from Western visitors.

Kay Danes has spent the last ten years living and working in some of the most dangerous places on earth. Here she uses the insights gained in that time to penetrate to the heart of Afghanistan and to demonstrate that even in the harshest environments hope springs eternal.

The international media tells one story of Afghanistan; a story centred on crisis, war and suffering of unimaginable quantities. From the safety of the West we might imagine that only soldiers, doctors and engineers could make any difference on the ground. We might struggle to understand how agriculture, education, healthcare and culture can survive in such an environment. The reality, of course, is that they do. Books, food, arts and public health can all make a difference. Peace, prosperity and calm may still be distant aspirations. But as Kay explains, the determination to get there eventually remains utterly undiminished.

Plenty have tried and failed in Afghanistan. That makes Kay's partnership with the US State Department and organisations like the Childlight Foundation and Rotary so worthwhile. Their work includes reading rooms for girls and specialist women's prisons through to bulk supply shipments for towns where much of the population has been widowed by war. The efforts to promote healthy communities in the isolated Herat region of Afghanistan's west have been consolidated through a partnership with the local university. The gains have been locked in to local communities through empowerment and capacity building.

Kay Danes demonstrates here that good can prevail and that small initiatives can deliver life-changing opportunities even for those living in the harshest environments on the planet.

Dr Andrew Laming

Federal Member of Parliament (Australia)

Former landmine clearing doctor, Pul-i-khumri, Afghanistan

Testimonials

It's a shame so much reporting is done on Afghanistan and so little of it is from the Afghans' point of view. Thank God for brave people like Kay Danes who dare to venture beyond the safe zones to tell the stories of those who matter most in Afghanistan.

– Josh Rushing co-host Al Jazeera's *Fault Lines* series,
bestselling author of *Mission Al-Jazeera*

Kay Danes is one of those kinds of people who sees a need and then takes action. Her work assisting challenged peoples and putting herself second is the 'stuff' that makes the world a better place. Kay Danes' near death experiences have put some of my actions into perspective.

– Simon Westaway, Australian actor

The people of Afghanistan have endured hardship and conflict over many decades. In particular, the Afghan women have suffered terribly, including brutal oppression during the years of Taliban control of their country. During my visit to Afghanistan in 2008, it was apparent that the aspirations of the local people are the same as those of people throughout the world, and that is to live in peace and safety with the opportunity to provide adequately for their families. Many nations of the world are working in Afghanistan to bring peace and security and we must hope that mission is an enduring success.

- The Hon. Julie Bishop MP — Deputy Leader of the Liberal Party
Shadow Minister Foreign Affairs of the Australian Government

Courage, stamina, bravery in the face of fear, hope when the dark is deepest ... that's Afghan women. Because Kay Danes, from her own life experience, shares these characteristics, they talk the same language. Afghan women open up to her. Remarkable stories; an eye-opening book.

– Bill Rowlings, CEO, Civil Liberties Australia

In a country with few paved roads, a dirt poor, illiterate population blighted with poverty, disease, and violence, it is rare to find foreign reporters who will work outside the safe bubble of Kabul. As a result, Afghanistan's people, culture, and traditions remain unknown to the world, or reduced to crude stereotypes. Kay Danes is one of the few internationals who are determined to make a difference and brave enough to go outside the international 'security bubble' to see for herself how the ordinary Afghans are fairing in post Taliban Afghanistan. She brings us back a delightful, informative story with wit, charm, a little humour and a lot of important information. One can only hope there are more people like her setting their sights on making a difference in difficult lands like Afghanistan.

– Tim Lynch, Vigilant Strategic Service Afghanistan

Kay Danes is an inspiration for giving a voice to the oppressed and unjustly accused of the world, and for shedding light on the struggles faced by the Afghan people, particularly women and children.

– *WHO* magazine

A brave book written by a brave woman, but it is the courage of the Afghan women in the face of so many social atrocities that tugs at the heart and makes one reflect on the many aspects of the desperate situation that exists in that country. Nothing brings it home more than the words of those who are living the nightmare. Kay brings the confronting issue of what is happening to the Afghan people, and most particularly to its women, well and truly to the fore in a way that's not been done before. A very thought provoking book.

– Yasmine Grey, Director, Gray Media Services

Chapter 1

Kidnapped!

The danger of travelling beyond Kabul is partly overshadowed by the excitement of seeing the wonders of Istalif, a mountainous village 28 kilometres northwest of Kabul. Istalif's location is both scenic and strategic. From 1979, Afghan resistance fighters used Istalif as a base from which to launch attacks on the Soviets in the valley below. More tragically, Istalif later became a site of major fighting between the Taliban and Northern Alliance Forces, as the Taliban advanced north out of Kabul. For months, the front line moved back and forth across the area, destroying crops and homes. Once the Taliban finally took the town, they forced all of its residents out and began systematically burning down all the buildings. Most Istalifis fled elsewhere with little more than the clothes on their backs. Others became refugees in Pakistan and Iran. Tens of thousands were displaced or slaughtered.

Since those bloodied days, and with the fall of the Taliban in 2001, many Istalifis have returned home but still, the township is far from safe.

Sitting in front of me is our guide, who is taking our group of five intrepid humanitarian aid workers to Istalif. She is a young Swedish woman of slim build with short-cropped brown hair and startling blue eyes. Her name is Ester. She spent most of her childhood in Pakistan with her missionary parents. Now in her twenties, she works for the Turquoise Mountain School of Ceramics, established to restore the city's former beauty and to keep its famous craft skills alive. It is also a place where young students develop a sense of pride in their historical culture.

I know very little about pottery but I am intrigued by the way memories of Istalif affect Ester. When she describes the place her face becomes animated like a child waiting to open Christmas presents. She reminds me of the way some women back home talk of diamonds. I listen to Ester's lyrical descriptions of the Koh Daman

Valley encircled by hills dotted with masses of mulberry groves, the picnic grounds of Emperor Babur, the terraced gardens and the most famous attraction of all, Istalif's blue pottery.

'This is something you will never forget,' she said. 'It's more beautiful than anything you will ever see. Istalif is simply just to die for!'

It nearly comes to that.

Our mini-van slows as we approach a police checkpoint with heavily armed uniformed men pointing their AK-47 Russian assault rifles straight at us. Our young Afghan driver ditches his Camel brand cigarette out the window and steers the mini-van off the dusty bitumen road until we come to a sudden stop. My hand grips the edge of my seat to stop me from crashing into Judy.

Within seconds of stopping, our driver is showered in the babble of the local Dari language, which we five Western passengers don't understand, though it doesn't take a genius to figure out that something is wrong. Even our tour guide, Ester, appears nervous and she's travelled this route many times.

'Français?' the young officer barks as our driver reaches nervously for the cigarette packet carelessly thrown on the dash. Is he chain smoking for a reason?

What's the officer's interest in French nationals?

Ester intervenes in Dari, which she speaks fluently, telling the young man we are not French. She quickly turns back to us and tells us to get out our passports.

'Hold them up please.'

We hold them up: two Australians and three Americans. Ester also displays hers, a burgundy Swedish passport, and she keeps up the patter in Dari. The young officers flash a glance to each other while the one doing all the accusing seems increasingly edgy. I take no comfort when Ester tells us that they reckon they are the Afghan National Police (ANP). I take no comfort because many of Afghanistan's citizens reckon the police are as scary as the rebels. Their black eyes roam from each one of us to the next. Do they have to point that gun at me? Surely they are legitimate police? They could be Taliban insurgents in disguise or bandits. God I hope they're not from that insidious group involved in the sale of illegal human organs. I guess we'll find out. My only consolation is a tiny voice of reason that tells me that Ester has checked her employer's security network, but of course, no system is infallible and this is Afghanistan. Still I can't ignore the sickening feeling slowly descending on me as I recall Kerry's words: 'Be careful you don't become complacent'.

All five of us have been very cautious having been in Afghanistan for a month. We have been careful to stay out of trouble. Sure there were a few close calls but for the most part we have maintained a constant vigilance. We have blended in, and avoided behaviour likely to arouse suspicion. We have moved quickly whenever our in-country guide says 'it's time to go now'.

We remained in the relative safety of our compound when an explosion ripped apart the building two doors away, and when two foreigners were gunned down by their own security guards in the compound next door, we were sipping tea on the back deck of our own accommodation block. We avoided the suicide bombers who blew themselves up and killed five people at the Information Ministry that Diana and Judy had only just left. We also steered clear of the shopping centre when heavily armed militants pitched battle there. Now, here we are again, in another precarious situation. I'm beginning to feel that it really is time to go home!

An older, surly officer strides towards our mini-van and in one fluid motion, grips the handle and rips the door open. He leans his beefy upper body inside and takes a long look around. The smell of stale tobacco and body odour invades my nostrils. I am rigid with dread. His dark eyes sear through us. I lower my gaze, and bite the inside of my lower lip, hoping this isn't the beginning of another nightmare. He barks something at our driver. His deep voice bounces off the interior walls of the mini-van like blasts of thunder. I glance up slowly only to find his dark brooding eyes staring at me, stripping away my defences. He stares at each of us one by one in complete silence for what seems an eternity. I am certain Judy is praying to Jesus. Though I'm not a Christian, I do too.

The seconds tick by. I'm holding my breath. The surly officer mutters something we can't follow but it becomes clear that he has ordered her out of the vehicle when her blue eyes flash me a serious look before she slips quietly through the open door. I see her tug her headscarf back in place as she scampers behind the surly officer striding to the back of the mini-van. Meanwhile other cars are stopped at the checkpoint and ushered on, some without as much as a glance at the occupants inside. Why us? I feel an old anxiety creeping in. Subconsciously I feel for the wooden Buddha prayer beads nestled against my right wrist, a gift from a political prisoner I met in the landlocked communist country called Laos. 'They will keep all evil away from you.' he said. A pity I didn't have them before I was taken hostage that Christmas ... but they've worked well so far. I reach for the iced bottled water at my feet. The ice has melted. The young policeman looks on. I twist the pale blue lid. His eyes shift from me to Chris. I note a tiny droplet of sweat slides slowly down the left side of his cheek. He wipes it away. It is nerve-racking not knowing what's happening, and then Diana suddenly gets to her feet.

'I'll see what's going on,' she says as she slides past me and through the door the surly officer had just tried to break. The young officer says nothing as she whips by him and heads towards the rear of the mini-van where she joins the negotiations and explanations. The rest of us just freeze despite the warmth inside the mini-van. Judy and I sit absolutely still. Chris is saying nothing. And Diana's 76-year-old father John is silent too, alone in the front passenger seat. I wonder what he's thinking. He survived the Korean War. Does he imagine he could die in Afghanistan? Surely the thought must have crossed his mind. I know it's crossed mine.

'Maybe they're just going to hit us up for a few bucks,' I whisper under my breath and shrug, hoping to lighten the mood.

'Maybe,' says Judy, without enthusiasm.

Muslim's warning comes to mind.

'Even those who are supposed to protect the people are often the most corrupt,' he says. 'It is not uncommon to be stopped at a police checkpoint and then be kidnapped for ransom.'

'Even though you are an Afghan?' I ask our in-country guide.

'Yes even so. I tell them I am a farmer because if they knew that I am educated and have a job, they may assume I have money.'

The young officer standing guard over us is dressed in a heavy grey wool Afghan National Police uniform. He casually leans a little closer. I've got nothing else to do but check him out. His AK-47 is slung over his shoulder and thankfully pointing down at a safe 45 degree angle. The green ballistic vest shields his wiry frame and I count three ammunition pouches and one for his radio. A black silky scarf hangs loosely around his neck almost like a cravat. His dark hair is cut short in a typical army style with his fringe cut straight across, probably by either himself or one of his friends. His dark brown eyes meet mine. The soft orange and cream tones of my headscarf catch his eye. The silk fabric was made in India and has generated quite a few complimentary remarks from other Afghan people I'd met. Most likely the young officer had never seen a headscarf as pretty, or perhaps an Australian woman like me who looks very much like a high caste Kazakhstani, or so it has been said to me on at least a dozen occasions. Must be the high cheekbones.

'*As-Salaam Alaykum*,' (peace be upon you) I say to him quietly.

He looks intrigued then he smiles crookedly. Is he calculating my value?

'*Wa alay-kum As-Salaam*,' he responds (the same upon you).

I adjust my headscarf respectfully in place. According to his culture, he *should* see my wearing of a headscarf as a sign of respect for his country. Shouldn't he? Hopefully, this might convince his comrades not to harm me but then again, I am still a foreigner regardless of how I dress and desperate times can make people do desperate things, unimaginable things. I think of another time where I'd seen people, so-called police, do all manner of torturous evil things. I can still hear the screams of those who were dragged into the torture room ... their genitals burnt with fire, their bones broken ... my husband among them ... Pushing these dark thoughts from my mind, I throw an anxious glance over my shoulder. I see the pale yellow of Diana's scarf. I'm sure she and Ester are doing their best in the *discussions* to secure our safe passage to Istalif. As for Chris and John, well I have resigned myself to the fact that they will have to fend for themselves. This is after all, *a man's world.* I look back at the young officer and ask him if he really is the police. He nods in affirmation but then why wouldn't he? I ask if he wants his photo taken with me. Lesson 101 if you are taken hostage: try to humanise yourself. Reason being, it's easier to harm or kill an object than a person. My survival instincts automatically kick in, as a result of my previous experiences working security in hostile environments. It may be totally useless but it's worth a try. I endured torture in a communist prison and it was there I learnt that you do whatever you need to do to stay alive. His smile broadens. I call Chris for assistance then hand him my camera.

Snap!

When he sees the picture of me and him on my little LCD screen, our little cop insists on another, by holding out his mobile phone and saying 'cam-era' in broken English. And so we pose like a happy couple as I try to ignore that there are still four days until Holy Friday when all good Muslims bath for prayers. Chris takes our picture again and laughs nervously. 'Another prospective husband, Kay?' he jokes. The mood is slightly more relaxed. Some commotion catches the young man's attention and he quickly grabs his phone and joins his gun-toting comrades. Diana and Ester return looking sombre, as does our Istalifi driver.

'What's going on?' whispers Judy.

'We have to go back,' says Diana now seated next to us in the rear of the vehicle.

'Why? What's happened?' I ask.

Ester squeezes past the surly officer to jump in beside Chris who hands her a bottle of water.

'Thanks,' she says almost breathlessly and twists off the lid. She takes a large gulp to clear the dust from her lungs.

'A French NGO worker has been kidnapped in Kabul,' she says. 'They've been ordered to close the city. We have to go back.'

'When did it happen?' Judy asks.

'About an hour ago ... '

The side door slams shut.

As our driver starts the engine I notice the machine gun-mounted jeep, filled with armed Afghanistan police, waiting across the road. Ester follows my gaze.

'They will make sure we return to Kabul,' Ester explains as the checkpoint police stop traffic long enough for our driver to do a U-turn across double lanes. The armed escort waves him off.

'We need to get back to the compound quickly,' she explains. 'These situations are very dangerous.'

Where there's one incident there are usually several more to follow. No, we're not going to die today. That's what the armed escort is for *... to prevent that ... right?*

My blood pressure returns to normal a half hour later when we arrive safely back at Ester's compound. We are met by her employer's security guards, who rush towards us when they hear all the vehicles pull up out the front. More guns! They quickly usher us inside the compound. It's dark and I have no idea where to go so I just follow Diana, who's being led by Ester. The guards want to see our passports.

'Please sign your passport number in the book,' the NGO worker requests politely as he issues each of us with a visitor's pass.

The police mob leave their machine gun-mounted jeep outside to follow us in. The tiny room feels claustrophobic all of a sudden. I spot the young police officer again seeking me out with his curious dark eyes. No doubt as to what he's thinking. He flashes me a smile then licks his dry, cracked lips. His boss, the surly officer, issues instructions to the NGO security that, given the kidnap of the last few hours, we are not to venture outside Kabul again. I stand quietly beside Diana who, on behalf of our group, thanks the surly officer for taking our safety so seriously. She tries to tip him but he throws his hand up in refusal and then lectures her on this being his *duty* and not a *service*. After a brief exchange with the NGO security staff, the surly officer raises his hand in a curt salute and disappears outside. The young police officer touches two of his long brown fingers to the brim of his hat and bids me a private farewell.

I barely notice I've held my breath the whole time until Diana squeezes my arm and says, 'You can breathe now.'

'Come,' says Ester, 'let's eat.' She motions us to the doorway leading into the main compound.

'And he wouldn't even take a tip ...' I laugh with Diana as we follow Ester to a small courtyard at the edge of the compound.

There's a small wooden table and chairs nestled in one corner underneath a pergola laden with bright purple bougainvillea. It's a lovely spot that overlooks the city.

A gentle breeze blows.

We remove our headscarves and sit at Ester's invitation. I can tell she is badly shaken by the experience but is putting on a brave face. She has a faraway look in her eye.

'Tea?' she asks Judy.

'Oh, that would be lovely,' Judy replies and we each nod in agreement. While drinking the tea, we find out the details of the kidnapping.

At 9.15am a young Frenchman was walking along Qassabi Street on route to his office at the AFRANE Educational Centre in the Kart-e-Parwan suburb where we are staying. He was ambushed by gunmen. He had only been in Afghanistan a week. According to reports, a passing driver working for the National Directorate of Security intelligence agency, tried to intervene and was shot dead. That's when the government ordered the masses of catacomb streets surrounding Kabul to be closed. This all happened shortly before we arrived at the police checkpoint and why they were so edgy.

Two Afghanistan Defence Force helicopters are currently circling above us. Their gunners scan the streets for the kidnappers who would have by now, well and truly disappeared. The mood at our table is quiet concern. Someone's life has been taken in a most horrific way. As I break off a piece of naan bread I feel for that terrified young Frenchman. I sure know what it's like to be abducted and held for ransom! It is gut-wrenching. I remember the gunships that frequently flew over the communist prison camp where I was held and wondered if they were coming to rescue me ...

The Afghan helicopters circle back and forth until they finally disappear.

As I dip the naan into some spicy chicken curry I become lost wondering about that Frenchman's fate. Is he married? Does he have kids? There are over three million people walking the dusty streets of Kabul, all going about their daily business. Here we are enjoying a meal. Does he have anything to eat? I remember the political prisoners in Laos offering me giant-sized river rats and skewered toads. When you are hungry you will eat *almost* anything. I hate my thoughts. I wish I could forget.

Most likely the Frenchman will never be found. Or worse, he might be sold to the Taliban or extremists who might even feature him in their political videos before executing him with a blunt machete. Or hand him over to any number of young boys 'in training' to behead foreigners and suspected spies. Official figures say that this year alone 118 business people have been kidnapped in Kabul and Herat. No-one really bothers to report what happens to local Afghans because media interest remains focussed on the misfortune of foreigners who make for great headlines.

Since we arrived in Kabul there has been an endless spate of killings and kidnappings of foreigners. Three Turks were kidnapped and two Bangladeshi aid workers were among dozens of foreigners abducted recently. Militants kidnapped 30 bus passengers who were found mutilated and beheaded. They had been killed after the militants accused them of being soldiers travelling in civilian clothing. The bodies of at least 20 others are yet to be found.

What hope for one young Frenchman? But not everything bad that happens in Afghanistan can be attributed solely to the Taliban, despite it being a convenient truth. The National Directorate of Security (NDS) launched an operation to break up the criminal network operating in the country, responsible for the increased number of kidnaps, murders and armed robberies. They posted a reward of 500,000 Afghani (AFN) (AUD$12,000) to anyone who could provide information leading to the capture and arrest of such network members. Considering that the average salary in Afghanistan is only AUD$40 a month, it is quite an incentive for ordinary citizens to act. Why they don't just arrest the Kabul gang leader? In many cases these criminal networks have connections, relations and support in the Government itself. Some locals say that whilst they have no desire to return to the fanaticism of Taliban rule, some aspects are preferable to the chaos and fear that shrouds their lives today. The criminal networks now dominate the city and no-one is safe.

Here I am just an ordinary Australian and mother of three, smack bang in the middle of it.

What a day! It began early as we travelled north towards the desolate snow-capped mountains of the Hindu Kush. We passed by hundreds of martyrs' graves, green flags flapping in the breeze. Their significance is lost to anyone visiting for the first time but we knew them to be markers. Loved ones rotted away beneath the cracked patches of stony soil covered by dull grey rocks.

Our dark maroon mini-van sped along the Shomali road where once both young and old men died together in what was once a bloody battleground. They were Mujahedeen resistance fighters, backed by the United States and coalition, who took up the fight against the Afghan Communist Party, backed by the Soviets to ensure a pro-Soviet regime came to power in the country. Between 1979 and 1989, over 620,000 Soviet soldiers served in Afghanistan and with them a trail of destruction ensued. Farmers who were able to fled their fields as millions of bombs were dropped in a carpet bombing campaign over Afghanistan. Many were killed outright, millions were maimed or wounded. Livestock was slaughtered. Irrigation systems obliterated.

Thousands of Afghan women were made widows and those who weren't were left to fend for themselves when the male members of their household were recruited into the Mujahedeen or taken away by the Soviets. Many did not return. Some of these widows were raped, young girls violated and countless young children were blown to bits by carefully laid Soviet landmines made to look like colourful butterflies.

The losses on both sides were colossal. Many mothers in the Soviet Union wept for their lost sons and husbands. Many Soviet daughters too, who volunteered for service in Afghanistan in clerical roles, communications and as nurses, endured unspeakable hardships at the hands of their fellow compatriots. Many of these female soldiers were raped by Soviet male soldiers sent to Afghanistan instead of prison. It was the Soviet's equivalent of the United States' Vietnam War; a dirty war, a war that could never be won.

Millions of Afghan civilians were killed and official losses of Soviet troops were reported at 14,453 with 417 missing in action or taken prisoner, of which 119 were later freed. As for material losses, these too were significant. The Soviets lost 451 aircraft, 147 tanks, 1314 armoured personnel carriers, 433 artillery guns and mortars, 1138 radio sets and command vehicles, 510 engineering vehicles and 11,369 trucks and petrol tankers.

At the 1989 Soviet withdrawal, hundreds of tanks carrying soldiers retreated along the same road we travelled today. Some of these tanks were abandoned on the roadside. Mujahedeen horsemen watched their withdrawal from a safe distance, their rifles raised over their heads as a final signal of defiance. They then turned their attention to the collapsed Afghan Communist Party. The factional fighting gave rise to a warlord system of governance. Afghanistan remained in a system of anarchy.

A loosely organised group of *Taliban* (religious students) emerged as a united entity. They were a politico-religious force based on anti-Western, anti-modernisation, Islamic fundamentalist ideology and they were determined to rule. They set their sights on the tiny town of Istalif, home to peaceful potters, and after Istalif fell their fighters pushed forward to capture Kabul, which they did by September 1996.

Many Afghans elsewhere were relieved that the factional fighting had finally come to an end. Many began hoping for peace. The devout Taliban had some success in eliminating corruption and allowing commerce to resume. They held 95 per cent of the country's territory and wanted to establish the most pure Islamic state in the world. Activities considered to be frivolous were banned, like kite-flying. Non-Islamic influences like the internet, television and music were also banned. Men were told to wear beards and if they didn't, they'd be beaten. The situation for women, however, deteriorated. Women were forced to live their lives in secret and public executions and punishments (such as floggings) soon became part of everyday living.

The beginning of the end for the Taliban came soon after the terrorist attacks of 9/11 (11 September 2001) when the Taliban Government refused to hand over Osama bin Laden, the mastermind behind the attacks. Their decision to host bin Laden destroyed the Taliban's chance of ever attaining international credibility. They were ousted from power in December 2001 by the United States military and the opposition Afghan Government, known as the Northern Alliance. This had a significant impact on the entire country and for townships like Istalif. Soon after President Hamid Karzai's interim government was put in place, the Istalifi people slowly found the confidence to return to the ruins of their former lives. Most of the buildings that were once their homes had been destroyed. Most were just rubble and stone.

Even though a decade has passed, the Taliban are still out there, and so too are the Mujahedeen and warlords. But now so, too, are the foreign forces: Canada, the United States, the United Kingdom, Italy, France, Germany, the Netherlands, Belgium, Spain, Poland, and most members of the European Union and NATO including Australia, New Zealand, Azerbaijan, Turkey and Singapore. They make up the International Security Assistance Force (ISAF) in support of the Government of the Islamic Republic of Afghanistan. Aristotle said that we make war so we might live in peace. Yet after all these years of constant fighting, the Shomali road still remains so treacherous and today, impassable.

The Turquoise Mountain training centre in Kabul is keeping alive the traditions of old. I wander its retail store and marvel at the intricate pieces on display. I wish I had the money to purchase some of the Islamic calligraphy. It's so beautiful but also so expensive. I decide instead on a brilliant blue-turquoise glaze hand-thrown bowl with incised ornamental decorations. I am told it is crafted on a very old local design. This will be a lovely reminder of our day's adventure.

As for Istalif … it will just have to wait.

Chapter 2
The Philanthropic Journey

In most societies, getting through wars, famines and environmental disasters largely depends on the generosity of its support groups, which comes down to acts of human compassion. It's all about the age-old saying, 'treat others as you would have them treat you'.

When I was 19 my mother and father sold everything they owned and travelled thousands of miles away to help impoverished people in the Philippines. They exchanged the comforts of a Western civilisation for a single, modestly furnished room in an isolated mountainous village just north of Manila. The post office was a half-day journey so Mum infrequently wrote, but her letters were filled with anecdotes about her amazing discoveries, the spectacular countryside and the generous nature of the people she met. Even after reading her jottings, I still couldn't picture Mum taking a shower from a drainpipe that ran from a nearby rice paddy. She sent a photo of the makeshift shower to prove it, and I still didn't believe that my mum, who despite not having the easiest life, would have the guts to.

The only time I was ever concerned about my parents was in the aftermath of a coup against the Aquino Government. I got worried when they asked us to send T-shirts bearing the words 'I am Australian'. What did they want those for? Mum said she didn't want people mistaking them for Americans. Americans were a target because the United States military supported the Aquino Government under attack from soldiers loyal to former President Ferdinand Marcos.

During my parents' stay in the Philippines, they helped to build a one-classroom school and renovate a little mud brick church. They stocked it with musical instruments, probably because my father had once been an entertainer, with the belief that 'music heals all wounds'. For transport, my parents bought a Jeepney, a flamboyantly decorated vehicle converted from a leftover World War II US Jeep. The villagers used it to transport their food and supplies from the nearest town back to their mountain village. My parents helped for as long as they could afford to, but since they had neither any sponsorship from their church nor any other organisation, they stayed until their money ran out and returned home penniless. Given that my parents were in their mid-forties, it was a challenge for them to start again from scratch, but they did so and quite successfully too.

When they were 60, they retired to a beautiful country setting just a few hours north of Brisbane.

My parents derived enormous satisfaction from their adventure in the Philippines and talked about it for years to come. They made lasting friendships in the Filipino community back home and I have wonderful memories of chatting with lovely Filipino ladies in my mother's kitchen, learning their phrases and eating the most delicious food.

Throughout my life I've been attracted to philanthropic people like my parents who have a strong desire to help others. Altruism is driven by a complex set of factors and every person who does humanitarian work has a unique motivation. Some, like my parents, do it for religious reasons. Others are called to act, sometimes because of their own wounds, or through empathy for the suffering of others, or a desire to make a difference. My personal philanthropic side most likely developed partly because of how I was raised and partly because of the people I was drawn to. One of my earliest inspirations was my friend, Norma Jamieson. She's always running around raising money for one charity or another and making people feel good about themselves. Her zest for life has had a significant influence on me, though at times I don't know where she gets her energy from!

'Kay, it's better to wear out than rust out,' she says.

Like me, Norma is an author and married a career soldier whom she followed to the ends of the earth. Like me, she loves people from other cultures and has fond memories of living in exotic places, like the Kashmir and Thailand. Norma loves adventure and in the early days, her stories inspired me to see life beyond my home (then) in the affluent Perth suburb of Swanbourne. Images of Norma dressed in a beautiful Indian sari or sitting high on the back of an elephant, trekking through the Kingdom of Mysore and helping impoverished people impressed me so much that I wanted to be just like her. She always said that there is nothing we cannot do, if we set our minds to it. So that became my philosophy. I began living my dreams of travelling to exotic places. I even rode high on the back of an elephant in Thailand, plus I climbed the ruins of Angkor Wat in Cambodia!

I threw myself into countless charities, just like Norma. I emulated her desire to make a difference in other people's lives, which led me to mingle with some of the most influential Australians, and soon I was on numerous committees and participating in countless fundraisers.

In the late 1990s my life took a rather dramatic turn when, after 20 years service in the Australian Special Forces (SAS), my husband Kerry decided to take a leave of absence to work in Southeast Asia. He was appointed managing director of a British-owned security company in Laos, providing security services to the international community and foreign investors. I too had a security background and was employed as the company's Administration Manager, although I was given an active role training guards in security procedures. In fact, Kerry and I wrote the country's very first bilingual security training manual. I later ventured into the close protection industry and started my own bodyguard company with special tactical police as my subcontractors. The 1997 Asia financial crash brought an increasing number of expatriates to Southeast Asia to provide expert debt restructuring services on behalf of the major creditors and banks. Business for me was lucrative, albeit dangerous too.

On 23 December 2000, Kerry was abducted by Lao secret police, who took him to an undisclosed location, in defiance of International law. There they tried to physically force him to sign a false statement against his client, Gem Mining Lao, a US$2 billion dollar sapphire mining concession. Kerry refused and was beaten. The secret police then detained me, hoping that my arrest may force Kerry's hand. It didn't. The matter escalated into an international incident after it became public that what the Lao secret police were attempting to do was illegal. Our Government and the Lao Government became embroiled in a diplomatic face-saving standoff with each side trying to gain the upper hand. At times I felt that our government should have just sent in the SAS (Australia's elite Special Forces Unit). They didn't. They sent soft-soled shoes of a special diplomatic taskforce instead. We spent almost a year in a filthy prison wondering if they would succeed in their negotiations.

Our two children, Sahra (11) and Nathan (7), were secreted out of the country following Kerry's disappearance and my subsequent unlawful arrest. The embassy sent them home to Australia where their older sister, Jess (14), was completing senior studies, as the International School in Laos only went to year 9. Jess lived with my parents, Ernie and Noela, and visited us on school holidays. I had no idea if we'd ever see our children again after our abduction. This terrified me more than anything else.

Over the next 10 months, Kerry and I endured torture, ill-treatment and mock executions. There were many times when I thought I wouldn't survive but for Kerry, who said we just had to. We were forced to witness the endless suffering of many political prisoners who were detained indefinitely without charge.

In the cramped confines of the 3 x 3 metre cell I shared with five other inmates inside this place they called a *death camp*, I lost my freedom and almost my hope. There's a concrete sewage tank stamped with my footprints inside the prison. Day after day, week after week, month after month, and despite the foul vapours it emitted, this grubby tank was my form of escape. God, did it stink. After three months of confinement I was finally allowed outside my cell to exercise, thanks to some rather tough lobbying by the Australian Government and my compliance to the Lao authorities' communist indoctrination. I'd jump on the tank for an hour every morning and another hour in the afternoon and I'd run on the spot, always visualising myself in another place. I could tell you exactly the journey I was running, the people and the places I could see along the way. My mind took me far beyond the prison and even further beyond Laos. It was here I ran and won my first Olympic marathon. I could actually hear the crowd cheering me on as I entered the stadium. I crossed the finish line just in time to return to my stinking cell for another 16 hours.

We knew we were innocent and the Australian Government knew we were innocent. That's why our foreign minister, Alexander Downer, sent a taskforce to negotiate our release, the first time an entire government had been activated in such a high level way to get its citizens home. Yet for all that, there was no concealing how dismal the situation was for us. So I ran on the spot on that sewage tank to maintain my sanity and to build up my physical fitness. If our government couldn't get us out, if they couldn't find a way around the Lao Government's need to save face, there was no way Kerry and I were staying in that stinking hole. If there truly was no hope left, we would have done everything in our power to escape and be reunited with our children.

After 10 harrowing months we were finally released from the prison to be placed under house arrest at the Australian Ambassador's private residence. A month later we were granted an unprecedented Presidential Pardon. Since we refused to sign an admission of guilt, our Government got the Lao Government to agree that if we *said* we'd pay US$1 million dollars then that would enable the Lao authorities to save face to their people, and thus conclude the matter to everyone's satisfaction. The Lao Government was given no guarantee that we would actually *pay* the compensation and nor would the Australian Government enforce payment. It made for great news headlines, but the issue of the compensation was yet another non-event. We returned home to our three children on 9 November 2001 to face a 200-strong media contingent wanting to know why we hadn't just given in and signed the false statements, so we could come home. It's not as simple as that. There were never any guarantees that we would ever go home if we did sign. And what if they just killed us after signing? What then? Is that how our children were supposed to remember us? What a horrible legacy to them.

Kerry and I are two very determined people who are not prepared to compromise our integrity for anything. Thankfully we didn't have to. Our Government's lobbying made sure of that.

Such life-changing experiences have the ability to alter one's perceptions. Bad things do happen to good people. Some things are meant to happen. It's not *what* we do that defines us, but rather *how well* we rise after falling. Spending almost a year in a Lao prison did not change *me* as a person but it did make me more aware of my surroundings and to be more trusting of my instincts. I believe firmly that we can choose to fully live our lives without fear, or we can live in fear and only half live. I could have chosen to stay in the safety of my comfort zone and convince myself 'I have endured enough'; only I'm not one to sit in the shadows. I'd much rather turn what could have been a totally debilitating experience into a reflection of strength and determination to make a difference. I wanted to inspire people. I wanted my life to once again have meaning.

After our Laos ordeal, however, I was constantly hindered by the debilitating effects of post-traumatic stress disorder (PTSD) and depression. I was prescribed medications that were supposed to make me better but my recovery was slow. Certain anti-depressant medications have serious side effects and the potential to make you an 'accidental addict'. It was the darkest time of my life. Yes, even darker than the interrogations because I had almost no control over what I was feeling now that I was free. All the effort it took for me to focus on surviving in that prison often meant that I had to suppress emotions like fear and anxiety. I eventually began to unravel and at one time, ended up in an emergency hospital room crying, 'Please help me'. I didn't want to die. I just wanted to free myself from my skin crawling. I felt overwhelmed by everything that had happened to us in Laos. Mostly that our reputations were attacked so publicly and we were hardly in a position to fight back. I also felt survivor guilt for surviving when others didn't. Then I felt guilty about feeling guilty. It was horrible. I frequently suffered flashbacks, night terrors and anxiety attacks. These were so intense that I could barely breathe. Kerry would wake up to find me hiding in the corner of the room. He said I looked like a deer caught in a car's headlights, totally afraid. I was exhausted from surviving. But through it all, self-preservation, meditation, exercise and Kerry rescued me.

By 2005, I no longer had as many nightmares, although I was frequently plagued by an uncomfortable tightening in my chest. Although the depression lingered, it was no longer accompanied by hallucinations. I began to think *thank goodness I survived* and decided to make the best of my life as a tribute to my survival and to those whom I know continue their struggle to survive. I was now recovered to a point where I could begin to look beyond myself, so I began looking for ways to fulfil a promise to raise awareness for the political prisoners in Laos.

I entered 'foreign prisoners' into an internet search engine and the Foreign Prisoner Support Service came up. The website promoted human rights and information on foreign internment issues, mainly relating to Australians detained in Thailand. I emailed the owner of the site and within hours Tony Fox emailed me back.

'Go ahead and create the 'Laos Prison Pages' and I'll upload it to my site,' he invited.

That was just the beginning. We built an extensive database of vital connections so that when families with loved ones detained or missing overseas contact us, we connect them to specific experts. This is how I met Martin Hodgson, a fellow Australian with extensive academic qualifications and knowledge of international politics and affairs. The three of us, still to this day, work tirelessly as volunteers and together, networking with others, we have helped reunite hundreds of families. It can be a frightening situation when your loved one disappears or is arrested in a foreign country. Most of what we do is behind-the-scenes work with very little public recognition. Most of the families we deal with are just grateful to connect with someone who has empathy.

In early 2008, my second book was released, titled *Families Behind Bars - Stories of Injustice, Endurance and Hope.* I based this book on dozens of real life stories of people I have been either directly or indirectly involved with as a human rights advocate. I wanted this book to help prepare families, to give them ways of coping, managing or simply surviving as we had survived. In many ways, *Families Behind Bars* is my way of taking a horrible personal experience and transforming it into something positive. Having a public profile, coupled with the integrity that I regained through my work in human rights, has opened quite a lot of doors for me, particularly within government, although I've turned down several invitations to become a Member of Parliament both at a state and federal level. At this point in my life, I much prefer focussing on my humanitarian projects. There's a certain freedom in not marching to the beat of someone else's drum. Besides, I still had a few personal challenges to deal with.

Still facing memories of Laos, I began writing about my horrible experiences in that Laotian jail, hoping to unload a lot of things that were burdening me. My story ended up being published, although there were many things I didn't include. I just couldn't face some of those memories. My book was titled *Nightmare in Laos* and it didn't do nearly as much for me emotionally as I had hoped. The timing was all wrong, but I was quite fortunate in late 2007 when an Australian publishing house bought the Australian rights to my story and released another updated edition.

A year later, I completed *Standing Ground: An Imprisoned Couple's Struggle for Justice Against a Communist Regime*. At last I felt the closure I longed for after which I no longer felt a victim. (The UK edition of *Nightmare in Laos* was updated in 2010.)

Several years ago, I broadened my interests beyond Laos and was appointed an honorary Ambassador to the US-based International Relief Centre that assists thousands of impoverished people throughout Southeast Asia, particularly displaced refugees in Thailand and Cambodia. Together we generated awareness and built drinking wells, immunised children and established schools and medical facilities.

Through this association and my previous experiences providing security to a number of United Nation development projects, I have learned many things about poverty. In fact, half of the world's population lives in poverty and as much as we may not want to look at it this way, the other half invariably profits from their poverty. One hundred and fifty-eight million children under the age of 15 are trapped in child labour worldwide. Over 640 million people throughout the world are without shelter and 400 million are without safe water. Two hundred and seventy million are without any form of healthcare, three billion live on less than two dollars a day and one billion live on less than one dollar a day. In the UK alone there are 4.4 million apples a day that get thrown away. Most are binned without even being touched. We are a wasteful society yet we know that people are starving.

Wouldn't the world become a better place if we each did *something to help someone less fortunate? Can the world become a better place?* On our own I'd say no but together, maybe – if we all steadfastly persist, hence why I joined Rotary International, to follow in the footsteps of those who live by the motto — Service Above Self.

On 9 April 2008, while sifting through my emails, one in particular caught my eye. It asked if I was involved in any campaigns for women prisoners in Afghanistan, signed Diana Tacey, Mesa Arizona, USA. I cast my eye over my campaign files marked 'Prisoners Overseas' and had to respond, 'No … we have very little information on this, other than what we access from the US State Department.'

Diana and I emailed back and forth and I learned that she was planning to take a team of five to Afghanistan in October 2008. The Nangarhar women's prison in Jalalabad was one of the places they planned to visit. I was instantly intrigued. Unless they've been picked up by the police, few foreigners have seen the inside of a Middle Eastern prison. And, having had quite a bit to do with the inside of a foreign jail cell myself, I was curious about the trip. I was curious about Diana too. What makes a 53-year-old American grandmother risk her life for people who are located half a world away? What drives her to care about people she doesn't know? Shouldn't she be angry instead, about the tragic events of September 11, 2001 when Al-Qaeda destroyed the lives of 4000 Americans? What motivates this woman?

Is Diana religious?

Is she a do-gooder?

Or is she just nuts?

At the time many Americans were paranoid about their own security, and with good reason. Diana on the other hand couldn't bring herself to stop thinking about the hundreds of thousands of orphaned Afghan children who had no-one to protect them after their parents had been killed. In her world the concept of 'freedom' was associated with the United States of America. By its very Constitution, freedom was something that all Americans had, and there were laws that prevented those freedoms from being taken away. All Americans enjoy the right to free speech, to bear arms, to preach, to write about any topic in which they believe. And they have the right to disagree too. Many Americans assume that people in other countries had similar rights, and if they didn't, they should. What rights did the Afghan orphans have? Diana was so driven by this question that she decided to raise funds to go to Afghanistan herself and start an orphanage. She came across a woman from the San Francisco Bay area who had just returned from her first trip there. She suggested Diana get in contact with her cousin Baraylai, an astute businessman and community organiser. Through him, Diana was introduced to what would become a longstanding devotion to the people of Afghanistan. Baraylai's first email to her began with the words, 'First of all, thank you for trusting us.' And so in the summer of 2002 Diana and her team boarded a plane to Peshawar via Chicago, London and Dubai. They disembarked in Kabul on a hot, muggy day and were greeted by a large crush of people. 'I knew I wasn't in Kansas anymore,' she said.

Chapter 3

Self-Doubt

Six years after that first mission Diana asks me to join her Childlight Foundation team. I take the offer seriously and consider its implications. First up, do I really want to go to this dangerous country? My husband Kerry is halfway through his second tour of duty in Afghanistan with the Australian Special Forces. I email for his opinion. I write, 'Honey, I've been invited to Afghanistan on a humanitarian aid mission. What should I do?' He isn't surprised at this turn of events. He knows I'm an adrenaline junkie.

His answer comes back: 'Whatever you want to do is up to you.'

In the days that follow, I have a heightened sense of news from Afghanistan. It's like when you decide what make of car you're going to buy, you see that same model car everywhere you drive. On TV there's a documentary with footage of young Afghan girls setting themselves on fire. I open a newspaper and see photos of child victims of landmine explosions. They have no arms. Another photo: an elderly man dragging himself along a dirty street on the stumps that were once his legs. Every image is graphic and disturbing. The radio broadcasts are filled with discussions on whether or not Coalition troops should be in Afghanistan and if so, for how long? I think about Afghanistan constantly. Something is pulling me towards a country with which I have no prior experience, except that my husband is risking his life there, trying to stabilise it so its people can rebuild their shattered lives.

Late one night Kerry phones from Kandahar. 'What are you going to do?' he asks.

'I really don't know,' is my response.

A little voice inside my head whispers, 'There's a reason for everything, nothing happens purely by chance ...' yet this monumental decision will affect not only me, but my family too. 'What should I do Kerry?'

'Why not speak to one of the boys before you decide,' says Kerry. ('The boys' is what he calls the enlisted men!)

He puts me in touch with Captain Reece Dewar, who has recently returned from a tour of duty and is one of the commandos' most experienced officers. Initially I expect Reece to say, 'Kay, you're insane,' but he doesn't. Instead, he advises that if I decide to go, I should exercise extreme caution at all times, take nothing for granted and if it feels wrong, get the hell out of there – to safety! He reminds me of basic security protocols and situational awareness. He says, 'Be ready for the unexpected and always have an escape plan.' I feel a surge of excitement when he talks, especially when he adds, 'Afghanistan is an amazing place. Very few people get an opportunity to do what you will be doing.' I gain some valuable insights from Reece. More than anybody, he knows the difficulties and cultural differences that will confront me there, as a woman.

A few days after my discussion with Reece, I contact the Australian Ambassador in Kabul, Martin Quinn. Getting in touch with him is difficult but it turns out he's already heard from the Department of Foreign Affairs and Trade that I'm *thinking* of going to Afghanistan. He provides some good advice on personal safety and says he is keen to meet me if I do decide to go. I make contact with various others working over there, just to ensure I have as many options as possible. I'm running out of time. A decision has to be made.

'What do you think?' again I ask Kerry, in one of our long distance phone calls. I begin rationalising the sequence of events that have happened so far. The Ambassador, Reece, Kerry, Diana …

'I'll be home soon and we can talk more about it then …'

There is no doubt that Afghanistan is one of the most dangerous places in the world and being the wife of a Special Forces soldier, I understand that better than most. We have had many friends killed in service to defence and dozens more who live with serious disabilities. There are close to 80 Australian soldiers who have sustained serious wounds from within Afghanistan alone. It's best not to think about such things, particularly when you're the one home waiting.

When Kerry eventually comes home we talk for days about what I should do. Part of me wants him to make the decision for me, but I know he never will. Instead he reiterates, 'It's up to you.'

Several weeks later I decide that I'm going. Just like that. I book my flight. There is no turning back now. 'Just don't tell Mum I'm going to a war zone,' I whisper as Kerry kisses me goodbye at the Brisbane Airport departure gate.

'Why on earth would you want to go there?' The Australian Immigration officer enquires as he flicks through my passport.

'The skiing is fantastic!' I joke. He is not amused.

Of course the skiing is fantastic but who would risk being killed by insurgents just to ski on virgin slopes? He doesn't laugh. So I continue, 'Actually, I'm working with a US charity providing humanitarian care and support to the women and children of Afghanistan.'

He pauses momentarily, as if searching for an appropriate retort, then picks up the heavy stamp and presses it firmly on the page before handing my passport back.

'Travel safe,' he says, with a puzzled smile.

He probably thinks I'm a lunatic; my friends do. I smile at him then walk through to the duty free area of Brisbane's International Airport. I'm totally absorbed in my thoughts. I live in a nice brick home in an affluent suburb overlooking a beautiful bay; I have great neighbours, wonderful friends, financial security, three beautiful children (Jessica 23, Sahra 20, Nathan 16) and a loving husband, oh ... and a Cavalier King Charles Spaniel named Sunny.

'Haven't you been through enough already?' said one of my friends after I announced where I was going. 'Why don't you just live a quiet life?'

'Isn't your husband worried you'll get yourself killed?' said another.

Actually I never ask Kerry if he worries, the same as he never asks me if I would be okay if he didn't come home from one war zone or another. Mostly I never knew where he was going or what he was doing because that's the nature of Special Forces. Though I'd never deployed on military operations, I had conducted a number of bodyguard activities in some otherwise semi-permissive environments when I'd previously worked in security. And I had experienced several life-threatening situations. One time a device exploded at a diner across the street from where I was eating lunch. I saw the fragments of human flesh splatter on the tree outside.

It had been promoted in the news as a rebel insurgent attack on the government, but who really knew for sure or who the target was?

'What about the military? What do they think about you going?'

Soldiers' wives aren't supposed to go to war zones. They aren't supposed to be in the spotlight at all; however, because of my social justice profile I have been extended a few liberties and this is one. So the question is irrelevant. I am not required to inform the Department of Defence. And to go to Afghanistan, I certainly don't require their permission.

'What did the Australian Government say?'

The Department of Foreign Affairs and Trade was less enthusiastic when I told them of my plans and sent them a copy of my itinerary. Many of them know me personally and some tried in earnest to dissuade me from going. Of course, I never sought their permission. I only wanted to know who to contact in-country if there was a problem and the location of the nearest Australian Embassy. I got my answer with the usual: *We strongly advise you not to travel to Afghanistan because of the extremely dangerous security situation and the very high threat of terrorist attack.*

The travel advisory for travel from Australia to the United States is worded similarly but with a softer tone (given that the US is one of our main trading partners): *We advise you to exercise caution and monitor developments that might affect your safety in the United*

States because of the risk of terrorism. Similarly, the travel warning for Laos is much the same, hence why I question the accuracy of these travel warnings, and especially since arbitrary secret detention and torture is prevalent in Laos.

'Do you think you can change anything there?' said another of my friends who went on to suggest I was going as a human shield to prevent US-led coalition troops from bombing certain locations, as others had done in Iraq.

'Oh come on, ...' I laugh, 'I've no intention to deliberately put myself in harm's way by making political statements ... *they're nuts!'*

'Do you have a death wish?'

Some people just don't get it. I replied, 'Absolutely not!' On the contrary, I have a life wish. I want to get as much as I can from life. I want to live life to the fullest and not be afraid of shifting beyond my comfort zone. I hand over my boarding pass to the Royal Brunei Airline staffer who directs me to the business class section. Kerry upgraded my ticket for my birthday. Still lost in my thoughts, I find my seat and get comfortable. Maybe it's that word 'comfortable' that starts me thinking how sad it is that our society has lost the art of being kind to each other. We can revive it can't we? Surely we can, if we each show genuine compassion for others, even in a small way.

With the seatbelt fastened tightly around my waist and the big jet engines roaring in my ears, I push away my thoughts and just smile. There's an announcement from the Captain, 'Cabin crew prepare for take-off ...'

This will surely be the most amazing experience of my life.

Chapter 4

Getting There

Diana's talented team for the Sixth Humanitarian Mission to Afghanistan are also Rotarians herself, her father John from Arizona, Judy from Texas, Chris a fellow Australian, and me. (It's a shame that Anne Mickey from Atlanta, Georgia, isn't able to go as Diana said that Anne and I had similar personalities. She is a tremendous amount of fun, and very generous and caring.)

Diana's father, John Dell, is a very fit-looking 77-year-old former US marine and veteran of the Korean War, who conducts study tours throughout south-western United States, Mexico and several other countries. He has worked for 30 years with the US Forest Service in California and the Pacific north-west regions and has authored more than 50 professional papers and articles on fire ecology and forest protection. John has a wealth of knowledge and knows a thing or two about survival and adapting to harsh environments. His experience and wisdom will be invaluable.

Judy Hutcherson is a retired registered nurse from Fredericksburg, Texas. She is the international chairperson for her Rotary club and the World Community Service chairperson for Rotary District 5840. She actively volunteers to support low-cost clinics in her hometown and has visited Guatemala and Russia on a number of humanitarian missions. Judy also frequently travels to Mexico. One of the committees she is on has helped set up seven villages in Northern Mexico with water, medical and agriculture needs. They built a clinic in a village about half a mile from the Rio Grande River, just south of Big Bend National Park and they are in the process of providing more aid to those regions. Judy wants to go to Afghanistan to conduct maternal child health education. She also wants people in that region to know that not all Americans want to harm them.

Chris Dickinson is a fellow Australian public servant, with a deep interest in the way crime interacts with economic and social justice issues. We first met when I was speaking at the 2006 Writers Festival in Perth. At the time, Chris was working with Rotary to raise the quality of life of the female prisoners in Kerobokan jail (Bali) – in particular, to improve their sanitation and water supply. He was instantly intrigued when I told him about our pending mission to Afghanistan and the work we would be doing for women prisoners in Nangarhar.

Our itinerary is fairly well thought out with a reasonable amount of flexibility. Chris will meet up with me in Brisbane and we'll fly together to Dubai. Diana, John and Judy will meet in Phoenix, Arizona, fly to New York and London and Dubai, where we'll all meet. Why Dubai? We chose Dubai because it is the most stable Arab state in the Middle East and, despite the diversity of its population, there has only ever been minor and infrequent episodes of ethnic tensions, primarily between expatriates. It will be a good place to regroup and, if we have time, take in a little sightseeing.

We fly Royal Brunei from Brisbane and Chris and I leave on Friday 17 October. We arrive in Dubai just after midnight on the next night, which is the 18th and Eid ul-Fitr, the holiday that marks the end of Ramadan, a busy time to be travelling to the Middle-East.

Dubai's Terminal 1 Airport is massive. It caters for more than 34 million passengers and over 260,000 flights on average each year. Not only is it the busiest terminal I've ever seen, it is a shopper's paradise with over 5400 square metres of luxury merchandising floor space. There are thousands of travellers everywhere around us and I imagine a significant number will be making their way to the taxi area. Having relied on public transport in countries like China, where there are millions of people, I know that it isn't beyond logic that 20,000 people can be queuing for taxis. On seeing all that human chaos, I fully appreciate the advanced booking I made (on hotel.com.au) knowing that our own private driver will be waiting in the arrivals hall.

We don't even make it to the arrival's hall before I spot our driver holding a sign waving to us. He stands frontline in a sea of people waiting in line to get their passport stamped. I estimate it will take us another hour or two before we make it to the customs area but our driver tells us to follow him and – incredibly – he fast-tracks us through the entire process and we are at the baggage carousel within 20 minutes! Then it takes next to no time to collect our bags because he's already had someone put them aside. So we follow him outside into a throng of travellers patiently sandwiched together in the nearby taxi area. Our driver manoeuvres us and our bags to the other side of all the traffic and he gets us into a private car park where a luxury Toyota mini-van is waiting. Twenty minutes later and we are pulling up outside the Versailles Hotel on 15th Street, Al Rigga, Deira.

I've never been to Dubai before but that was the best service I've ever received and all for only AUD$12 per person.

It is now around 1 am and I am overdue for a good night's sleep which won't take long once my head hits the pillow. I check in easily because I've already paid for my room in advance. All I have to do is hand over my passport and collect my key. Chris, on the other hand, has trouble with his booking. The Versailles doesn't have any record of his reservation despite the copy of the receipt he shows them. With Ramadan all their rooms are fully booked. With a sinking feeling I sit back down to watch Chris haggle with the night manager over the mistake. Poor Chris, he's as tired as I am but the night manager keeps telling him the hotel is full. Backwards and forwards they go until finally the manager's final check of the reservations reveals a vacancy. It's a rather expensive suite on the third floor and almost double the price of what I'm paying, but Chris has no choice but to take it. He says he doesn't mind because the alternative is to sleep in the foyer!

I think our six-hour flight from Brisbane to Brunei, a three-hour stop-over, followed by a seven-hour flight to Dubai is long enough. I can't wait to get some sleep. Poor Diana, John and Judy's flights are almost 48 hours in total. Before they arrive Chris and I will have two full days of rest and plenty of time in between for sightseeing. We drag our bags from reception to the lift, declining the manager's offer to call concierge. Who knows where the bell boy is at this late hour or how long he'll take to respond? I'd rather just carry my own bag and get to bed. Chris agrees.

'I'll see you in the morning,' I tell Chris as he staggers from the lift on the third floor.

'Sleep well,' he smiles.

'I already am,' I laugh, pushing the button that will take me to floor six.

I am relieved to be far away from the ground floor given that several nightclubs in the lower part of the hotel stay open until six in the morning. I wonder if Chris will get any sleep down there. In minutes the blanket of darkness envelopes me.

Next morning, when we meet for breakfast, Chris pours a strong cup of coffee and says, 'Thank God for earplugs!'

On our first day of sightseeing we do the Big Bus Beach Tour, which gives us a chance to see Dubai's famous white sandy beaches and glistening turquoise waters. It is a pretty full-on tour, jam-packed with many interesting things. We see about 20 different places along the way, including the world's tallest hotel, the Burj Dubai, shaped like a giant sail.

We drive by the Jumeirah Mosque, the most beautiful mosque I've ever seen. It looks like an intricately carved, giant sandcastle. The tour operator says that it is usually open to non-Muslims for special tours 'to give insights into Islam,' but unfortunately it isn't open today. We drive along the coastline to the Palm Islands and World Islands. These are the most innovative manmade structures ever created. They are also home to the famous Atlantis Hotel that reduces the Bellagio Hotel Las Vegas to 'a Best Western Hotel'. At AUD$7,000 a night (for the Presidential Suite), you would expect the Atlantis to knock your socks off. For that sort of money I could feed an entire village in Afghanistan for a whole year!

The bus winds its way through the streets of the city centre and we get to see what was once a small fishing village lost to modernisation.

We stop at the Dubai Museum and in the stifling heat of the day, we scamper around the inside of the old Al Fahidi Fort, believed to be the oldest building in Dubai. Neither of us is particularly interested in the underground merchandising store or the multi-media presentation, but the eclectic collections of artefacts are fascinating. There's also an impressive display of weaponry on show including several ancient curved daggers, swords, intricate shields, axes and pistols.

Chris discovers an ancient wind tower made from giant hessian bags, an ancient but very effective form of air-conditioning that was developed from early wind scoops first built around 2000 years ago in Iran. It brings a welcome relief to the heatwave that engulfs us. As I start to figure I could stand under it all day, we are told to get back on the bus. We forgo the typically tourist Abra boat ride across the busy Dubai Creek, and the walk through gold and spice markets, to delve instead into the Bastakia Quarter, a town built in the late 19th century by Persian merchants. It features popular courtyard cafés and art galleries and is near to Sheikh Saeed Al Maktoum's palatial home.

Much to our disappointment, we're informed that our tour is about to finish so we can't see Maktoum's palatial home after all; maybe tomorrow?

Reluctantly we return to the hotel to wait the remaining four-and-a-half hours for Diana, John and Judy. The time goes by relatively quickly on the rooftop entertainment area as we drink ice-cold Heineken beer with a friendly young Arab named Faris. The legalities of consuming alcohol in Dubai mean that it is usually banned in most Islamic countries. Even where laws are written, there are often differing interpretations of those laws. I assume it is simply safer to abstain but according to Faris, Dubai's licensing laws for hotels and private clubs means they can legally serve alcohol. It is only illegal to drink in the street or in a public space.

At 10 pm we decide to head downstairs and wait in the foyer for Diana, Judy and John to check in. Much to our surprise when the elevator doors open, there's Diana and John standing there before us.

'Hey, there you are!' says Diana as she greets us both with a friendly hug. 'We were just asking about you.'

'We were waiting upstairs with a lovely young man,' I respond, looking around for Judy.

'She's just gone upstairs and should be down any minute. Kay, Chris, this is my father ...'

'So good to meet you, John,' says Chris on a handshake.

'Well, hey there, Miss Kay!' I hear the words over my shoulder and spin around to find Judy standing there. I feel an instant connection. We hug like best friends reuniting after many years apart. Everyone is smiling and chatting about our day, their flight, the hotel service, and everything else we can cram into the first five minutes of meeting.

We enjoy what is left of the night and decide tomorrow's activities, and soon it is time to retire to our rooms. Chris has vacated the expensive suite to bunk down with John in the room he booked from the States. I move from my room to the suite booked by Diana and Judy. It is so much bigger than mine and even has its own lounge room where a foldout bed is made up. I decide to sleep there and as soon as my head hits the pillow I'm gone.

The next morning it is Monday 20 October. It begins with a light continental breakfast and plenty of freshly brewed coffee in the downstairs dining hall. Diana, John and Judy are happy to pick up touring from where Chris and I left off yesterday. So we actually do get to see Sheikh Saeed Al Maktoum's palatial home. It isn't, of course, anything like the magnificent Hotel Atlantis, but it is interesting nonetheless. The temperature is in the high forties and the humidity stifling. I can feel the sweat running down my back. By noon I can feel the heat sapping my energy and, judging by the expressions on everyone else's faces, they too are ready to call it a day.

We are running low on water and there are no shops in sight to purchase more, which is odd for a city renowned for its shopping. We decide to head back to the Versailles Hotel or risk heat exhaustion. Unfortunately the taxi driver will only take four of us. I volunteer to remain behind with Diana and John while we send Judy and Chris back to the hotel. For the next hour we try to hail a taxi without success then the big red bus eventually comes, so we board it and make our way back as close to the hotel as we can. Relief washes over us when we see the Versailles Hotel roof. I know exactly where I am because I have a city map. Although the driver says there are no designated stops along the way, I convince him to let us off the bus in the middle of the busy afternoon traffic so we can cross the three lanes of traffic to the other side. Although somewhat treacherous, I convince Diana and John that it is better to do it this way than to walk back a dozen blocks without water. Judy and Chris are anxiously waiting inside the hotel reception and rush to greet us.

'Thank God you're okay!' says Judy. Her face full of concern as she takes in the sight of us, red-faced and drenched with perspiration.

'Quickly, come inside!' says Chris.

The temperature instantly drops two or three degrees as we hit the air-conditioned foyer and immediately head for the restaurant on the ground floor. Chris begs the hotel staff for some water. The manager takes one look at us, snaps his fingers and a staff member scurries into the kitchen.

'Please, madam. Sir, please sit,' he ushers us to a near table. 'I've ordered ice-cold mango juice in extra tall glasses for you all. It will rehydrate you much faster than water.'

He is so thoughtful. We drink the mango juice followed by a jug of cold water. We rest an hour or so before being collected for phase two of our Dubai adventure.

At 3.30 pm a young Arab man waits by a modern four-wheel drive in the Versailles Hotel car park. Dressed in a white kaftan he looks as if he has stepped straight from the movie set of *Lawrence of Arabia*. He is taking us on a desert safari. Everyone is fully recovered from the afternoon's adventure and is excited about our desert safari, but none more than I. What better way to spend your birthday than an evening in the beautiful Arabian Desert, a magical midsummer's night under a thousand stars. I'm expecting it to be fantastic. I only wish Kerry was with me.

We drive steadily along the Al Awir Road towards Oman. It is incredible to see the changing sands of the desert glow from pale cream to soft gold and then later it will turn to deeper shades of burnt orange. I frequently hit the record button on my mini DVD recorder to capture what I can of its magnificence.

An hour or so later we stop at a roadside store that sells everything tourists could want: bottled water, ice-cream and Coca-Cola. There is also an abundance of traditional Arabic kaftans, brightly coloured shawls and the usual 'Welcome to Dubai' postcards, miniature toy camels and bottled sand. We get into the spirit of things and allow the sales staff to fit us out in the brightly coloured Arab headdress. Mine is purple checked and my travelling companions reckon it suits me magnificently, so does the sales staff. Getting into the theme of the occasion I also purchase a lavender-coloured belly dance coins hip scarf and giggle along with Judy, John, Chris and Diana at my sudden transformation. John jokingly dubs me 'Little Egypt'. I tell him he looks like Yasser Arafat.

A half hour later we set off on our 30-minute dune-driving adventure. Judy and I sit in the back squealing with excitement. Chris and Diana are in front of us, while John is up the very front with the driver. I imagine the experience to riding a magic carpet across the very top of the ancient world.

'Faster! Faster!' I can't get enough of this! 'It's like being in a washing machine!'

I soon realise the only thing holding me firmly to my seat is the seatbelt strapped tightly across my waist. Our driver is skilful and I feel completely at ease as he manoeuvres his way across the shifting desert sands. Briefly I hold my breath as we are thrown this way then that way. I can imagine the bruises I will have afterwards but at the time I don't care. It is a mystery to me how the nomads ever found their way to wherever they were going. Then suddenly my mind goes blank as we plunge momentarily down the side of an incredibly steep sand dune and then the engine roars as we tear back up to the very top of the next. *Whoosh.*

When the ride is finally over we stand on the top of the highest peak and look as far as the eye can see. There before us in all directions is a sea of beautiful deep orange sand, peaking and falling like soft folds of endless silk. I turn a complete 360 degrees and drink in its beauty. We marvel at the most beautiful sunset, which is a breathtaking experience no words can describe.

Then reluctantly, after a few photo opportunities, we climb back inside our four-wheel drive chariots and cruise our way across the desert towards a distant Bedouin campsite. It is now dark and the glowing firelights of the camp are welcoming. Famished from our adventure, we are looking forward to the delicious barbecue dinner that is promised. We park just outside the campsite then walk to a line of six creamy seated camels beautifully adorned in red and gold satin saddle blankets. Judy and I are the first to climb on board at their handler's instruction. Chris takes the camel behind us. Diana and John opt to walk to the entry only a few metres away. Their stomachs have taken all they can of the rocking sea-like four-wheel drive motions. Our camel ride isn't nearly as long as we hoped but it is all part of the experience. Judy and I have our photo taken to remember the occasion of us high aboard the great ships of the desert. The campsite is awash with tourists. Some are getting henna painted on their hands and feet. Others are sitting around a camp fire smoking a 'shisha', an Arabic water pipe, or hookah pipe, filled with a flavoursome mixture of molasses and other extracts. Judy and I head straight for the Arabic coffee *gahwa* and fresh dates. They taste so delicious we can't help going back for more. An evening of full Arabian flavour follows. Judy, Diana and I even get roped into doing a bit of belly dancing with a gorgeous young lady who is barely covered by several thin silky veils. Oddly enough she's Russian.

We leave the campsite at 9.30 pm to return to the Versailles Hotel, laden with so many wonderful memories that will last us all a lifetime. It is a wonderful birthday moment for me and a little ironic because in the morning I will mark Kerry's birthday with our departure to a war zone – Afghanistan.

Chapter 5

Welcome to the War

The plan is to fly from Dubai to the ancient city of Peshawar in the north-western frontier province of Pakistan, nearest the Afghan border. The city is set on the edge of a magnificent mountain pass, the Hindu Kush. Weaving through these majestic ranges, over 53 kilometres is the famous Khyber Pass. It connects all of the main trading centres on the Silk Road to South Asia, Central Asia and the Middle East. At its narrowest point, the pass is only 3 metres wide.

Peshawar is historically associated with Buddhism, which gives it great significance to me because I feel a personal connection with Buddhist thought. Contrary to what most people think, Buddhism is not a religion, it's a philosophy. Buddha was a person, not a God. He didn't create anything, heal the sick or make the blind see. Through his own experiences, the Buddha found certain things to be so. The essence of his teaching is simple: live a good life and don't hurt others in the process. This way of life is very appealing to me. It's a simple philosophy that's not complicated by stories that ignite fear or that pit one person against another. I think the world would be a better place if more people focussed more on improving themselves than judging others. But that's just me.

I love temples. They're such peaceful places and I am looking forward to seeing one of the greatest in Peshawar. Many travellers have said that of all the *stupas* and temples in the world, none compares with the Kanishka Stupa for its beauty, form and strength. At 210 metres tall, it was once the tallest building in the world and was covered in multi-coloured jewels. The jewels are gone now but I could imagine that it must have been a magnificent sight in all its glory. I'll bet that it's still magnificent! Unfortunately the insurgency problem has escalated following the resignation of Pakistan President Pervez Musharraf and Peshawar has become the frontline for extreme fundamentalists. The Australian Department of Foreign Affairs and Trade has issued a travel warning, advising all Australians to defer travel to Pakistan, citing concerns for safety and security. I imagine that means us.

A sinking feeling envelopes me when Diana says we cannot travel via Peshawar. It's not fair. I have really been looking forward to seeing all the amazing things I'd read about in the Lonely Planet guide book. The Kissa Khawani Bazaar, otherwise known as the 'Street of Storytellers', is supposedly a sea of multi-coloured flowing native robes, a place where bearded tribesmen bargain with city traders over endless cups of green tea.

For a brief moment we consider ignoring the warnings, but the matter is well and truly decided when the Australian Cricket Team cancels its tour following a wave of terrorist attacks throughout the entire region. Many locals are dead, tensions are boiling, and going anywhere near Peshawar makes no sense. Concerns for the safety of foreigners have never been higher. There are kidnappings and killings of aid workers in the city. Several journalists are slaughtered by militants who have resurged with a vengeance. From an economic point of view, Diana feels awful that we have to cancel our tickets. None of us can really afford to throw away AUD$700, but our own safety must come first.

Nothing we ever do in life is entirely risk free. You can't totally avoid the inevitable, but if you are aware of what may go wrong, you can anticipate and compensate accordingly. Someone once said: *The difference between a suicide attempt and a base jump is calculated risk.* I like that.

We decide to avoid the unnecessary risk of going via Peshawar and we'll fly directly from Dubai to Kabul. Our itinerary is dependent on constant review and I'll just have to accept that. I will have to content myself with my imagination of this almost-ancient civilisation co-existing with the modern world.

It is the morning of 21 October 2008, Kerry's birthday. I hope the kids give him a nice cake. I whisper 'Happy Birthday, Kerry' before stretching to enjoy the sudden rush of excitement that seeps into my veins as I welcome the new day. Today, our adventure really begins. In a few minutes we are leaving the Versailles Hotel; we're leaving early so we can beat the traffic.

'The shower is free now!' I hear Diana calling out to Judy, so they're on the move. I get out of bed, put my toiletries bag on the coffee table, lay out a change of clothes and strip the bed. Next I check my travel papers and refold the US dollars in my wallet so only the small notes are visible.

'It's all yours, kiddo!' Judy calls from the hall.

'My turn, is it?' I pick up my toiletries and head for the shower.

Within minutes I am lathered in my favourite sandalwood-perfumed soap. I make a point of always packing a small bar because the smell of sandalwood reminds me of Buddhist temples and I like that. Its sweet-smelling fragrance never fails to calm me, even when I've got troubled thoughts. The hot water cascades down my back gloriously and for a few selfish minutes I relish these sensations, not knowing whether or not simple luxuries like this will await us in Afghanistan.

'This is it, Kay …' I tell myself. Live every minute of whatever comes next.'

Diana, Judy and I do a last minute check of our room before leaving it to the maids. We head for the elevator where John and Chris are awaiting us. This is it, I guess.

A buzz of excitement fills the air, a knowing look passes between us and we quietly walk into the lift. John presses the button for the ground floor. Forget breakfast; our driver is already waiting in the foyer. He takes my bag, hoists it into the rear of the mini-van and comes back for Chris' bag, then Diana's, John's and Judy's carry-on bags.

'What's the plan?'

'Okay, first we drop John at Terminal 1, the rest of us go to Terminal 2' Diana explains.

'Lead the way!'

John's, Diana's and Judy's bags didn't arrive with their plane from Heathrow but Diana confirmed with the airline that the bags were on their way and would be stored at Terminal 1 where we could pick them up when necessary. They didn't see any point getting them before now.

Fifteen minutes later we arrive at Terminal 1.

'Don't be long, Dad,' Diana to calls to John as he strides toward the big glass doors. 'I'll send the driver back to get you.'

Five minutes later we're at a rather deserted Terminal 2. We pay the driver and send him back for John. Diana suggests we wait inside while Chris goes to the main doors to keep an eye out for him. Minutes tick by and there's no sign of John. Our departure time is 6.30 am and by 7 am we are all eyes glued to the terminal entry while waiting in the check-in line. *Where is he?* There is only the one flight to Kabul and if we miss it, we'll be in all sorts of bother.

'I'm going to check on Chris,' I tell Diana as I push my bag closer to Judy's before heading off.

I find Chris where we left him, still waiting by the door just outside the terminal, ready to help John with the bags. He looks anxious.

'Any sign of him?'

'Nope,' Chris replies.

Another taxi pulls up. 'Maybe that's him?' It's not. I keep looking for John's short crop of white hair but he is nowhere to be seen. Ten more taxis, but no John. Chris paces around. 'Here's another one,' he calls to me as I chew my bottom lip.

'It's *him!*' Chris and I let out an audible sigh of relief. It's him all right, waving to us from the back seat of the approaching vehicle! John's smile is triumphant. I can almost hear the cavalry charge bugle call.

'Oh my God! I was so worried about you,' I hug him before he's properly out of the cab.

'It's okay,' he laughs, then goes on to explain some mix up. 'I had a devil of a time locating our bags.'

We pay the bemused driver, load the bags onto a trolley and head towards security. Check-in is easy.

'Oh, you made it!' cry Diana and Judy.

'Yeah, I made it,' John smiles and hugs his daughter. He hugs Judy too.

'The marines always come through ... hey, John?' I add, thinking of my Kerry and the Australian commandos. They laugh.

We laugh our way into the departure lounge, where, to our relief, the passengers are still waiting for our boarding call. Our flight has been delayed. We needn't have panicked about John after all. An hour later we are shuffled onto the tarmac. 'Like sheep are the words that flash to mind. Somehow that conjures an image of an Afghanistan shepherd with his staff and his herd. And that's when it hits me – what I am doing here?

I wish Judy could take my photo to mark the significance of the occasion but I don't want to draw any attention to our group. People are already looking at us curiously most likely wondering why on earth we are travelling to Afghanistan. Back to reality: a young policeman wants to check my passport and boarding pass. I show it. He glances at it and waves me on. Judy climbs the stairs beside me, up to the plane. Diana is behind her and the men board after us.

'This is it,' I exhale.

Judy and I are seated towards the rear of the plane. We take our seats and watch other passengers squeeze down the aisle. We're hoping that a woman will sit next to us, not some smelly bloke. The plane already reeks of foul-smelling body odours ... or something. Judy jokes, 'We should have flown on the Friday – everyone would have been freshly washed for the holy day.' The plane stinks. I hold the soft folds of my headscarf over my nose and mouth. I've heard of 'boy germs' but this is ridiculous!

There's a commotion three rows back and that awful smell again! A steward is quick to ask what's going on. Someone is unhappy with something a male passenger's got. A babble of conversation breaks out. 'Okay, okay …' the passenger seems to be saying. He gets out of his seat, stands in the aisle and the steward checks out the problem. No wonder the place stinks; he's carrying fresh fish under his seat. They're still wet. No sooner has the steward got rid of that problem and there's another incident, this time in business class. Apparently one of the passengers is upset that his chickens are flying economy class. The stewards apologise and locate his clucking chickens in an overhead locker. I watch in amazement as they carefully pass the box over the heads of other passengers into the hands of the man, grateful his chooks are rightfully in business class.

Meanwhile, the passengers keep boarding. The Afghan passengers keep shunting towards the back of the plane until every seat is full. I grin like *Alice in Wonderland's* Cheshire Cat when suddenly a little old lady sits down beside me.

'Perfect,' Judy whispers.

The cabin doors shut and the engines roar as we taxi towards the runway. No-one says a word as the plane picks up speed. It shakes and shudders. I'm holding my breath. Then within minutes we lift off and are banking hard, upwards, towards the clouds. The monitor comes on and I watch it as the motion camera underneath the plane shows us which way we are going. In case I need to know, it even shows the direction of Mecca during the flight, the birthplace of the Islamic prophet Muhammad.

An hour or so into our flight we are given a soda of some sort and some crackers. Judy checks the used by dates. I don't care and crack mine open to the taste of apple cider. We have just crossed the border entering Afghan airspace. Judy and I clink our soda cans together. *'Salute'*.

I'm transfixed by the beautiful landscape below. Snow-covered mountains blanket the earth. They are endless. Judy is amazed that the first time I've ever seen snow is flying over a war zone. Every now and then I see little settlements and then more mountains. It is desolate, yet so beautiful. Discreetly I snap a few photographs, holding my camera close to the window, hoping not to be noticed. Curious eyes frequently meet mine. Time flies too, we are flying over Kabul already. The pilot requests the crew to prepare the cabin for landing. We start our descent. I imagine the pilot doesn't want to spend longer than necessary over the mountains and in the clearing, where the plane can easily be attacked by anti-aircraft fire. We bank hard again, drop another few thousand feet and without wasting any time, our pilot lines the plane up for the runway and we land within minutes. We arrive in Kabul with a thump.

I'm hoping the brakes work and we don't overshoot the runway like the US Navy Patrol plane did earlier this morning, attempting to land at a base just north of here. I sit mesmerised as the aircraft slowly taxies to the small terminal. Looking out the window I feel like I am looking back in time. I quietly adjust my headscarf so that I am utterly respectable. The plane halts with a massive jolt. The doors open and everyone inside quickly moves outside. I guess they don't wish to stay too long in such a large target.

We exit the aircraft too, although my feet barely touch the ground as we're swept along in the great sea of Afghan passengers. I try to stay closer to the women who are all covered from head to toe. I can see a white transit bus just in front of us. Judy follows me with Diana, John and Chris behind her. I don't say a word as I board the bus and make my way to the back. Judy's eyes catch mine and we smile in silent reassurance. We're here! We're in a war zone! It's utterly surreal. At any moment I'm certain Chuck Norris will squeeze his muscular frame on board.

Through the dirty glass window my eyes dart this way and that. There are dozens of military vehicles and men dressed in combat fatigues with guns. They're walking briskly in every direction. Overhead the helicopters come as quickly as they go. It's kind of an organised chaos and it's noisy. A large poster of the revolutionary martyr, Ahmad Shah Massoud (pronounced ma-sood), covers a giant billboard and above it the words 'Welcome to Afghanistan'.

Under Massoud's command the Russians were defeated but the day before the 9/11 bombings, Massoud was assassinated by Al Qaeda agents. A year later he was named 'National Hero' by the order of Afghan President Hamid Karzai. Now every year, the 10th of September is observed as a national holiday, known as 'Massoud Day.' Many say that the Nobel Peace Prize nominee had all the potential of becoming President had he not been assassinated. Many say Afghanistan may have been a very different place to what it is now.

I can't miss the telltale signs of war, the bunkers, the sandbags and the bullet holes sprayed into the concrete wall of the building we are heading towards. I spot two MI-35 attack helicopters with Afghanistan flags proudly displayed on each side, they are mounted with 57 mm rockets and 12.7 mm cannons. As if this is not oppressive enough, next we see several Blackhawk helicopters, an armed personnel carrier (APC) and a giant C-130H Hercules on the tarmac. At least a couple of dozen foreign troops are said to be stationed nearby. Welcome to Afghanistan indeed!

'You'll be fine, Kay,' I tell myself, 'you'll be fine.'

We line up in the Immigration queue behind a throng of people. Some look like US state department types. Others look like plain clothes marines and then there's the sea of Afghans. Judy, Diana, John, Chris and I, stand silently watching the comings and goings at the arrival hall. After five minutes we take a small step forward and then another. After a quarter of an hour, it is our time to be processed.

'Passports!' the official behind the counter calls.

Diana moves forward with John.

'How many of you together?' the officials barks.

'There are five of us,' John replies and waves for Judy, Chris and I to join him.

Three more officials rush over to the counter at the young man's request. They grab at our passports and flick through the pages. One says something unintelligible to the other older man and then the three of them are all talking at once. It's confusing. Our paperwork is not in order. The Afghanistan Embassy in our respective countries somehow failed to advise us that we required two passport photographs for a special ID card that will remain in our possession at all times for the duration of our stay. We are instructed to go into the city, to the Ministry of Interior, to get our papers in order or risk being detained by authorities. I have no idea what the inside of an Afghan prison looks like and I certainly have no desire to find out! The IDs are a priority. The big red stamp comes down hard on each of our passports before the official hands them all back to John and waves us on.

'Passport!' he calls to the next in line.

'Come this way,' John beckons.

We are shepherded into another darker room like sheep being led to the slaughter. Where did the lighting go?

'It's alright. Your eyes will adjust in a few minutes.' John gently grabs my arm and leads me forward. 'Here ... this way.'

I find myself standing beside Judy, who is pushed up against a large concrete pillar. Diana and Chris have thrown themselves into the throng of people grabbing at the suitcases on the conveyor belt. Within minutes, dozens of local Afghans swarm around us, shouting and waving frantically, all desperate to become our porters. I point to Diana. The men rush to her offering their help.

'It is madness,' I say under my breath.

One by one our bags are retrieved. John does a good job securing them in a pile until the wild porters return and converge on them with their make shift trolleys. Diana looks confident. She's making sure the porters don't run off with our bags. Getting out of the actual airport is easier said than done. It's like being caught in the middle of a Wall Street selling frenzy. Everywhere I look there are more dark brown eyes staring back. I hardly know where to look. I feel a little claustrophobic but I tell myself to remain calm. It's only chaos.

By the time we leave the arrivals area we have attracted an entourage of willing helpers, about twelve young men in all. Each one wants to be paid handsomely in US currency, of course. Diana? Where's Diana?

'There she is,' says Judy.

Diana is walking ahead through the crowded car park trying to locate our in-country language assistant, 'Muslim,' a young man who she knows from previous trips. I have no idea what he looks like so I can't help.

Eventually we push our way through the throng and out the double glass doors to another parking area. Still no sign of Muslim. More porters come forward wanting to help us but we wave them all away. I hang onto Judy's arm so we won't get separated. Diana walks just ahead with John. I give my camera to Chris, who films us. I talk to the camera: 'Well, we've arrived in Kabul and here I am with ...' I point to Judy beside me, dressed from top to toe in her salwar kameez. 'Sorry I don't recognise you in that get up ... *who are you*?' And we giggle like naughty schoolgirls. Cut.

Our entourage of male porters push our suitcases behind us. We walk into another car park and still no sign of Muslim! So we decide that Judy, John and I will wait here, while Chris and Diana go further ahead to look for him. Ten minutes later we spot Diana from 100 metres away signalling for us to join her. A young man is standing beside her, obviously this is Muslim. (The guards wouldn't let him into the airport area.) One by one Diana introduces us.

'Is that really your name?' I can't prevent myself from asking.

The young man smiles broadly to reveal the whitest and most perfectly aligned teeth. 'Muslim by name, Muslim by nature,' he jokes.

Later he explains that his family tree is traced back to the Holy Prophet (Peace be upon him) via Hazrat Ali (May Allah be pleased with him), the Holy Prophet's cousin and Son-in-Law and Hazrat Fatimah (May Allah be pleased with her), the Holy Prophet's daughter. So when using his name, it should be said in full. This might be too much of a mouthful for us.

'I think it will be easier for you to just call me Muslim,' he says.

Good grief. I never knew you had to give the translation whenever you used a name. Muslim would definitely be easier! Actually I encountered something similar when I first moved to Thailand. I learned that the ceremonial name of Bangkok City was in fact *Krung Thep Mahanakhon Amon Rattanakosin Mahinthara Yuthaya Mahadilok Phop Noppharat Ratchathani Burirom Udomratchaniwet Mahasathan Amon Phiman Awatan Sathit Sakkathattiya Witsanukam Prasit* ... Try saying that to a taxi driver every time you want to go to the city. Bangkok's easier.

To our relief our transport is just beyond the blue wrought-iron gates. Our wild porters carry our luggage and pack them in the back of our Toyota mini-van. We pay them five US dollars apiece and we're off. I am so pleased to be sitting beside Diana as we finally leave the airport and are on our way – at last – to our accommodation. It is so reassuring being with someone who has done the trip five times before.

'Some of those porters wanted to be paid twice!' I complain to Diana, as we make our way along the gleaming black asphalt of the airport road to Kabul City.

'Yeah, they'll try it on,' she smiles and gently squeezes my hand.

Embassy flags fly high above the rooftops. I can identify the flags of Kazakhstan, Belgium, Bulgaria and the United Kingdom, and then we turn into Sherpur Square. The embassies of Iran and Turkey are immediately to our left and the famous Flower Street runs parallel all the way into Chicken Street and then into the main road where our accommodation sits next door to the United Nations High Commission for Refugees (UNHCR) Headquarters. Had I known that, I would have considered moving to another hotel. But nowhere in Kabul is really safe. The Taliban are encroaching from all sides.

We're going to the Gandamack Lodge, recommended by Heather Fitzgerald, who works for the Great Game Travel Company. I made contact with her prior to making my decision about coming to

Afghanistan. She said the lodge is one of the safest places to stay even despite being next to a UN building. Its founder, Peter Jouvenal, a journalist, established the Gandamack Lodge shortly after the fall of the Taliban Government. I'd read a great deal about Peter Jouvenal, who filmed the BBC's *World Affairs* editor, John Simpson, walking into the city after the Taliban fled in November 2001. Jouvenal has spent more time in Afghanistan than most foreign journalists. He is probably the only cameraman to have filmed both Mullah Omar and Osama bin Laden.

When it comes into view, the Gandamack Lodge complex doesn't look as nice as it did on the internet booking site, but then again, nothing ever does. Our mini-van stops inside a steel door where it is checked by security guards packing AK-47s and 9 mm handguns. We are escorted on foot through a second steel door that takes us to the entrance of the Gandamack. Our luggage will follow after our mini-van passes inspection.

Walking up the inside stairs, I imagine Osama bin Laden walking these very steps. I imagine this because Osama bin Laden used this very place as a home for his fourth wife and family. They left suddenly in the middle of the night and the hearsay is that the landlord who lives next door is still angry because he's owed AUD$500 in back rent.

John and Chris are accommodated inside the main lodge overlooking the garden. The Gandamack allows its guests to stay in either the main house or in the garden rooms, all of which are unsuited and have internet and satellite TV. Judy and I are led down a winding walkway towards the edge of the complex where we have agreed to share a garden room. Diana takes the single accommodation a few doors from ours. The rooms are surprisingly elegant. Our room is comfortable and clean. We are pleased to see white linen bedspreads with delicately embroidered floral patterns covering our dark antique-framed, single beds. Soft mood lighting washes the room in a golden glow. A bookstand takes up one corner and a TV and satellite system the other. Heavy drapes shield us from the outside world and make a lovely backdrop to an oak desk and chair, obviously the basic essentials for any writer.

We set about unpacking some of our things but we don't dally because we still have to go to the Ministry of Interior to get our ID cards. So it is a quick visit to the bathroom, a spray of deodorant and a light coat of lip gloss, then out the door to meet up with Diana and the others, hopefully waiting in the reception area. Through the dining room doorway I can see the staff preparing the dining room. Dozens of white tablecloths and fully laid tables are adorned with delicate crystal holders and candles. It looks so intimate.

'Let's go,' says Diana.

Adjusting our headscarves, Judy and I fall in quietly behind her. John and Chris are two steps behind us. The mini-van is waiting in the drive. As we discover when leaving the Gandamack Lodge, the traffic in Kabul is chaotic at all times. Traffic police wave cars this way and that. Horns blare. Animals cross the road at inconvenient times, while their keepers herd them back in the direction they want them to go. Toyotas are everywhere; the big sport utility vehicles (SUVs) as well as bulletproof UN cars. They are all Toyotas. I wonder why that is, but as back home I am the proud owner of a Toyota Camry, I assume it comes down to affordability and economy. Remember home?

There is some sort of military presence on every corner. There are armoured trucks with troops on the roof, machine gunners ready to shoot, and security guards and police with automatic, high calibre weapons seemingly outside every building. If a gun battle began it would be difficult to figure out who fired first and, more of a concern to me, who would fire last? With all that firepower, I can't imagine that anyone could be left on the street! We spot the red and white barriers around the DHL building two doors down that had been the scene of a violent murder a couple of days ago. The men were shot in their car as they were pulling into the DHL office. There were blood stains on the ground and two bullet holes in the window of the DHL office.

'The journalist at the Gandamack told me that after the security guard killed them, he then blew his own head off with his Kalashnikov,' I said.

We drive by in complete silence after that. The city is enveloped in a constant cloud of dust and I frequently find myself in a coughing fit before tossing another throat lozenge in my mouth. Along the roadside are single-storey buildings, some dilapidated tin sheds used as workshops, others open spice stalls selling pomegranates of the brightest red. It's a sad sight.

Burqa-clad women walk alongside dirty shoeless children. Their filthy hands beg passers-by for anything they can spare. They're lucky if they can earn AUD$1 a day and most don't even earn that. Child beggars endure insults and threats. They are often beaten for not earning enough. All of us are deeply affected by seeing this sudden rush of poverty despite the fact that some of us have seen similar devastation in other countries. Diana says she would like to come back to Kabul, find all the little children and buy them all shoes. As a former hairdresser I am more into shaving their heads and scrubbing their scalps with disinfectant. Judy, being a nurse, wants to immunise them. And John, the doting grandfather, wanted to hand out toys and bags of candy. Chris is deep in thought.

As our car comes to a halt mid-traffic, children aged eight or nine tap wildly on our windows. There are so many of them. Little brown eyes stare at us sweetly. They should all be in school. Most likely their parents can't afford school. Half of these children are probably the sole breadwinners of their families, assuming they have families. How many of them might be sold into the sex slave trade? I recall a report I'd read about an 11-year-old girl who had been molested by a legless man. This is a ghoulish story. He had lost his legs to a land mine. She and her friend felt sorry for him and used to take him tea and scraps of food. One day he forced himself on her. Afterwards he paid her five dollars, and that was how she started selling herself for sex. The irony of that story was that by the time she was 13 the girl was fluent in four languages including English. The sad reality was that her own parents had encouraged her to sell sex. When she stopped doing it, her parents sent her 10-year-old brother to the legless man in her place. The young girl was never seen again. Ugly weird stuff. After only one day in Kabul I understand what motivated Diana to start the Childlight Foundation for Afghan Children. If anyone ever needs the miracle of her selfless support, it is certainly these darling little dirty children tapping at our car window.

It takes less than 30 minutes to get to the Ministry of Interior or Foreign Affairs. We get body searched then an administrator directs us to a nearby store where we get photographed. Shortly afterwards we return to the Ministry and subject ourselves once again to the body searches. The female policewoman smiles broadly and says, 'Welcome'. Another lady, sitting in the corner of the tiny strip-search room is curious to know why we are in Afghanistan. When we explain that we have come to help the women and children through our aid programs, she smiles rather cynically and tells us that we should go home and come back when Afghanistan is not so serious. The only thing certain about this place is that any day in Kabul could be your last.

Chapter 6

Blue Burqa Women

The morning traffic is as usual, chaos, with cars, bicycles, trucks and buses all merging left, right and forward. A herd of scraggy-haired goats takes their time to cross the road but no-one worries. A bony brown horse adorned in red tassels pulls a turban-headed man in a cart filled with cauliflowers. Horns blare into the air. On this typical morning everyone on the street – mostly Afghan men – appears to know exactly where they are going, even though everyone is going in all directions at once. There is a familiar foreign presence too. It occasionally filters in between the scenes that flash before me, like a *National Geographic* documentary. I keep expecting some Hollywood director to call out 'cut', but it never happens – this is real life unfolding before my eyes. A white four-wheel drive vehicle passes. It has the bright blue letters 'UN' blazoned on every door panel. It sticks out like a neon sign flashing 'We're here to help'; insurgents might see it instead as 'aim rocket here'. Next, the intimidating attendance of Afghan military convoys, loaded to capacity with dark-haired, bearded soldiers adorned with every conceivable bit of combat apparatus from ballistic vests, assault rifles and ammunition rounds to seemingly countless grenades. On their passing, a sense of foreboding lingers heavily in the air, as if a fog of fear had rolled in.

Our Toyota mini-van is parked at the curb outside a small naan bread bakery. We wait for Diana to return from the pharmacy. John, her father, is feeling unwell with a sore throat, chesty cough and blocked sinus. I suffered the same symptoms in Dubai but I feel much better now. The sliding door is left unlocked. I decide it is better that way, in case there's a bomb blast. I'll be first out the door. I scan the street for anything suspicious. My fingers fidget with a digital camera. I hope the batteries last longer than the last lot. For some reason I only get three or four photos then the batteries die. I am glad of my video camera as backup.

A young boy whose brown hair looks unwashed and matted, sits bestride a wooden shoeshine box across the road. Not more than 10 or 12 years old, his hands are already weathered, cracked and dry, and the face is serious, far too stern for one so young. As he scans the pavement for business, the eyes miss nothing. He looks patient, tiny. Today, he will eat very little, if at all. He will work all day, hopefully earning a few rupees, perhaps enough to buy naan bread from the baker. I snap his picture when he looks away. As my gaze continues down the street, I see a dozen or more boys just like him, the future fodder of war. Every day, countless vagabonds and streetwise kids roam grimy streets and rat-infested bazaars, scrambling for a few rupee.

The Lonely Planet guide book on Afghanistan says that, on such busy streets, life and death is completely unpredictable. I hope that, so long as we sit quietly and don't attract too much attention, we will be safe. As usual, I get to thinking about the political situation. The United States Government says that women's rights are a central part of its foreign policy with the new Islamic Republic of Afghanistan Government, aside from the war on terror and Al Qaeda that is. But I imagine it's not just a matter of wearing, or not wearing a pale blue burqa. There's more to it than that. Under the Taliban Government women weren't allowed to be educated or play musical instruments. Our car radio is playing as I watch the chaos of traffic coming and going. I wonder what it would be like not to be allowed to listen to music, or being banned from riding bicycles, driving cars and from riding unchaperoned in a taxi. The Taliban even prevented women from travelling on the same bus as a man! (I wonder what Rosa Parks would have thought of that. Rosa Parks was a black woman who, in December 1955, refused to give up her seat on a bus for a white passenger and in so doing sparked the Civil Rights Movement in the United States.)

I look through the window and watch the people going this way and that, oblivious to my curious stare. It's unsettling to think that women were once hidden from sight, forbidden to appear at public gatherings. How much of this has really changed? I don't know. I look at the guide book nestled in my hand and think how lucky I am that I can read. The Taliban prevent women from being educated. What do they fear?

Judy silently prays beside me that we will come to no harm. I begin to wonder how many women fall ill on these dusty streets as they scratch around in the dirt. How many must have contracted scabies and infections under the Taliban, who banned them from attending the public bathhouses when most had no other access to running water. How many were unable to bath, and therefore unable to offer their prayers to Allah? Islam prohibits women from praying without a bath. Life must have been horrendous. Looking around me, is it any better? The woman in the dirt looks as if she hasn't bathed for *years!* What will become of her?

Prior to the Taliban taking power, male doctors were allowed to treat women in hospitals. After the Taliban gained power, however, they were forbidden to and there was a shortage of medicine. With fewer female health professionals in employment, coupled with the distances many women needed to travel for treatment, thousands of women and their unborn babies died. But even under the present government these difficulties remain. Women still die prematurely and there is still a shortage of medicine.

I suppose at least women are now allowed to go to a hospital for treatment, and at least, they are allowed to go to a Mosque for worship. As for the public baths, something tells me they have not reopened.

The minutes tick by in slow motion. I become transfixed by a woman on the opposite side of the road. Heavy mesh-like kitchen curtains are sewn into her pale blue burqa to shield her eyes from sight. How can this woman see anything at all and why is the burqa always pale *blue*? Answer: no particular reason: it's just a common material colour, the guide book tells me. To be honest, I know very little about why Afghan women wear burqas at all, except for what I am told by other Westerners, see on documentaries or read in books. In fact everything I've read suggests that burqas are a symbol of female repression. But the Taliban are no longer in government, so is it still compulsory for women to wear the burqa? No, I'm told ... but what is the truth?

Diana, who has already been to Afghanistan a number of times, informs me that we don't have to wear the burqa. They're not compulsory for visitors and in many parts of the country, they're not even compulsory for Afghan women to wear. In fact, wearing of the burqa or full face covering is generally only reserved for the most repressive regimes. In the holiest place in Islamic society, Mecca (Kingdom of Saudi Arabia), the wearing of full face covering is actually prohibited for security reasons when women walk with men around the holy kaaba (black stone) at al Haram mosque. Indeed, in Islam in general it is permissible for women to wear any women's clothes she pleases so long as they are modest and are not tight-fitting or reveal her womanly form. Out of respect for their culture we wear the salwar kameez and headscarf. The salwar are pyjama bottoms, full and floppy like pantaloons; the kameez is a tunic, long enough to wear as a dress in the West. Actually I find the local dress very comfortable, as opposed to squeezing into a pair of tight jeans.

I get thinking that I have never known a Muslim except for a young man I met in the Lao prison, who was detained two cells down from mine. One day I offered him half my ham and salad roll, hoping to take his mind off the torture he'd suffered over the past four hours. He smiled but refused and said he didn't eat pork.

I shrugged. 'It's not pork, mate ... it's ham!'

He laughed. At least I made him laugh. I couldn't do anything about the burnt genitals or broken bones he sustained in interrogation. Sadly that young man died in that prison. For no particular reason, he was beaten to death. His story never made the news unlike the hundreds of stories of brutal killings in Afghanistan. Stories such as the execution of a 35-year-old woman convicted of murdering her husband who tortured her all the days of her marriage. The husband convinced himself that she was an adulterous. After his murder, Zarmina's elder girls and son were given to her brother-in-law, according to tradition. He was Taliban and demanded blood law refusing to let her escape death. Then, two months before the execution, he told Zarmina's mother he had sold Najeba (14) and Shaista (16) into sex slavery.

I watched Zarmina's public execution on YouTube. She was dragged in front of 30,000 spectators at Kabul's Ghazi Sport Stadium, made to kneel before the goalposts and shot in the back of the head. Her pale blue burqa, covered in blood, her body slumped on the stadium ground. Her executioner was her brother-in-law, who afterwards exited to Pakistan with the proceeds of the sale. This tragic story can now be read in full here: http://www.rawa.org/zarmeena2.htm.

Looking through the tinted glass window of our mini-van, I can't help thinking of that young woman, known only as Zarmina, as another pale blue burqa passes me by. Such barbaric public executions may have stopped under the present government, but the abuse of women and children continues as a legacy of ignorance and unfettered violence. I get to thinking about my own country and thinking that domestic violence is not limited to religion, race, income or culture. Domestic violence is an issue that affects everyone, directly and indirectly. It should not be considered a private matter to only be dealt with behind closed doors and it is ridiculous to think that getting rid of the Taliban will guarantee that women's rights will suddenly be restored, or anyone's rights for that matter! Men and women have been abused in every country in the world, in their homes, their workplaces, on the streets. They have been trafficked across borders and sold as sweat-shop slaves, drug mules, and prostitutes, and many have become victims to the widespread and systematic sexual violence in conflict situations. It isn't any wonder people want justice, particularly against those who perpetrate such incomprehensible deeds, and especially when they involve crimes against our most vulnerable. Finding the balance can be difficult and clearly Afghanistan is very much a man's world!

It is steeped in tradition and far removed from the modernisation I am familiar with. But looking around me, I think it must be changing. I ponder this as I spot a woman walking unaccompanied *and* smiling. I see another woman wearing fashionable high heels and tinkering bangles. She is wearing light-coloured make-up, dusted eye shadow and lip gloss. She is so beautiful. Some women look modern with their Gucci handbags and mobile phones. Some opt only for the hijab, a thin veil worn as a head covering that sits firmly in place without any need to readjust. I see one woman wearing a bright green hijab with sparkling silver sequences. I check my headscarf hasn't fallen again and wish I could swap with her. Then I notice her feet are adorned in matching silver strappy shoes.

I am even more surprised by her red toenail polish! I point this out to Judy, 'Hey, check that!' Judy looks at me and with her fine eyebrows raised says 'Women's Lib?' which sets us both laughing. Then we spy another woman, sitting in the dusty street, metres away. Just sitting in the dirt. Judy and I wonder why. Has she committed a crime and, as a consequence, become an outcast? Is she a heroin addict? Has her husband been killed in the fighting? Or perhaps *he* is a heroin addict and cannot support his family? One thing is for sure, no woman would choose to scratch around in the dirt all day long unless that was her lot in life. I will never know this woman's story, despite my curiosity, but I do notice the silky apple green material of her salwar kameez. Her pale blue burqa slips slightly, leaving her undergarments momentarily exposed. It is an odd contrast against the dirty grey of the Kabul pavement and fascinating to know that even while trapped in such abject poverty, this woman wears brightly coloured clothes under her burqa – almost festive attire.

I read somewhere that scientists have ascertained that colours transmit a unique message to the brain which impacts our moods. For example, my favourite colour red is a stimulating colour that enhances self-assurance. Yellow is reflective and is supposed to enhance optimism. Orange is meant to act as an antidepressant to stimulate the mind. Blue is associated with depth and stability, symbolising trust, loyalty, wisdom, confidence, intelligence and truth. Green is said to be relaxing and also a colour that represents faithfulness, unity and hope. It really doesn't matter what colour her clothes are. The woman in the dirt is still destitute. My heart fills with sympathy for her and for the countless others like her who endure hardships as part of their normal everyday lives. I can't help but think that women who beg on the street were once beloved mothers, cherished wives, devoted daughters and treasured sisters, yet here they are reduced to crawling filthy pavements. Why?

War, war and more war!

A little boy approaches the beggar woman and stands beside her. He is dressed in canary yellow pants and a tunic top. He looks no more than seven years old as he hugs the wrought iron street barrier with his dirty little fingers tucked firmly into his mouth. His baby brother, a grubby slip of a child, dressed in orange and black, lies cradled in the folds of his mother's pale blue burqa. The street is awash with litter. Grey puffs of dirt envelope the abandoned family. A mangy dog walks past without looking at them. I watch quietly and like a thief, I steal their picture with my digital camera. It doesn't seem right that the tragedy of their pitiful existence has become a photograph to me, the passer-by. I could have handed her the loose change in the bottom of my pocket. I don't.

I merely sit, ignoring the tapping on the car window as other beggars peer at us imploringly. I see a group of young women walking together, dressed in blue denim jeans. It is a rather peculiar sight in Kabul, probably frowned upon, which somehow gets me thinking about my mother. In her day, blue denim jeans were frowned upon too, and only worn by bodgies and bikers. It also reminds me of when we lived in Laos and the government gave approval for girls to wear blue denim jeans on the weekends. It is interesting that despite our cultural differences, blue denim jeans are a universal image of freedom. However, despite such signs of modernisation, the damage from the already-inflicted violence and degradation remains.

What happens to Afghan women when life gets too much? Does life get too much for them? Do they suicide? Sadly, many Afghan women do take their own lives just the same as other women in the world do. They face the same struggle of not being able to manage the traumas they have endured or are continuing to endure. They face the same heartaches and despair, and just like many women who suffer in a domestic violence situation, they suffer in complete silence.

In another time when I and no-one else are witness, an oil lamp sits on a makeshift table a few feet away from a smouldering fire. The water bubbles and boils in the big black pot. The smoke rises up the mud-caked chimney until it finally escapes to the blue sky above. The sun is shining and in any other place, in any other time, the young woman sitting near the makeshift table would be cherished as she once was when she was a little girl playing with other little girls. Now she sits and quietly sobs, nursing her bloodied beaten face in trembling hands. She doesn't know why her husband beat her. All she knows is that she cannot take any more of the shame it has brought to her life. She stands quietly in her pale blue burqa and lifts the oil lamp and without warning, pours its flaming contents over her body. Her husband stands still and doesn't do anything to stop her. He just watches without expression. If she is lucky she will die, but today she is unlucky. The flames don't burn brightly enough or nearly long enough. In the hospital she is a mass of charred flesh but she is breathing.

Scores of young women have set fire to themselves believing that they are guaranteed to meet their death. Many don't die, however, and are forced to return to the humiliation and hell that they were trying to escape. I am becoming consumed by my thoughts. My mind is racing a hundred million miles an hour as I try to absorb the world beyond the glass window. These women walking beneath the pale blue burqa are so vulnerable. Those who are badly burned are hidden under the folds of pale blue material and so too is their plight. Those who are beaten are hidden also. They have no one to champion their protection. They have no white knight on a trusty steed to race them off to the sanctuary of a fairytale castle. But there are those too, under the pale blue folds, who are beautiful, untouched, young and ready to begin life. Without the anonymity of the burqa they risk being exposed to many dangers, including rape. The burqa offers them some protection at least, and this is vital if they are to survive in a society where the most sensitive social issue is the honour of women, who represent the honour of the entire Afghan family.

At that moment, the sliding mini-van door is thrust open and momentarily I am startled from such deep thoughts. Diana has returned with John's medicine and within minutes we are making our way back to the Gandamack Lodge. We engage in idle chit-chat on what's going on outside. There are no real in-depth discussions about free-range animals, shoeshine boys or the constant stream of beggars. The pale blue burqa women pass by. They are everywhere. Women, who just like the rest of us, simply want the freedom to live without fear.

Chapter 7
Kabul to Jalalabad

F lying is a dangerous business in Afghanistan. The terrain and weather are even more hazardous and unpredictable than the insurgents. Back in 2004 an airplane, landing at Kabul Airport, slewed off the runway for no apparent reason. A few months later, another flight inexplicably vanished from the radar screens as it was preparing to land. The wreckage of that plane was eventually found at 11,000 feet on the peak of the Chaperi Mountain, 32 kilometres from Kabul. It was completely destroyed and all 104 passengers were dead. At the time of the incident, the weather conditions were horrendous; in fact, it was recorded as being the worst snowstorm in five years. But the actual reason for the loss of communication and subsequent crash remains unknown. The media said the pilot had placed an urgent call saying the plane could only remain in the air for a further 15 minutes. He requested permission to land at Bagram Airbase where US forces were stationed. The request was denied. The US troops would not risk allowing the plane to land and the tragic air disaster was the result.

It took rescue teams 11 gruelling days to get to the treacherous crash site. At least 20 foreigners were reportedly killed. Most of the bodies were not retrieved and the crash became known as one of the deadliest air disasters in Afghan history. One TV cameraman, who reached the site on an Afghan military helicopter, described a woman's corpse strapped to a seat in the tail area of what was left of the plane. It was dreadful. She was later identified as a Russian flight attendant.

When we ring to confirm our flight to Jalalabad, we are informed that all flights are cancelled. Diana, who has to deliver much-needed supplies, immediately investigates alternative travel arrangements, even if it means chartering a light aircraft. Judy and Chris both agree with this decision. The UN offers a small charter service but the cost is AUD$600 each way. Then we find another charter company who say they can take us but just as we are about to make the booking, they advise that the single engine Cessna's engine has just blown up. They do, however, have a larger aircraft. So it's back to square one and we negotiate on price. To our surprise, they agree to transport our persons and luggage for considerably less than the original quote. Call it kismet or karma but the day before our scheduled departure, our flights are no longer available. We are bumped off the plane by another group, who obviously flashed more dollars. Even so, Diana is still committed to making the road trip, alone if need be.

'The cost of turning back now is too much for me,' she explains. 'We've already spent a small fortune getting here. I must get to Jalalabad; people are counting on these supplies.'

'I'll go with you, Diana,' says John. (Of course he will. He's her father!)

Diana tells the rest of us to think very carefully and not feel pressured in deciding our intentions. I can hear Kerry's voice of reason ringing in my ears telling me 'don't take unnecessary risks'. But we can't turn back now, we have to reach Jalalabad. There must be some way of minimising the risk!

'We must let God take the lead,' says Judy. 'If he wants us there it will happen.'

Judy, a Methodist, has tremendous faith in God. She continues: 'Over the years, I have learned that God will protect me, if I am about what he wants me to do.'

I admire her commitment to her faith and she actually *lives* by example, as a good Christian should. But all reason tells me that if God is watching over us, then there is a good possibility that, at a critical point, she/he could be distracted by all the madness that's going on. I will make my decision purely on logic. I will decide what risks I am prepared to take after listening to reliable sources and taking advice from locals like Muslim.

Diana explains over dinner that the road trip to Jalalabad takes about three-and-a-half hours. This is considerably shorter than the eight hours it used to take before the international community upgraded the road. But the journey is just as treacherous and frequently prone to insurgency attacks. Decisions, decisions. There's a travel alert and it advises strongly against any road travel.

Travel Warning: The road from Kabul to Jalalabad is a dangerous road with high incidents of robberies, kidnappings, IEDs (improvised explosive devices), and suicide bombings. We do not take our guests anywhere near this road and those of us who live in Kabul avoid the area as a general rule, even when security is relatively good. The past couple of months have seen a marked decrease in security in the areas surrounding Kabul, making this road an even more dangerous route to travel. At the moment we are seeing a trend of insurgents targeting international aid workers throughout the country. We would strongly discourage travel along the Jalalabad road, and would even recommend that any travel to areas outside Kabul be done by plane if possible.

Heather Fitzgerald — Administrative Director
The Great Game Travel Company Kabul, Afghanistan

...The insurgency problem has escalated along the road to Jalalabad ... Two American marines are dead and four others are wounded ... in a recent attack ... A suicide bomber rammed a car full of explosives into their vehicle ...

According to these reports, the possibility of being kidnapped or killed is now 'high-risk'. That is difficult to gauge because we don't have an obvious target on our heads. The insurgents obviously want to kill as many soldiers as they can but we are not driving military vehicles. We discuss the travel report amongst ourselves and the verdict is: it's certainly *risky*. But no-one can provide information to formulate an accurate risk assessment, i.e.: risk level = hazard severity x likelihood of occurrence.

When we retire for the night, I go to sleep thinking about the scale of what the average person would consider 'risky'? Thinking about home too, of course, I recall Kerry and I working in security in Southeast Asia. We were often surrounded by the threat of violence. The Hmong Insurgency continued to be in conflict with the Laos Government that was endeavouring to track down the remnants of a 'Secret Army' which supported democracy, the US and its allies. Then there were the gun runners, gangsters, drug dealers and lots of other unscrupulous people intent on kidnapping or killing others, some to whom we were providing security. Our workplace was risky but the precautions we took enabled us to remain relatively safe. That we were taken hostage was unpreventable. Some things just happen at random. How you react is often what's important. Panicking may only make matters worse.

I thought about the media reports that I had seen leading up to our journey to Afghanistan. I also thought about the news reports in the *Kabul Times*. How accurate were they? The journalists I saw staying at Gandamack Lodge rarely strayed beyond the compound. I got chatting and asked one of them how he got his information. 'I get most of my information from paying a local outside source,' the journalist told me, 'I don't want to get killed here!'

The embassy staff rarely venture outside the safety of their fortified green zone. Understandably, as they are high on the insurgents' kill list. For the foreign aid workers and NGOs in Kabul, tensions are at an all-time high, especially after the murder of a British woman who worked for a UK charity known as SERVE Afghanistan. Only days ago she was shot dead in broad daylight on a street in Kabul. It is no surprise to hear that the Taliban claimed responsibility, but it is shocking that they should target a woman who was merely helping educate and train people to live a better life with their particular disability.

A Taliban spokesman explained to the media that the woman was killed because she was working for an organisation that was preaching Christian faith. But 'preaching Christianity' is not part of the SERVE Afghanistan charter. Its projects focus on community development through education and vocational training for Afghans with disabilities. Written on their website are the words of an Afghan proverb: '*Qatara qatara, darya mesha!*', 'Drop by drop, a river is formed!' which summarises well an important principle for SERVE.

Many believe more attacks are imminent.

The decision to travel by road to Jalalabad need not be decided straightaway. We have a few hours till morning.

Following breakfast, Judy and I sort through the suitcases that contain the dozen or so newborn and hygiene kits to be delivered, donated by Diana's Church of Jesus Christ of Latter Day Saints. We are scheduled to take these kits across town to Fayrene (Fay) Spencer, a judicial advisor for the US State Department's Correction System Support Program (CSSP). Diana knows Fay from her previous visits to Afghanistan and I know of her through correspondence.

'What do you think about doing some driving, Kay?' Judy asks as she hands me the suitcase and turns to lock the door of our room.

'I don't know,' I reply quietly, setting the suitcase down. I don't have to decide yet; we're being driven to Fay's premises. I reply, 'I'm still not 100 per cent sure. I'll wait to see what Fay reckons.'

Fay is expecting us. She is a lovely woman with dark curly hair and olive skin. Her face lights up the instant we step from the mini-van and walk towards her. She comes down her steps and shakes each of our hands. It's always difficult to get a feel for people over the internet but the minute I shake her hand I know that she is one special woman. We waste no time mounting the six or seven steps of the white-painted brick building, surrounded by the usual thick compound walls and topped with razor wire. We head through a narrow doorway to a stairwell that takes us downstairs to a basement-type boardroom.

Fay invites us to make ourselves comfortable around the big wooden conference table, which five of us do. Muslim positions himself at the end of the table. He quietly observes. Each of us takes a few moments for introductions and an exchange of business cards. Fay is a particularly fascinating lady with the warmest of smiles that draws me in and leaves me wanting to ask a billion questions. As she explains, the CSSP is responsible for providing training and mentoring to the Afghan corrections system. Its role is vital in aiding the development of infrastructure, specifically with the refurbishment of prisons. With my security and social justice background, I am interested in her organisation's correction programs. I'm a little disappointed that her superior, Delbert Moad, isn't available. It would have been good to meet, particularly given his reputation as an expert in corrections and training. There are so many good people here doing amazing things. I want to meet them all. I love networking and sharing ideas, especially if it means keeping up to date with the latest in the security industry.

As I listen, I recall a time when Kerry and I first went to work in Laos. Some of what Fay is describing is comparable to what we encountered, working in an environment that has also been ravaged by war. It was like starting from scratch, in Laos. There was an abundance of unskilled labour, just like here. The justice sector was (and still is) in particular ruin, just like here. In fact, in the early days when the international community endeavoured to introduce justice reforms to Afghanistan, the people didn't understand what it meant or how it would benefit them, just like Laos.

Afghan prosecutors lack basic equipment such as paper and pens. Judges' salaries are roughly one-quarter of the country's national average income. None of the justice institutions sing from the same songsheet; however, the United States has convinced them that it is vital to do so. Hence for the first time ever, the three key Afghan justice institutions – the Ministry of Justice, the Attorney General's Office and the Supreme Court – have agreed to develop a unified program to rebuild the Justice Sector.

'It is quite an undertaking but obviously an essential one,' says Fay, 'particularly with the level of crime that has consumed Afghanistan following the fall of the Taliban.' And, as the program develops, so too will the number of persons prosecuted for criminal activity and hence the need in 2006, to establish the Corrections System Support Program. The majority of Afghans are accustomed to resolving their differences under a less formal system.

Fay explains that her team works closely with the Ministry of Justice's Afghan Central Prison Directorate to provide guard training, records and information management, and infrastructure and equipment support. There are over 30 US advisors in Kabul and four other provinces. Over the last two years they have been kept extremely busy and have trained over 1400 corrections officers. They also work with Afghan engineers to develop a prison model that is suitable in design to meet international standards and is economical enough for the Afghans to build and operate themselves. It is more than just 'important' work, it is vital. They are starting at the beginning and it is overwhelming to put the enormity of what they are seeking to achieve into perspective. Without a fully functioning justice system it will be impossible to promote rule of law, which leads to stability. Yes, they are tackling those issues with determination.

I could have stayed in that boardroom for hours listening to Fay talk about the wonderful progress they are making. Listening to her is such a pleasant change from the typical doom and gloom we hear about. Downstairs, in a communal games room, we meet Fay's staff. They sit as a group and listen as one by one, we introduce ourselves. In turn they introduce themselves too. They are missing their loved ones back home but dedicated to making a significant difference in Afghanistan. They tell us that they appreciate the risk we have taken getting to Kabul and hope our journey will continue to be safe.

The afternoon has snuck up on us so quickly, it's time to go. With tremendous admiration for their efforts we farewell them, before moving into the adjoining corridor that leads back to our mini-van.

Muslim and our driver have brought the boxes of hygiene kits into the foyer and are waiting by the door for us.

'Oh wonderful!' Diana exclaims, cracking open a box and handing a plastic-wrapped bag to Fay. 'These are the newborn and hygiene kits for you to distribute to the women prisoners. They were put together by the Church of the Latter Day Saints (LDS) in Salt Lake City, Utah.'

'Oh my ...!' Fay sighs with gratitude.

Diana rattles off the contents of the packages. 'Each kit contains two bars of soap, two wash clothes, four toothbrushes, toothpaste and two combs.'

'This is unbelievable ...'

'They also provided us with these newborn kits,' she holds up another package. 'That contains soaps, baby blankets, nappies and pins, washcloths, little baby clothes and matching booties and caps ...'

'LDS, Salt Lake City ... thank you so much!' cries Fay as she holds up one of the kits for Chris and me to admire. Both of us are filming this with our separate DVD cameras. 'You just don't know how much they're going to appreciate what you've done.'

Fay tells us that she has 19 female prison officers looking after all the women in Kabul Prison, the largest female prison in Afghanistan. Sixty-two children also reside in the prison. What a difficult job she and her team are undertaking but what amazing courage they show, when every day, they face insurmountable heartache. The expression on Fay's face is priceless. She is completely overjoyed. We stand around with great big silly grins on our faces, basking in the feeling you get when you do something really nice for someone. Momentarily I look at Diana who is positively glowing. How lucky am I, to be part of something so wonderful?

That evening at dinner, back at the Gandamack Lodge, surrounded by the sweet-smelling roses and the ghost of Osama bin Laden, Judy, Chris and I make the decision to accompany Diana and John to haul the supplies on the road from Kabul to Jalalabad. As I go to bed and pull the crisp white bedsheet over me, I wonder if this journey isn't about to introduce me to another of those defining moments in my life.

To justify my time here, I really don't have to go on this trip. I could meet up with the Australian Ambassador, Martin Quinn, and do something equally worthwhile in Kabul. Or I could stay in bin Laden's underground bunker of the Gandamack Lodge, transformed to look like the inside of a fully stocked British pub, and sip my usual Bailey's on ice, courtesy of a lovely, hearing-impaired Afghan bartender! He's a sweet little man with a quirky toothy smile.

I don't really have to go on the road trip, except I do. I can justify not going, but what I can't justify is loosening the bonds of loyalty and friendship that have been built up between Diana, Judy, Chris, John and me. We are all in this together. When Fay described the drive to Jalalabad, she made it sound amazing. She has driven the route numerous times and says that it is no less safe than any other part of Afghanistan, excluding Kandahar of course. I did receive an invitation from the commanding officer of the Australian Reconstruction Taskforce to visit and liaise with AUSAID staff in Oruzgan province, but that part of the world is far too dangerous at present so I respectfully declined. *See, Mum, I do know when to say no to adventure!*

Everyone must decide for themselves. I must admit that I am intrigued, nervous and excited, all at the same time. Tomorrow will be breakfast of cereal and toast, after which I will send Kerry an email to reassure him that I am safe and being safe. I will tell him that I will email him again once we arrive in Jalalabad. The details of how we are getting there, I will tell him some other time. Just as I will, upon my return to Australia, let my mother know that I lived through these amazing experiences. I think I just made my decision to go. I'll make a plan tomorrow. It will be fine.

Chapter 8
Equality

For our journey from Kabul to Nangarhar Province our personal safety and security is largely dependent on advice of Muslim, our guide. He takes his place in the front seat, beside the driver, and we all scramble into the back.

Muslim interests me lots. Physically he looks like any other young Afghan man: dark hair, dark eyes and a black beard. He is taller than I, solidly built and quite handsome. It's difficult to tell how old he is, but Diana tells me later that he's 29. I try to get to know him, first by making small talk because we are strangers, then gradually inching towards more contentious topics. From Muslim I learn that in this country, issues concerning personal freedoms, feminism and equality are multifaceted problems. Their complexities affect the deepest levels of the social fabric. There is no simple solution and reluctantly I am forced to admit to myself that I have a lot to learn. But I am eager to understand his culture, the politics of Afghanistan and the differences and similarities between our worlds.

My education is about to begin!

Muslim was born 3 March 1979 in the Pashtun Kama District of Nangarhar Province, with a population of just over 88,000. In Australian terms, that's about the size of Toowoomba, Queensland. As a consequence of the 1979 Soviet invasion, Muslim's family migrated to Pakistan where they spent six months in Peshawar before moving south-east to Jehangira. Here they remained for 22 years.

In Pakistan, Muslim's father was employed as a contractor for an engineering company. He earned a reasonable living, enough at least to meet the family's day-to-day requirements. As a young man growing up in a foreign land, Muslim was fortunate to attend high school and later, college. He studied hard and was considered to be among the school's most talented students in most subjects, and he enjoyed good relationships with fellow classmates and teachers. Muslim's life was mostly comfortable with simple comforts, and this was largely due to his father's work ethic.

Muslim dreamed of becoming a doctor. In fact he narrowly missed a golden chance of becoming a doctor in 2001, just before the American invasion of Afghanistan following 9/11. Muslim took a special examination at the Ministry of Higher Education and obtained marks high enough for medical school. But the then Higher Education Minister did not agree with his entry. He ordered Muslim to be enrolled instead in the Engineering College, which Muslim did not want to pursue. Muslim tells me that had the minister not meddled in his choices, or had Muslim agreed to study engineering, he would have become either a doctor or an engineer.

'I regret my decision. It was in the days of 9/11 when America was preparing for attack and everyone was fearful of the future. My chance to become a doctor fell into sheer darkness,' says Muslim.

When Muslim's father's contract with the engineering company ended, he set about making sure his family was not forced to face further hardships. He worked selling electronics, carpets and blankets with relatives but these ventures barely produced enough to sustain his family. To help out, Muslim travelled over 30 hours by train (1358 kilometres) to Karachi, twice, to look for work. He eventually found a labouring job but the salary was low. It paid between 1800 rupees (AUD$45) and 2500 rupees (AUD$63) per month.

In 2002, after the fall of the Taliban, 1.56 million Afghan refugees returned to their homeland under a special aid program sponsored by the UN Refugee Agency (UNHCR). Certain parts of the country remained dangerous and best avoided. Thousands poured into small border towns and, with nowhere else to go, they simply sat, slept or milled about along whichever roadside where they had stopped. Aside from the obvious dangers that gripped Afghanistan during this time (feuding war lords, opium traders and the Taliban) the worst drought in their history brought six million people to the brink of utter despair. The few aid agencies that were left, struggled. No-one seems to care about Afghan orphans. The skeletal frames of children clad in baggy clothes which offered little protection against the harsh wintery conditions, are never aired on TV. There are no famous celebrities advertising their plight like those in Rwanda, Malawi and the Sudan. As soon as they reach puberty, some parents, certainly not all, sell their daughters into loveless marriages because they need the money to feed the rest of their starving family. I try not to cast judgements; after all, I am an outsider.

On 14 July 2002, Muslim's family was preparing to return to Afghanistan. His father had gone ahead to prepare their lodgings. He sent word back that the house in Jalalabad was rundown but he would make it livable. Fifteen members of Muslim's family all live under the one roof in the house that his father renovated all those years ago. The family saved a little money to hire a truck that would upload them and their belongings. They left early the next morning for Torkham, the busiest port of entry between Afghanistan and Pakistan, to join the queue of hundreds of thousands of refugees also returning. I asked Muslim what it was like for his family at this time:

We returned by the middle of July 2002 so it was the season of extreme hot weather in Afghanistan. In fact, Jalalabad is among the hottest places in Afghanistan. We were all very sad to be leaving Pakistan where we had made many good friends and a comfortable life. We did not know what it would be like for us back in our homeland but we knew it would not be easy. The UNHCR did help us, as they do all refugees, with some fundamental needs, providing us with 2 x 50kg bags of wheat, a couple of soap cakes, 2 buckets, 2 lanterns and such other small basic necessities. Similarly, we were given a total of US$50 from their relief fund, and although we were very grateful, it didn't *go very far. This amount was given to all refugees at that time, although some families were paid slightly more.*

In the beginning, it was difficult for us to re-establish ourselves in Afghanistan because we did not know much about the environment. We had been away for so long, although I had visited Afghanistan alone prior to our eventual repatriation to see relatives. I was at least a little bit familiar with the situation there. My father worked hard to renovate the house so that it was liveable, but it was very basic. Yet I cannot complain because it was a little better in condition than others in our neighbourhood. The war had devastating effects. None of us were truly happy to return to Afghanistan. We missed our life in Pakistan. It was our home for 22 years. It was sad to think that we had come from a country that provided electricity 24 hrs a day, 7 days a week, to return to our homeland in ruins and no electricity.

We welcomed the end of each day that brought some relief from the heat but in the darkness, we were almost eaten alive by the mosquitoes. Most of us fell ill with malaria infection.

One or two weeks after our return, I was fortunate, with the help of my uncle, to secure a job in the Afghanistan Border Police as a captain even though I had no formal qualification in the army. I received a salary of 4000 AFN per month (AUD$100). Our battalion was posted to the Nazian District of Nangarhar Province, bordering Pakistan. The unit lacked discipline, however, and no-one wanted to be on guard duty at night. It was a difficult job.

After I finished my duty from the Border Police I sold carrot juice in town to help keep food on the table. The farmers working in our field grew wheat, maize, rice and vegetable, which they sold at the market and paid us a percentage of the profit. This helped our family a great deal but since I was working so much I could not establish relationships with my neighbours.

My younger brothers, however, made many friends with the local boys. So I am known through them and I've made many new friends through my work with the Abdul Haq Foundation and UN. In those hard times we were forced to rely on our neighbours power connection to supply electricity to our house.

After about 10 months serving with the Border Police, another uncle of mine was working with the Abdul Haq Foundation (Abdul Haq was the person who led the coalition into Afghanistan and was later assassinated by the Taliban). My uncle recommended me to the Deputy Director of the Abdul Haq Foundation (AHF). He told them that I was good in English translation. After succeeding in a written test I was appointed as a language assistant. The Deputy Director helped me a great deal. He instructed me on the basics of translation, finance and administration and under his auspices, I improved. Over time I was promoted to various higher positions in the AHF. I am still obliged to his guidance and attention.

Muslim is dedicated to bettering his life and that of his family. He continued his studies and became fluent in four languages: Urdu, Pashtu, Dari and English. He became the highest paid language assistant for the Abdul Haq Foundation until he left to work fulltime as an internet/ILC administrator to the Nangarhar University. After almost a full year, he was employed by the United Nations. This is what he was doing when we met. In his spare time, he assists the Childlight Foundation for Afghan children, which is Muslim's connection to Diana.

I am looking forward to visiting his family and especially his newborn baby son.

'I will be very happy for you and Judy to visit my son, and to give him a clean bill of health,' Muslim says, over a cup of tea.

A clean bill of health? He says this because Judy is a registered nurse and, like every Afghan father, Muslim is anxious about his baby's development. He has every reason to be. In this country, six per cent of newborns die each year, and one child in four dies before reaching the age of five. Muslim is anxious to encourage the visit so his baby can be examined by a registered nurse who may offer some precious advice concerning the baby's wellbeing. In this place, family is everything. It is the single most important institution in Afghan society. Frequently, three or four generations live in the one house. That includes the male head of the family, his wife, brothers, several sons and their families, cousins, cousins' families, plus unmarried and widowed females. The women have six to seven children on average. Muslim has five brothers, all studying at various local institutions. He also has four sisters of which two are still at school.

My husband Kerry was one of seven children in his family. I was one of three. Remembering older-style Australian families back home, as we continue our journey out of Kabul, I thoughtfully add, 'I think our family values are really quite similar.'

'Do you think so?' he asks, with inquisitive surprise, as if no Westerner has ever said that to him before.

'Yes, family is very important to most Australians and while our structures may be a little different, the principle of unity is there for many families.'

'Perhaps there are similarities …' he says thoughtfully, '… but your culture is based on Christianity, which makes a lot of difference.'

'True. But that doesn't automatically make all of us *Christian!*' I counter, possibly a little too sharply, as I recall many injustices perpetrated by so-called Christian people in my lifetime. Muslim ponders that paradox as our driver makes a sharp turn to avoid another nasty pothole.

We take time for reflection, as we drive this dusty road. The word 'Christian' evokes the religious differences between our two cultures, especially – in my mind – women's rights. Muslim doesn't strike me as the type of man who would violate any woman, so I ask him a question that's been bothering me. 'What about husbands, Muslim? What does the Holy Prophet say about the way they treat their wives?'

'Husbands are told to treat their wives with love and kindness,' he explains, leaning into the space that separates his seat from the driver's so I can hear him better in the back. 'Many Afghan men learn their values from people with whom they can easily identify – their father, uncles and teachers. Many are taught from a young age that the woman is highly valued in Islam as a mother. And, according to the saying of the Holy Prophet, if she is not happy with her son, due to his bad behaviour in this world, that son cannot enter paradise.'

Muslim is enjoying his religious instruction lesson. He is enjoying it because he wants to help me understand some of the preconceptions in my Western mind. 'There are hundreds of sayings and teachings of the Holy Prophets, as well as what is written in the Holy Qur'ãn, about dealing with women with due respect,' he concludes.

Yet one in every three Afghan women experience physical, psychological or sexual violence, at some point in their lives! The number of women dying in Afghanistan, as a result of domestic violence, is increasing! The silence surrounding the widely known problem of violence against women, however, is not isolated to Afghanistan.

Plenty of Christian men beat their wives, some on a daily basis. Women's issues plague my mind. I've got two daughters – Jessica and Sahra – I couldn't bear them having been deprived an education. How does Islam handle that? 'What are your thoughts on sisters and daughters? Must they forgo an education and simply marry?'

'The Holy Prophet says that women are to be valued and exalted, as sisters and daughters. If a person brings up two of his daughters in a good manner, and educates them properly and marries them well, then he will go to Heaven.' Similarly according to the saying of the Holy Prophet, which states *seeking knowledge is the duty of every* Muslim, *man and woman.*

Yet only 30 per cent of girls have access to education in Afghanistan and more than 80 per cent of women are illiterate. On a positive note, so long as the stabilisation of the country continues and fundamentalist are kept out of power, then those figures stand a good chance of changing upwards dramatically.

'In Western society, women can juggle a career and family. Is this the same for Afghan women?'

'Yes, but women take the role of motherhood more seriously. It is an important role,' he remarks most sincerely. 'A woman has the right to work provided it is within the framework of modesty and does not jeopardise the happiness and contentment of her husband or her family.'

I ponder these issues of gender equality; Western women today put themselves under tremendous pressure to advance careers over motherhood. Many women CEOs are driven to compete with men for equal salaries and rightly so because remuneration should be performance-based and not gender-based. During the late 1950s and early 1960s, there was no equal pay for women in Australia. Equal pay legislation didn't come until 1972. Back in the 'old days' (early 1970s), Australian women couldn't make decisions about their own bodies (contraception). They were not encouraged to attend universities. There was even a time when women couldn't have bank accounts in their own right. It was lawful in those days for a man to beat his wife so long as he did not use a stick thicker than his thumb. Plus, it was taken for granted that men should, at all times, have sex with their wives on demand, regardless of consent, simply because they were married. Even in relatively recent times, rape victims were sometimes told that it was their fault and they must have 'led the man on.' In those dark days of Western society, men fretted about how society might change if women stepped outside their traditional motherhood role. It's scary, allowing people to be free.

'Give them an inch and they'll take a mile – that's what men in my country would say back then,' I tell Muslim.

'Most likely it is true!' he laughs.

'Most likely!' I agree.

'The situation in which women in Afghanistan find themselves today has little to do with Islam and more to do with politics,' Muslim continues, still anxious to undo the impression that his culture represses women unjustly.

'Politics?' I ask.

'Yes, because Islam does offer rights to women, as does the Constitution of Afghanistan. It is usually the politics of the day that undermines how these rights are interpreted.'

A woman has the right to expect her husband to be faithful and loyal to her, and vice versa. She has the right to expect her husband to provide adequate funds for her housekeeping so that she can manage the household efficiently. A woman has the right to expect her husband, as the head of her household, to treat her with respect and love. She has the right to expect him to not become tyrannical. Men and women have the right to have their sexual desires satisfied within the marriage. Neither has the right to cause pain or be abusive to the other. A man has the right to expect his wife to care and cherish him and their children, to protect his good name, and provide him with support and comfort. A woman is permitted to engage in political activity and many women have participated in public protests and street marches.

My heads swims as I struggle to make sense of what Muslim says is so, and what I've heard others say is so. I have to remember that it's all about perspective and access to education. Certainly, as Muslim says, his views do not represent everyone's. They're just *his* personal views based on how *he* was raised. Never underestimate the power of having an education, especially in Afghanistan.

'I hope that your little baby boy grows up healthy and strong and has as much respect for women as his father,' I smile.

'*Insha'Allah*,' says Muslim.

Chapter 9
Through Taliban Strongholds

The rain clouds gather;'a good sign' say the staff of the Gandamack Lodge as Chris, Muslim and I board our mini-van. Yes, rain. It hasn't rained for months and the dusty ground needs a good dousing.

Muslim laughs every time I mention the Taliban. He reckons that, with my dark hair and eyes, they will most likely mistake me for Chris' translator. That being the case, I'll probably get killed 'quickly'. (Stop teasing me, Muslim! This isn't a pleasant thought, though I'd rather a bullet than a slow chop with a blunt machete.) Besides, I've travelled this path before. When Kerry and I worked in the security industry, I experienced near-death situations. I'd endured mock executions at the hands of secret police. I'd effectively dealt with gangsters who tried messing up our security arrangements designed to protect our clients from their evil schemes. I came to the realisation long ago that when your number's up, it's up.

Hopefully it will be as Muslim says, *Insha Allah*; we will reach Jalalabad unharmed.

We're taking two vehicles. Diana, Judy and John are in the mini-van behind us; Chris and I are in the lead car with Muslim. He instructs the other driver to stay as close as possible so that we don't get separated. Heaven forbid anything goes wrong but if it does, then at least I am with Muslim, who can tell me what's going on, as well as advise me how to conduct myself. I feel safer with Muslim. Hopefully help won't be far away if we need it. We've alerted Fay's people in Nangarhar so they have a rough idea when to expect us. As our drivers head east, I sit quietly in the back of the Toyota mini-van, trying not to think too much about the dangers that lie ahead.

I say a silent prayer in my head. That's odd. I'm not religious.

Prayer: *May the change in weather make it too cold for the shadow people to interrupt our journey.*

It's a smooth drive because the international community has resurfaced the road that links Kabul to Jalalabad. It's still highly treacherous not only because of the insurgency problems; there are plenty of motor vehicle accidents as well as rock slides.

Our driver makes excellent time. He weaves the Toyota mini-van safely around each dangerous corner, and into long dark tunnels cut deeply through the formidable stone mountains. He carefully bypasses police checkpoints with little fuss. Most of the delays we experience result not from checkpoints but from the gaudy jingle trucks, common in these parts. We get stuck behind them but our driver manages to find a way around. They are called 'jingle' because of the sound they make driving past. Jingle trucks are painted in mosaic patterns of colourful landscapes and exotic animals. Chains, tassels and pendants often dangle off the front bumper (thus the name). They remind me of enormous Indian elephants, covered with thick shiny silver chains and glorious pendants that hang from the fringes. These beautiful road-trains are a breathtaking sight.

We come across a US military convoy. Horns start blasting, their cars surround us. *Bullies!* Our driver slams on the brakes. The convoy force us off the road towards the mountain edge. Chris, help! My eyes fly to Muslim's face, trying to read what he's thinking. I turn and look behind and the convoy of military Humvees and other vehicles is gaining on us, travelling in single file. I am terrified! They must have no idea that two Australians are in our vehicle and three Americans are not far behind. Apparently one key to staying alive here is to avoid the Americans.

I spot Diana, John and Judy's dusty blue vehicle 100 metres behind us, trailing along the side of the road. I wonder if they are okay. Muslim tries to ring them but he can't get a signal. Damn that mobile phone! At least the checkpoints aren't that far apart, two or three kilometres at best. That's a distance I can easily run if I have to. *God. What a thought!*

The US troops are an intimidating sight. I'm used to being around military but I'm not used to staring back at a fully armoured turret

charging after me. Our mini-van would be cut to shreds if they decided
to arc up their 50 calibre heavy machine guns and 40 mm grenade
launchers. We sit in deathly silence and wait. I don't think any of
us even exhales. Forget the Taliban, Al Qaeda, drug cartel syndicates
and various opportunists who routinely attack travellers on this road.
These US troops are far more terrifying. I guess generally that's a
good thing but not at the moment.

It seems like an eternity, but I wait and think. I wait for an explosion and
I think of Kerry, who has completed two tours of duty in Afghanistan.
I reckon at some point he must have driven in a similar convoy, only
months before. It is sobering to think of Kerry in such a dangerous
zone. It is one thing to sit back home and 'know' your husband is in a
hostile environment but to actually see it for yourself brings home its
reality. *And* to be travelling similar routes, knowing that one wrong
move by either the US troops or our driver, could be end me.

Somewhere in these thoughts it dawns on me too, that our tyres and
the weight of our vehicles can trigger roadside improvised explosive
devices (IEDs), common in these parts. Roadside bombs cause 75
per cent of casualties to coalition forces in Afghanistan. I notice our
driver is careful to drive in the tracks of the jingle trucks. Thank
goodness, I tell myself, we have experienced guides who know how
best to avoid such hazards. Here's a place where overtaking is easy,
vmm, vmm, vmm, the Americans flash past. I breathe a sigh of relief
when I see the last of the Humvees. They thunder down the road and
disappear into the next tunnel. Our driver falls in with the merging
traffic as Muslim tells me that the US troops are not the only targets
here. Bandits, kidnappers and insurgents frequently travel this road
and ambush anyone they see as even remotely suspicious or valuable.
They overtake vehicles or run vehicles off the road, then either
kidnap their occupants if they think they'll get some money for them,
or if it's not money they're after they may brutalise, rape or even kill
their victims, depending on the purpose. It's a bit like *Mad Max 2*
really. An Australian blockbuster film that depicts a community of
settlers defending themselves against a roving band of marauders,

violent battles and chase scenes set on the backdrop of Australia's vast desert landscapes. Seeing the expression on my face, Muslim explains to Chris and me that as our guide, he is actually more at risk of being harmed than we are.

'If they find me helping foreigners then I will surely be punished and even killed,' he says. 'If they don't kill me, perhaps they may hack off my ears and part of my nose. There is no discrimination.'

It is a sobering thought. I rub my nose, which is still there. A car zooms by. I'm not sure what to say next. 'I try not to think about such things, Muslim,' I mutter. He agrees that it is best not to dwell on all the 'what ifs'.

'We will be fine – *Insha'Allah*,' he smiles.

'*Insha'Allah*,' I quietly repeat.

I have never seen anything so terrifyingly beautiful as this part of the journey! The landscape that engulfs us is incredible. We are ringed by magnificent cliffs that plunge into small valleys. It's difficult to know where one mountain ends and the next begins. The stone face is a real palette of colour. Gun-metal grey tones are softened against paler shades of grey then splashed with earthy tones of the darkest brown, rusty reds, pink and creamy beige; and all this is framed against caramel and honey tones.

As we hug the hairpin corner, I press my face against the window and marvel at the 600-metre roadside drop. Adrenaline courses through me. Looking at heights like that gives most people vertigo. It makes them dizzy but not me, I enjoy heights. I imagine swooping and soaring above this impressive landscape in a hang-glider; what an exhilarating experience that would be. Imagine the tourism potential of these parts! The road coils around the mountain like a giant snake. My eyes survey the aqua stream that dips, plunges and twists its way along the banks of the road. I make out the white breaks of icy water that crash into jagged rock formations jutting out from several of the river bends. Further downstream, I see the road snaking its way around the mountain and into another twist, another bridge, another tunnel. It's incredible. Here comes yet another hairpin bend! Beyond that there's a double-lane bridge supported by twin archways that allow the river to continue unimpeded. My eyes cross the bridge and follow the road to an opening of a tunnel and then the road is gone.

'In one single day over a two-hour period alone, there were a dozen or so accidents on this road,' says Muslim. 'Nearly all of them fatal.'

It was a sobering thought. The two-lane highway is barely wide enough for two cars. There is virtually no room for error.

'You can only go into the wall, over the edge, or into each other,' says Muslim.

'Great.'

What on earth possessed the Soviet military to imagine they could pass through this particular stretch and invade Kabul? It's bad enough now, but Muslim reckons that in those days, the road looked more like a goat track. The Soviets lost 15,000 troops in these perilous peaks. Many thousands of Afghans died too. Over 17,000 British troops and civilians were massacred as they beat a retreat from Kabul at the end of the first Anglo-Afghan War in 1842. The sole European survivor of that conflict, a doctor, rode into Jalalabad on a horse. The history of this particular area is incredibly interesting but amidst it all, an extraordinary amount of beauty. Muslim proudly states that this part of the journey is his favourite despite the fact that it is also the most dangerous. Being overwhelmed by its beauty, I'd completely forgotten about the danger. For the next few moments I don't want to think about Al-Qaeda. And then Muslim reminds me that the Americans almost caught Osama bin Laden escaping through the Tora Bora Mountain Range less than 100 kilometres north-east of here. How could all this beauty offer sanctuary to such a man?

I don't want to think about Al-Qaeda. I'll contemplate the possibility of a hang-gliding holiday in a new Afghanistan instead; one that is stable and can attract thousands of people to see the natural wonders surrounding us. Eco-tourism would explode, if this were safe. I rattle off all sorts of marketing ideas to Muslim, who laughs at my girlish enthusiasm for something that might never happen – but *Insha'Allah* it will. Every Afghan person I've met since my arrival here wants to improve his or her social and economic conditions. They want the same as you and me. They are hardworking people, intelligent and resourceful but caught in depressive conditions. Their struggle is unnecessarily made worse by the damned insurgents. I take another gulp from my water bottle. At least the bottled water industry is booming here. *That's alright so long as you can afford it!*

Sorubi is the halfway point between Kabul and Jalalabad. This place has an obscene history. It was previously the home of Hezbi Islami Commander Faryadi Zardad who, with his militia, captured and tortured people who passed through. According to locals, Zardad named one of his strongmen the 'human dog' because they kept him in a cave with a chain around his neck and released him to bite the prisoners and even to eat his victims' testicles. In 2002 the 'human dog' was executed by the Afghan Government. In 2005 Zardad was captured in the United Kingdom where he was living, and sentenced to 20 years jail for crimes committed during the 1990s, including torture. It's horrible to think that humans can be so decisively cruel to each other. Throughout history we have been shocked by the way people treat others. I just hope there's no-one else around here like Zardad. Two and a half hours pass without incident. We finally make it through the treacherous mountains and the township of Sorubi, where we stop briefly to purchase delicious red pomegranates (for Muslim's family) and to call Diana's mini-van.

'I still cannot reach them,' Muslim explains, waving the mobile phone at Chris and me.

'They should have been right behind us.'

'I will try again soon; don't worry. Let's wait here for them; they shouldn't be long,' he smiles then he turns the conversation to something pleasant.

'You know, Afghanistan is plentiful with some of the best pomegranates in the world,' He opens the bag and offers me one, which I accept. 'Take another,' he adds. They look mouth-watering.

'Thank you.' I smile. 'I tried these in China, when I was travelling around Xi'an with my neighbour Alyson last year. They're nice.'

'Oh, but these are the best I think, and quite cheap too,' he laughs.

It is slightly larger than a lemon but smaller than a grapefruit. It has thick reddish skin. Muslim breaks one open. Inside are deep red seeds, called arils, surrounded in pulp. You eat the arils.

'*Mmmm*, they're good,' I tell Muslim, as I wipe my mouth.

We sit there eating pomegranates, waiting for the other driver to catch up. I think I need a bathroom, but I don't let on. Muslim finally gets through on the mobile and says they are only minutes away. However, after being parked in the one spot for this long, we have attracted the attention of the locals. Several young boys tap on my window. Muslim shoes them away but they're persistent. A minute later they're on Muslim's side of the mini-van, at least a dozen young boys now peering in, and quite a few older men too. Muslim engages them until one by one the older men move away, disinterested, and the young boys begin to scatter too.

'I think we must get going now,' Muslim cautions. 'You are too interesting for them.'

'Yes, Kay, they might like to make you one of their wives,' Chris laughs.

'Very funny.' I poke my tongue at him then wail, 'Muslim, I really need to use a bathroom!'

Muslim shakes his head.

'Oh, Muslim!'

He says it is unwise for me to get out of the car.

'And besides, there are no toilets for you to use here.' He rings Diana to let her know we've had to move again.

My bladder is shouting, 'All I need is a tree on a quiet part of the roadside!'

As the mini-van starts up again, Muslim puts down his phone and reaches for another pomegranate. He breaks it open and passes some arils to our driver.

'We will stop at the university and give Diana time to catch up properly,' he says.

'Will there be a toilet at this university?' I ask. I am greatly relieved to hear there is.

'It's only another hour away,' I add, sarcastically.

Muslim instructs our driver to ease off the accelerator. He doesn't want to attract too much attention or run over anyone. I bite my lip, wishing him to just hurry up! Another half hour passes and with it the landscape changes dramatically. The mountains are now in the distance. To our left and right it appears completely desolate, like someone has ripped up all the grass and replaced it with dirt and sand. Every now and then we catch sight of a clump of mud houses that form a compound, or a cluster of martyr's graves. The aqua river flows along beside us, presenting a vibrant contrast to the sandy banks embracing it. Muslim suddenly stops speaking. He turns his full attention to our driver. Something is wrong. I can tell by his change of tone and the dark expression shadowing his usually smiling face. The sound of horns blaring from behind almost makes me jump into the front seat. Not those damn Americans again, I think to myself but I must have said it out loud.

'No, not Americans,' said Muslim.

I am almost too afraid to turn around. Chris, who is seated in front of me, moves ever so slowly to see who is coming.

'Definitely not the Americans,' he says.

I move my small handheld video camera slightly higher to use it like a compact mirror. Cautiously, I press play so that the image behind me is captured in the fold-out LCD screen. When the tiny camera finally focuses, I barely breathe at the sight of dark green machine gun-mounted vehicles coming towards us. Headlights flash on and off. The faces of the men behind the guns are partially covered by black fabric.

'Is it friend or foe?' I ask Muslim as I try to keep the camera steady.

'I am not certain,' he responds. 'Might be the Afghan army, Afghan police or bandits. We cannot be sure.'

I pray silently that they are not bandits and stow my camera under my seat while I still can. I make sure too that my head is fully covered and gently pull the material across the bridge of my nose so that only my dark eyes are showing. I hold my breath not knowing if it will be my last.

Chapter 10
The Taj

Muslim stares at the convoy behind us. There's a long silence as he tries to figure out who's on our tail. Slowly he leans a little closer to our driver who says something to him in Pashtu. Muslim is careful not to make any sudden movements. My dark brown eyes stare directly into his even darker brown eyes.

'It looks like Afghan Police,' he says.

'Looks like?' Chris bleats, nervously.

'Let us hope it is,' says Muslim just loud enough for us to hear.

The dark green machine gun-mounted vehicles close in on us; they are now directly behind us. We're unsure what to expect. The first vehicle draws level, checks us out. Our driver holds a steady course, eyes constantly darting to the side mirror. His knuckles turn white as he grips the steering wheel. Muslim talks calmly to him in words Chris and I don't understand. His steering becomes less erratic. I begin thinking about how terrified he must be, not knowing if this will be his last journey anywhere. I try to think of his name but my mind goes blank. The vehicle passes inch by inch then overtakes us completely. Another dark green machine gun-mounted vehicle draws level before it too passes, followed by another. Time stands still. These few minutes seem like hours. My throat is dry but I'm too nervous to drink. The convoy keeps moving in front of us until finally it disappears into the distance. I am glad to see the back of them.

'God is watching over us,' says Muslim, 'They are not insurgents.'

'Thank goodness for that!' I reply, breathing a sigh of relief.

We see them again, 20 minutes later, when we arrive at the next checkpoint. There, they have three men on their knees with hands secured behind their backs. The policeman doing the questioning has his pistol out pointing directly at the man's head. We don't know what's going on. We certainly aren't stopping to find out.

As we near the township of Jalalabad the landscape changes from desert to palm trees and brightly coloured gardens. It's so picturesque. I begin to see why Muslim says he would rather live here than in Kabul. Jalalabad has none of the urban sprawl we left behind, although it is a city nonetheless. We drive through its outskirts where I notice streets are lined with single-storey shops, billboards and roadside markets where the locals sell their vegetables and spices. Stray dogs scurry between the traffic. Honking horns sound off. The roads are populated with Toyota cars and a variety of bikes. Just like everywhere else in Asia, everyone is in no hurry. Almost everywhere I look I see reminders of past and present wars; crumbled buildings that have been bombed, burned-out cars perhaps once owned by a suicide bomber, and plenty of bullet holes in the compound walls we drive past. Nangarhar Province is no less dangerous than other parts of Afghanistan. That is my first impression. 'Things didn't seem nearly as daunting in Kabul,' I tell Chris.

Jalalabad is the entrance to the Laghman and Kunar Valleys, a leading trading centre, particularly with India and Pakistan. Most merchants trade in oranges, rice and sugar cane, which grow in the fertile plains around us. Within the city the people have a cane-processing plant and industry for both sugar refining and papermaking. Muslim says it also boasts the Nangarhar University and a medical school that Judy would, I'm sure, love to visit. Jalalabad is well known as a resort for monarchs and aristocrats but, like everywhere else in this country, it suffered a great deal during the Soviet invasion and the civil war. Now everyone is simply trying to rebuild.

'How many districts are there in this province?' I ask.

'Jalalabad is one of 22 districts in Nangarhar, which is one of 34 provinces in Afghanistan,' Muslim replies. 'We are mostly Pashtun here, although there are other types of people too because this road that we are travelling on is the same Silk Road that connects Kabul with Peshawar.'.

'So about how many people live in the province?' asks Chris.

'About one and a half million,' Muslim replies. 'You know, Jalalabad was once a notorious Taliban and Al Qaeda stronghold. Nowadays the Americans and the Afghan Army maintain a large presence here, so it is relatively more stable than other places.'

Taliban, Al Qaeda and drug barons have all had a stake in this part of the world and some years ago, black market organ harvesters were notorious for kidnapping young children here. Hundreds of children went missing. Many to become drug mules and sex slave, others sold for their organs. But in 2004, the Nangarhar provincial government worked hard to raise awareness across the province so that people would become more vigilant about their children. This campaign was reportedly successful and such kidnappings were greatly reduced.

'Those occurrences are now rare,' says Muslim.

Underneath the surface of any culture you will find the darkest stories that are almost too horrific to be told. After all, human beings can be so incredibly cruel. I shudder to think of those innocent young children literally gutted for their organs, like whales gutted by the Japanese in our southern oceans who claim it's all in the name of *research*. The ugly truth is that the whalers and the Afghan organ harvesters do what they do for money. It's all about creating wealth for those self-interest groups. And what's left of the *carcass*, both human and animal, is dumped for the birds and other species to feed off.

Who hears the children's cry before that last breath is taken?

Silently I sit contemplating this thought as the world keeps turning.

On the surface the scenery before me looks magnificent.

What lies beneath the surface is what frightens me.

Muslim is a virtual encyclopaedia of knowledge. He tells me a story about the water that we are drinking. 'According to a legend, the water from the Hozret-Ayub-Paigambar spa was said to cure lepers ...'

'I must tell Judy that one for her medical journal!' I laugh, holding my aching bladder.

'Soon we will arrive at the Nangarhar University and you can use the bathroom there,' says Muslim. 'But you should not waste time there because it may attract too much attention.'

Nangarhar is not for the fainthearted he says. We must be prepared at all times and follow his instructions without question – if we are to stay alive. I think of the insurgents waiting to ambush us. There are so many places for them to hide. Muslim informs me that many of the casualties are not from insurgents.

On 2 May 2007, 500 students from Nangarhar University protested against the alleged killings of six civilians by US-led Coalition troops a few days before. On that same day, just west of Nangarhar, Afghan and UN teams accidently killed 52 civilians in a day of ground fighting and bombings. Such incidents inevitably create tension between the foreign countries and the government of Afghanistan. Even President Karzai announced that his patience was wearing thin with US errors. Two days later, 4 March 2007, at least 33 civilians were injured and at least 19 civilians killed by US marines in the Shinwar District. The incident is referred to as the Shinwar Massacre. Reports after the incident state that Haji Ihsanullah, a member of a terrorist group, drove a mini-van filled with explosives into a US convoy. One US marine sustained injuries. Witnesses said the US marines responded with excessive force, firing indiscriminately at civilians on the busy highway. One local reporter claimed the marines sprayed civilians with machine gunfire even though they were not under attack. Sometime after the incident, an angry demonstration broke out in the region. Hundreds of Afghans blocked the road and threw rocks at police, with some demonstrators shouting, 'Death to America! Death to Karzai!' (President Hamid Karzai.)

The investigation into the incident later revealed that both the Afghan Commission and the US military supported the findings that US marines had in fact sprayed civilians with machine-gun fire even though they were not under attack. It resulted in the removal of an entire company of marines from Afghanistan. Compensation payments of approximately AUD$2000 a piece were paid to the families of those killed or wounded and a formal apology from the Pentagon was issued, and then dismissed.

'Some people do not care for foreigners because of these incidents. They may think wrongly that you are American,' Muslim explains.

'Don't worry, Muslim, I'll be very quick to use words like *mate* and *g'day* ...' I promise him. 'And I won't say *buddy.*'

On a more serious note, who could blame the Afghan people for distrusting anyone, foreign or otherwise?

At last we arrive at Nangarhar University. Our driver pulls up by the roadside. Chris waits with him in the car while Muslim escorts me along a dirt road lined with pine trees. I could easily duck behind any of them, and I hope the walk won't take forever. I listen to Muslim explaining details about Nangarhar University. It is one of the largest in Afghanistan with over 3500 students, mostly males, and 250 faculty members. Hopefully this will brilliantly translate to an abundance of ablutions for me to choose from.

Wrong!

Muslim enters the small toilet block first to see that no-one else is inside.

'Be careful of the open window and lock the door behind you,' he cautions.

I step inside and cross the once white tiled floor now covered in brown scuff marks. There are only two toilets. Muslim's right about the first one. It's disgusting. The second is not much better. A putrid smell hangs in the air. Faecal waste covers the floor, the toilet, the walls and I'm sure, my lungs. Its stench makes me dry-retch. 'Don't breathe, Kay,' I say to myself.

As carefully as I can, I manoeuvre my way over the muck and suspend myself mid-air over the toilet and pee until I feel my bladder completely empty. It's absolute relief. Then I carefully step back down and pull up my knickers. I push the door open with my elbow, carefully to avoid touching any parts of the wall any more than necessary. I reach into my bag for antibacterial wash and I scrub my hands thoroughly. I want to bathe in it! Instead I step outside and find Muslim waiting patiently. He says nothing as I walk towards him and avoids all eye contact. I don't know which is more daunting, the filthy toilets or the hundreds of male eyes that descend on me. Quietly I keep my head down as I follow Muslim back to the mini-van.

'How was it?' Chris asks upon my return.

'You really don't want to know…' I reply, pulling a face and climbing into the backseat.

The driver starts the engine immediately. He says Diana, John and Judy are minutes away.

'Did they stop for pomegranates?' I joke.

'I think maybe Diana stopped to take some photographs along the way,' Muslim responds thoughtfully.

Our destination is the Taj Mahal Guesthouse, located just off the Kabul-Jalalabad road. Our accommodation is about halfway between Nangarhar University and downtown Jalalabad. According to its website, the guesthouse is secure, comprising a guarded compound with 14 rooms in two spacious buildings. It has the only international bar in the region – the Bamboo Bar – as well as the only pool where the international community can sun, swim and relax without offending local sensibilities.

'Swim?' I laugh. What foreigner ever packs a bathing suit for a trip to Afghanistan!

I am hoping the Taj has internet connection so I can tell Kerry I've arrived safely. Keeping in touch by phone is almost impossible because I don't have one and Muslim's phone keeps dropping out.

Diana's vehicle is right behind us. We turn onto the dirt road that leads to the Taj. There are a couple of compounds down the end of the rubble drive; everything else looks as if it has been bombed or bulldozed. Our driver stops briefly to talk with armed guards and agrees for them to run a mirror under the chassis to check our mini-van for wires and exploding devices. 'Strictly routine,' they say.

The distant mountains are awash with pale pink as the sun moves through white clouds. A dusty haze begins to envelope us. The heavy gates are pushed open by armed guards who wave us through. This disturbs a stray dog that scurries into the bushes. We are directed to a parking bay. I climb out of the mini-van, knowing we won't be doing any more driving today. Our second mini-van pulls up alongside and everyone tumbles out – Diana, Judy, and John – hello! Diana is quick to busy herself at the rear of the mini-van. I hear her giving instructions to John, 'No Dad, ...', he picks things up then puts them down. 'Leave the boxes there for now; we'll just grab our cases.'

'Judy!' I run to her and we embrace like schoolgirls. 'I missed you!'

'Oh, my Lord, weren't those mountains incredible?' she hugs me.

'They were amazing! Muslim stopped for pomegranates and ...' I drift into a full description of events, especially about being tailgated twice.

As it turns out, the internet at the Taj Mahal is lightning fast but we have no way of accessing it as none of us brought our laptops. The entire hotel is wireless. Luckily we meet someone who can resolve this issue. Dr Dave Warner, a medical neuroscientist from San Diego, California. We make our introductions in the communal kitchen. Dr Dave is tall and solidly built. His hair falls well below collar length. He wears a pendant with an emblem of a squiggly man around his neck and his conversation is way over my head. Yet there is something very humble about Dr Dave. His kind smile puts me instantly at ease. And with my curiosity piqued, it doesn't take me long to learn that Dr Dave and his dedicated team of volunteers have been working hard since 2004 to get much needed education, medical and internet supplies to local communities; in particular, in Jalalabad.

On the afternoon of the following day, Dr Dave invites me to go with him to the rooftop of the Taj. He points out the Tora Bora Range, the Surkh Rud River, the Kabul River coming out through the gorge.

'It's *gorge...ous*!' I laugh.

This prompts Dr Dave to point at the ranges, and say 'The Spin Doctor of the Spin Ghar ranges.'

I giggle, 'You're so funny ... you must be Australian.'

'Hey, do I look like a convict?'

During the late 18th and 19th centuries, large numbers of convicts were transported to the various Australian penal colonies by the British government, many for petty crimes resulting from poverty. All my family came to Australia years later from Northern Ireland. Not a convict amongst us.

'Well ...' Dr Dave eyes me curiously.

Playfully I slap his arm.

'*Ouch*!' he feigns pain then points out a Buddhist cave system across the river, not far from where we are standing.

It is the same age as the Bamiyan caves in the Hazarajat region (Central Afghanistan). The actual Bamiyan caves are located 230 kilometres north-west of Kabul and are home to two monumental statues of standing Buddhas, carved into the cliff face in the Bamiyan Valley. They are listed as a world heritage site by the United Nations Educational, Scientific and Cultural Organization (UNESCO). The Taliban dynamited the two giant statues in 2001, claiming that they were idols and therefore against Sharia Law. Islamic, Buddhist and the UN perspectives contrast greatly with the views of the Taliban's former supreme leader, Mullah Mohammed Omar, who ordered the destruction of the relics.

Egyptian Muslim intellectual Fahmi Howeidy: *'Islam respects other cultures even if they include rituals that are against Islamic law.'*

Iran News: *'Islam has never preached the destruction of objects that embody the belief and history of millions of people throughout the world.'*

Phra Wipatsri Dhamaramo, secretary to Thailand's chief Monk: *'As Buddhists we are not allowed to criticise anyone, but good religious people should not destroy world heritage.'*

United Nations Secretary General Kofi Annan: *'The unique and irreplaceable relics of Afghanistan's rich heritage, both Islamic and non-Islamic, is the strongest foundation for a better, more peaceful and more tolerant future for all its people. Destroying any relic, any monument, any statue will only prolong the climate of conflict. After 22 years of war, destruction and drought, there can only be one priority for the government: to rebuild the country, to renew the fabric of society, and to relieve the immense suffering and deprivation of the people of Afghanistan.'*

According to Dr Dave, there are many Buddhist relics in the caves along the Silk Road and in Jalalabad itself. I find this intriguing. Some we saw coming into Jalalabad, caves with a history dating back to Alexander the Great, who invaded Afghanistan more than 2500 years ago. The mountains surrounding Jalalabad and eastern Afghanistan are one of the great centres of Buddhist culture from centuries 2–7 CE, a treasure trove to anyone interested in Buddhism. It is why thousands make pilgrimages from every corner of the earth to visit its many holy temple sites.

The city of Hadda was once visited by Buddha and boasts thousands of stupas and Buddha relics, including the staff, robe and one of Buddha's very own teeth. It's fascinating! It's history. It's more than just stones despite Mullah Omar saying that's all they were!

Chris joins us on the rooftop and becomes intrigued with Dr Dave's commentary on the caves and the possibility of there being some really impressive, undiscovered archaeological finds. Then the conversation shifts to a special project known as the Fab Lab (Fabrication Laboratory).

'Amy Sun is the team leader for the Fab Lab but she's not here so you're stuck with me,' says Dr Dave casually. 'This is our not-so-secret weapon ...'

Intrigued, I direct the lens of my video camera to where Dr Dave is pointing. It's an abandoned building beyond the razor wire.

'It looks abandoned but looks in this giant sandpit are often deceiving,' Dr Dave points out, 'This is the Fab Lab, a small-scale workshop with an array of computer controlled tools that aim to make almost anything ... and has the ability to literally transform lives!'

'Okay, I'm totally confused,' I say in response.

'Not totally ... that comes later,' Dr Dave laughs.

Incredibly I learn that the building below is a hub of creative activity. The concept was developed by the Massachusetts Institute of Technology (MIT) to advance knowledge and to educate students all over the world in science, technology, and other areas. High speed internet is being made readily available to the local community of Nangarhar. So the idea is simply to develop communities that can be powered by technology at the grassroots level.

'Khyber Pass meets the Cyber Pass,' Dr Dave eloquently adds. 'We can use communications and information technology to empower people to make informed decisions about their quality of life.'

'I don't get it,' I respond still confused. 'Are you're saying that instead of fighting the war with guns, we would be better to link people to people through modern technology?'

'No,' he grins. 'You're saying that.'

Like a school girl I poke my tongue at him.

'One objective is to give Afghans access to the internet so they can learn new ways and enhance current skills that will help them create new opportunities.'

Example: an Afghan man might be interested in medicine but has absolutely no access to any information on the subject. A simple Google search for 'health' puts a wealth of information instantly at his fingertips.

'We're able to introduce people living in remote villages to the rest of the world through the internet and that's pretty significant when you consider that many of them live their entire lives in the one village.'

'That's amazing!' I say as I begin to calculate the endless possibilities of the Fab Lab.

'Exciting hey,' says Dr Dave. 'And that's not even the half of it.'

Those working in Afghanistan know that it is a country that needs a multi-layered approach, combining military, diplomatic, civilian and humanitarian support. The Taj Fab Lab in Jalalabad is one of 40 such labs around the world, all of which are established with minimal funds and sustained by eager volunteers. These volunteers present a very strong argument that the Fab Labs are a compelling alternative to the current model of foreign aid – much of which attempts to throw money at the problems. Just look at Africa. Billions of dollars have been given to countries in Africa as an initiative to help restore their failing economies. But the giving of 'loans,' which these countries will never be in a position to repay, is hardly an effective strategy for reducing poverty. Africa is no better off than it was a decade or two ago. I could go on and on about our governments wasting foreign aid and failure to ensure aid accountability but that's a whole other story.

Since the opening of Jalalabad's Fab Lab in 2008, as many as 240 local residents access the facility on a daily basis. They are learning to become entrepreneurial and innovative. They are being educated in how to develop economic fundamentals and to make choices that will affect them personally and their community. They are doing all of this in a secure environment and it is giving back hope to the community.

So if local Afghans can advance their skills and knowledge quickly, in order for them to tackle more complex issues, then they will further develop a highly skilled, local workforce.

'I think I get it,' I say to Dr Dave.

'Don't think too hard!' he laughs. 'Just absorb!'

I laugh too as I watch him make circling motions around my head with his hands.

Fab Labs in Jalalabad are creating a range of opportunities; local telecoms infrastructure, prosthetic limbs, and products that can be made locally and sold locally. Then there are the improvements being made to existing services like the public library, where Fab Labs are making bookcases and creating study areas and providing much needed training so locals can gain desperately needed skills. All this will help rebuild Afghanistan. And why not? Herders in northern Norway erected a telecommunications network to track their sheeps' wanderings with radio antennas and electronic tags. Villagers in Ghana harnessed solar power to make electricity to cook food rather than relying on firewood. Fab Labs in South Africa are creating simple internet-connected computers that hook up to televisions and cost just 10 dollars each. With technology, anything is possible. It's almost mind boggling to think of mud brick villages in the remote regions of Afghanistan having access to wireless networks. Even more mind boggling to think that the Fab Labs are able to shoot high speed internet to people all over Jalalabad using not much more than a pile of wood and chicken wire. The idea being to get as many people in the country to access online educational, medical, and other vital resources. Imagine if a local midwife in a remote village is able to access lifesaving, instant online medical advice? Perhaps the rate of infant fatalities could be drastically reduced.

'But it all takes money,' says Dr Dave. 'So if you have some lying around we need it.'

The Taj Fab Lab has very little funding to maintain its operations. After talking with Dr Dave, I'm thoroughly convinced that these Fab

Labs offer long-term solutions in Afghanistan. Clearly they are making significant inroads. (See more at: http://fablab.af/)

Never doubt that a small group of thoughtful committed citizens can change the world; indeed, it's the only thing that ever has. - Margaret Mead, an American anthropologist.

After our discussion on the roof, Dr Dave led us back downstairs to the kitchen. This is where I met Todd Huffman, a young man from Arizona who, on his web profile, lists his interests as: neuroscience, molecular biology, cryonics, body modification, reality hacking and disco. Todd has a Masters Degree in Computational Biosciences, a Graduate Certificate in Entrepreneurship and Innovation Studies, and a Bachelor Degree in Neuroscience. I've never met anyone like him and probably won't again. The guy's a genius! But it is his simple life philosophy that I find most appealing: 'Don't wait until you're fully qualified to do something before starting down that road. If you want to do something find some small thing you can do, just do it. Learn by doing. Get qualified later'. Todd offers our group the use of a spare laptop so we can connect to the internet. Since my travel companions are suffering mild internet withdrawals, poor Todd won't see his laptop again for the whole time we are here. *Hello Kerry, I love you. Tell the kids I'm safe.*

The Taj Mahal Guesthouse, or simply the Taj as it is affectionately known, is a great place for foreigners. While relaxing at the Bamboo Bar with Judy, I meet many interesting people. Like Joseph Daniel Mooney from Guatemala.

'Just call me Dan,' he says.

Dan has the typical physical features that reflect his Spanish ancestry- fine dark hair and light olive skin. He has warm brown eyes and, as Judy agrees, is most charming. We hit it off instantly and as the night wears on I learn that Dan works with a British NGO 'POM354' founded by James Brett (the founder of Pomegreat), who is working with Afghan farmers to replace their heroin-producing poppy fields with pomegranates. His aim is to turn Afghanistan into the world's largest pomegranate orchard.

It's a fascinating story.

'You should come to Guatemala,' Dan invites. 'It's an amazing place too and I can be your guide.'

Judy agrees, having been there on holidays.

'Maybe we will.' I smile at Judy who nods. I've never been to South America. We sit and chat with Dan about all the things he is doing and all that we have yet to do. It's a comfortable way to spend an evening in a war zone.

Since there aren't any Afghan people at the bar, Judy and I opt for a little Western freedom as a reward for having spent so much of our time adopting local customs and wearing a headscarf all day long. Throwing off our scarves and donning our Western clothes, we feel liberated. I put on some lip gloss and Judy perfumes her wrists. We sit sipping cool lemonades with just a hint of gin. What a pleasant way of getting rid of the dust in our throats. We toast another successful day.

Our delightful bartender, Tim Lynch, is in fact the Executive Vice-President of Vigilant Strategic Service Afghanistan (VSSA) and a former 16-year veteran US marine. He has *Semper Fidelis* written all over him or as the marines do say: 'Semper fi – Always Faithful'.

During the evening I learn that Tim has spent the last several years working in some of the hottest spots in Afghanistan. He's pretty much seen it all and more than likely, a fair bit he'd have preferred not to have seen. He has a fairly simple view on life in Afghanistan; 'Everyone's fighting for different reasons. Sometimes they work together, sometimes they don't. If they 'succeed' in kicking us out of Afghanistan, they will probably end up fighting each other.'

He's a family man with, judging by the photos, three gorgeous-looking children now adults, Megan, Kalie and Logan, a photojournalist who runs photography workshops in Nangarhar. Tim is a no-nonsense-kind-of-guy who'd be right there for you in a jam. Instantly likeable, and not just because he resembles the stereotypical blue-eyed, muscle -bound fighting machines that girls drool over in action movies. Tim has a gentle and caring streak and talks about the importance of nurturing the children, educating them, playing with them, showing them that we are not a threat or here to hurt them.

'They are Afghanistan's future,' he says.

At night Tim's team will be working the perimeter of the Taj so we can all sleep easier. If all hell breaks loose, I certainly won't be running to the bomb shelter located in the basement of the Taj. Given Tim's extensive arsenal of high powered weapons, and that I am familiar with some of them, I'll be right on his heels to help keep intruders out, if need be.

I make a gaffe when introducing John to Tim. I introduce John as 'ex-marine', which is how one would introduce someone who had once served in our elite Special Forces Units ('ex-SAS').

'We don't have ex-marines in our marine corps, Kay,' says Tim, his tone earnest.

I quickly apologise. 'Sorry, Tim. I meant no offence.' Then I bite my tongue to prevent adding an enthusiastic '*Ooh-rah*!'

John tells Tim how he fought in Korea, a real bloody battle. There, 36,516 US soldiers were killed, 92,134 wounded, 8176 listed as Missing in Action (MIA) and 7245 made Prisoners of War (POWs). Unfortunately few people know anything of the Korean War other than what they've seen on *M*A*S*H*. (An American television comedy series based on a medical drama/black comedy set in a Mobile Army Surgical Hospital).

'Man, there was some heavy shit there,' says Tim, as impressed with Papa John as we all are. He and John have a lot in common despite the fact that they are generations apart. There is tremendous camaraderie between marines and former (not 'ex') marines.

'Once a marine, always a marine,' says Papa John.

For the next two hours I sit perched on a wooden stool at the Bamboo Bar thoroughly engrossed in the conversations encircling my ears. It feels incredibly satisfying to not only witness but actually be part of this mini universe of interesting and creative individuals, all working with a common aim – to help the people of Afghanistan. In the centre of it all, Tim Lynch stands like the sun god, with everyone else gravitating around him. What an amazing man with a tremendous knowledge of regional politics and security. These are two things which I am deeply interested in and Tim has an obvious understanding of how things really are in Afghanistan. Most of which is not as unsafe as the media and embassy would have us believe.

'So long as you don't go out of your way to attract attention or look for trouble, you'll probably be okay,' he tells me.

'That's not what the embassy says.'

In fact, all the notices I'd read warn of imminent danger for anyone who dares venture outside a 'secure compound'. According to Tim, many Embassy staff lack true situational awareness because they rarely venture outside themselves! When they do, it is like a full-scale military operation. (This is later confirmed by someone working in the US Embassy who told me that they had never been outside the compound in the three years they'd been posted in this country. They only ventured out when it was time to catch a plane and even then, always under military escort.)

Through Tim, Dr Dave, Todd and a quietly spoken Canadian named Dan, I learn more in the space of a few hours than I did in the months leading up to my arrival with in-country foreign officials. I learn that there is not a car bomber waiting at every corner nor is there an insurgent lurking behind every shadow. I learn that most Afghans are grateful for any help they can get so long as their culture, elders and religion are respected. The majority of people are peaceful. Most are glad to be rid of the Taliban Government. Most are tired of hearing about Al Qaeda because it distracts the world from seeing the real Afghan people; those who don't kill others, don't become suicide bombers and don't hate all foreigners.

I learn that there are tremendous things happening in this dusty part of the world that people back home would never believe possible. I want to know so much more.

'Stick around, kid, and we'll make your head spin,' Dave laughs.

Given that our room is right next to the Bamboo Bar it's a relief to Judy and I that the Taj guests aren't night owls. After 11 pm all goes quiet, which is fine by me because there's nothing worse than being kept awake all night when you have to make an early start. I think everyone at the Taj is in the same boat. They all have to be somewhere early in the morning, so 'lights out after 11 pm' is an unspoken rule.

Over the coming week we have so many things planned, including the Women's Healthy Families Seminar, several art and computer workshops at a girls school and the delivery of my books from Australia to the Nangarhar women's prison and the Nangarhar University. We are also supposed to visit a number of other projects too and tour four poultry farms that have received funding from Diana's local Rotary club (Mesa, Arizona). It is a hectic schedule but we are all excited.

Next morning Judy gets up at 6 am to take a shower and I am up and ready to jump in when she is done. I am so eager to be heading outside the compound. We haven't been outside the wire since we arrived in Jalalabad. My feet are itching to get out there. This journey through Afghanistan has begun to mean so much more to me then a mission to deliver life-changing opportunities and aid to people devastated by war. I can feel myself getting emotionally stronger, more confident and certainly more courageous to really live!

Today we're playing chicken!

Chapter 11

Playing Chicken

I n their quest for self-sustainability, Afghans have achieved many significant milestones over the last decade. They have elected a president, introduced free elections and independent-minded legislature (albeit with some controversy), engaged the international community with openness and sincerity, rehoused millions of refugees returning from Pakistan, rebuilt many of the institutions that were destroyed by war, reopened universities to encourage higher education and they have importantly introduced a generation of children, including girls, back into schools all over the country. All of these efforts have been driven by the Afghan people's strong desire to become independent and sustainable. Of course it's not a perfect system but what system is?

Most people back home are harshly critical of Afghanistan. They think Afghans are either lazy or crazy. They think the country produces nothing but opium, refugees and terrorists. Of course, many of these critics form their opinions simply on what they've seen and heard on the news. They may be surprised to learn that the challenges Afghan people face, are not dissimilar to the challenges faced in our own Western communities. Many Afghan young people lack education and trade skills and find it difficult to access opportunities, just as young people in Western cultures are struggling to find their way in this very confusing time. A significant difference, however, is that most of our young men, our sons and brothers, are not facing the imminent life-threatening dangers of war.

Afghans are determined to utilise every available opportunity to get skilled, which they hope will lead to stable careers. Just as there are new opportunities developing in the West through government initiatives for young people, Afghanistan is also fortunate that many of its young people are now gaining greater access to education, training and incentive programs developed and supported by government and non-government aid. USAID provides apprenticeship programs in Afghanistan, so that some lucky young men can access on-the-job training in trades like tailoring, carpentry, metalwork, mobile phone repair and panel beating. Other aid agencies provide education and training in agriculture. The issue of gaining independence and freedom is intricately linked to developing sustainability. A main focus of the international community is to assist Afghanistan by putting in place a critical mass of infrastructure, markets and services to spur ongoing growth.

I read reports released by observers, like the World Bank, that encourage a more holistic approach to the current needs, with an emphasis on strong interventions that support and encourage development. Some are beginning to see signs of success with this approach in some areas but in other areas the *old ways* still very much dominate the way things are done and, of course, nothing is ever so simple. There are a number of factors that make the quest for new trends challenging; for example, the eradication of opium production in all of Afghanistan. Opium is still the main source of income for many communities despite the counter-narcotics programs established in 2005 that promote alternative farm development. Switching from opium production to other non-illicit produce is yet to really take off because farmers know they can make fast money growing opium (poppies) over alternate non-illicit crops. For every dried kilo of opium they might stand to make between AUD$40 to AUD$100. Naturally, the price is dependent on quality but regardless of quality, drug barons are more than willing to *help out* desperate communities by cutting quick cash deals.

You plant it, you sell it and you're done. But the farmers are getting just enough fast cash to buy meagre amounts of food to keep their families from starving. They're not the ones driving around in the flash cars and living in mansions. Like the heroin addicts, the poppy farmers just get enough to keep them coming back because they're unable to access an alternative. This AUD$65 billion dollar industry is thriving even with the International Forces embedded in Afghanistan. Isn't the situation supposed to be improving?

There was not always such a level of desperation or despair in Afghanistan. From the mid-1960s to the mid-70s many parts of the country flourished through the development of agricultural programs, parks, schools, major development of dams and canal systems and so on, all designed to create a rigorous agricultural areas and all of which were funded by USAID. Lashkar Gar in southern Afghanistan (Helmand Province) was one of those places. American aid workers transformed the province with houses and hotels, bridges and a hospital. The Afghan people who are old enough to remember have fond memories of America. In fact, Helmand Province was dubbed 'little America'. It was once a beautiful place to live. But then the Soviets invaded and the 'little America' concept ended. Everything deteriorated because no one took care to protect vital infrastructure regardless of who established it. The hospital that was once filled with state-of-the-art equipment is now empty. Its equipment looks more suited to a museum than a supposedly functioning hospital. Nothing has changed in 40 years.

Canals and dams that once held vital water supplies dried up. The land perished as a result and the salt content in the soil meant farmers were unable to grow anything but for the poppies that grow best in such poor soil. Poppies also require very little water so when faced with starvation, Afghan farmers turned to this crop as the only cash resource available. What we see now since the fall of the Taliban is the 'little America' concept being revived albeit ever so slowly. But in order to have development you need security. And in order to export non-illicit products to sellers, you need vital infrastructure. This perhaps best explains why the international community's assistance is needed as a matter of urgency. Once the security measures kick in the development should expand and so too should the entrepreneurs arrive, looking to invest in new markets. Among them, James Brett of POM354, the young British man I'd heard so much about from Dan Mooney at the Taj Mahal's Bamboo Bar. He is, according to Dan, trying to establish an alternative to opium production by way of pomegranates. After all, Afghanistan was once famous for its pomegranates, which were originally traded along the Silk Road to India and the Arab countries. Unfortunately, those ancient trade links are among the most dangerous in the world hence the need for security.

The pomegranate industry in Afghanistan is currently dwarfed by the billion dollar poppy-producing industry, but farmers have the potential of earning more than AUD$5000 per acre of pomegranates over the AUD$1300 dollars per acre earned from growing poppies (opium). In one year alone, the farmers currently growing pomegranates doubled their export quantities to what is now a multi-million dollar industry. The downside, of course, is that pomegranate production is a five-year investment. So in the short term, someone has to be prepared to sustain the farmers until their pomegranate crops can fully mature and yield results.

James Brett was fortunate to meet with over 200 tribal elders, who agreed to support the pomegranate scheme throughout Nangarhar Province. If they succeed, the program has the capacity to create a stronger, more sustainable economy and 1.3 million inhabitants will be opium free for the first time in a hundred years. To the village elders, James Brett is perhaps the first person most of them have ever met who comes to them as an ordinary man, not a diplomat, with a strong desire simply to see positive change. There are other entrepreneurs in Afghanistan like James Brett, who are making incredible inroads. With their assistance Afghan farmers are now exporting apples that fetch up to AUD$2 per kilogram, almost four times what they would in the domestic market. People are beginning to have hope. If they have stability then the resources will come, and with it, a restoration of valuable export industries that once sustained whole communities.

Major industries in mining and precious and semi-precious gems are slowly developing and Afghanistan does have extensive deposits of natural gas, petroleum, coal, copper, chromites, talc, barites, sulphur, lead, zinc, iron ore and salt. But understandably there is very little investor confidence. Once upon a time natural gas was exported to the tune of more than AUD$300 million dollars a year in revenue. Those gas fields, however, were capped during Soviet occupation to prevent sabotage by the Mujahedeen. The need to create greater sustainability on a localised level is of critical importance to ordinary families.

When Diana first came to Afghanistan, she learned pretty much what the United States Government learnt when it developed the 'little America' concept; that an average family needs to generate income and secure a food source. Through local families, Diana enquired as to any industries that might support these two critical needs, and enable women to gain valuable vocational skills and training. Contrary to what people may think in the West, women are actually allowed to work alongside their husbands, so long as it is within their family compound. Women currently undertake farming roles together with their children. They are the main tenders to their livestock. Though women are less visible then men in these roles, they are able to be useful and so make a valuable contribution to their household. Contributing income to the household increases a woman's confidence and involvement in active decision-making. At a community level, it helps expand the roles that society offers to its female members. Inevitably, men will continue taking the animals out to graze while women and their daughters will continue to collect fodder, nurse sick or injured animals, do the milking and feed the stock. It is as it should be.

As an aside, USAID is running some wonderful para-veterinarian training programs in Afghanistan where women attend classes in pharmacology, nutrition, disease identification, anatomy, and pathology. They receive practical training at rural veterinary clinics and they learn how to run small businesses through business management courses that prepare them to manage veterinary field units. A veterinary unit run by a woman is a great benefit to her community.

Poultry farming is also an ideal project that doesn't jolt the existing social encumbrances already placed on Afghan women. It is well-established in many parts of the country. It provides nutritional support to family members, as well as allowing women to learn vocational skills. It also gives older sons and husbands an opportunity to engage in the community bazaar and in this way it helps the family become gainfully employed.

Diana presented the idea of establishing several poultry farms for women to her Rotary contacts back home, from which support grew. The Mesa Sunrise Rotary Club, Mesa East Rotary Club, Jalalabad Rotary Club and the local Poultry Farm Association in Nangarhar collaborated and together they help to fund four new poultry farms operated primarily by women, with the support from their husband's and family. Two of the farms are close to Jalalabad but the third and fourth are relatively isolated. We will need to be very careful when visiting those.

Training and development in poultry farm management is provided for each of these families under the supervision of the Poultry Farm Association (supported by USAID) through a Rotary Matching Grant for AUD$15,000, designed to assist the self-sustainable programs, including veterinarian and skills training, ongoing support and follow up. But even with financial assistance, there are no guarantees in this harsh economic climate that any of these families will be successful.

On 23 October 2008, we meet with the members of the Poultry Farm Association at their office in Jalalabad. During this meeting we are updated about the progress made by our sponsored projects. All four farms are apparently working reasonably well, although further training is still required. Diana suggests we might be able to arrange for the Nangarhar University Agricultural Department to provide mentoring, additional communication and training for each of the families involved in the project. This is a welcomed suggestion. I try to follow the briefs that flow around the room during the meeting, but I don't follow it all because there is a good deal I don't know about poultry farming.

Muslim translates and I listen politely. One of the poultry farms has sustained losses due to bird flu. It has also been affected by some other unfavourable conditions to do with difficulties faced in everyday life. An additional AUD$1200 dollars is required to fully reactivate the lost farm with new feed, medicine and a new batch of baby chicks. The family is saving towards that goal but they barely have enough for food for themselves let alone the farm. These people are relying on us, who have come from half a world away, to try to help them. The feeling of responsibility is almost overwhelming but for Diana's commitment to offering realistic support over false hopes and promises. These farms cost AUD$8000 to establish if the buildings have to be constructed and another AUD$2000 for the first year's supplies, medicines, baby chicks, etc. It's a small fortune for most locals. Who has that sort of money aside from the drug lords?

As for the returns, farmers can earn a legitimate living and profits of AUD$400-$1200 dollars a month depending on how many chicks they have. The two most successful farms both had 2000 or 3000 chicks going at one time. There are chickens that grow up to lay eggs and chickens that are sold for their meat. The meat poultry farms are the most profitable but both types are essentially valuable to a family.

Most of the families who are engaged in poultry farming face many problems due to the lack of availability of modern technologies such as cold storage facilities, poultry vaccinations and the necessary training in the utilisation of modern agricultural and poultry farming equipment. Of course, when the batches of chickens are raised, the farmers have only one option and that is to sell them. The local market is unregulated and does not offer the seller reasonable prices. This damages the economy base for the industry.

I sit quietly in the corner of the room sipping hot tea but this time I pass on the sweets. I am sure that by the time I leave Afghanistan I will weigh at least an extra 5 kilograms. A pretty young Afghan girl sits opposite me against the wall. Her dark eyes smile at mine. Her skin is pale olive and smooth, not at all like the women we meet in the provinces. To only a female's discerning eye, there's the faintest hint of rose-coloured eye-shadow beneath her delicately shaped eyebrows, and a dash of lipstick too if I'm not mistaken. Her clothes are beautifully tailored in a fashionable three-piece suit in the palest of tea green and olive tones with a matching hijab. A young man dressed in a deep burgundy coloured long shirt over loose fitting pants (salwar kameez) sits to her right. He catches our silent exchange. I quickly lower my eyes hoping I haven't created a problem. Is he her relative or husband perhaps? Maybe he is the other girl's husband. She sits quietly behind a wooden desk and is impeccably dressed in a dark olive tailored salwar kameez with a contrasting white hijab, bordered with tiny embroidered flowers. Her intelligent eyes, framed beneath the tinted silver-rimmed glasses, quietly observe the men speaking.

I sip my tea. Through Muslim we learn that the projects have already enabled some of the families to make significant improvements to their living conditions. One home has installed new windows and a new carpet. While considered a luxury, windows and carpets are a necessity, considering how bitterly cold it gets in Nangarhar. In another household, each family member has been able to purchase a new set of clothes and second-hand rubber-soled shoes.

These problems are so far removed from situations back home, where folk struggle to make their lives better by purchasing big plasma TVs, fancy new cars, even bigger houses with two extra bathrooms, overseas holidays to exotic resorts and fine dining in world class restaurants ... I look at Diana scratching on the pages of her notebook and realise that this is more than just helping a family get on their feet. She is intimately involved with each family. She has taken on an enormous amount of responsibility. She becomes concerned with their other emerging needs such as medicine, school clothes and school supplies for children in the family, etc. It is more than just caring. It's a comprehensive commitment.

During the meeting, an invitation is extended to us to visit each farm, though one of the farms will need to be scheduled for the following day because of its remote location.

'For that farm we will need to arrange our security very well,' says Muslim wisely.

We are excited with how well everything is turning out and that the poultry farming projects are impacting significantly. At the conclusion of the meeting, as we are preparing to leave, Muslim makes the surprise announcement that we have been invited to lunch with members of the Spin Ghar Association. I glance towards the young girl who smiles ever so sweetly.

'We shall look forward to sharing more with you,' says the young curious man. His dark eyes look directly into mine.

'Come,' orders Muslim.

Silently I fall in with the rest of our group, making sure my headscarf is fastened securely. We head outside and within minutes are sitting in our mini-van following the other mini-van towards the centre of town. I have no idea where we actually are but it's somewhere between Chowk Mukhaberat (the Communication Square) and Pashtoonistan Watt (Pashtoonistan Square). As soon as we arrive we exit our vehicles and are rushed up a steep set of stairs and into a tiny room. We are accompanied by the two young ladies we met at the Poultry Farm Association office, plus another sister. I didn't catch her name but they said she is the second eldest and is equally as pretty as the other two. The men sit outside in the larger, more comfortable room.

Even though we women are more or less banished to the back room, we are still perfectly hosted. The room is clean and carpeted. A plastic sheet is placed in the middle of the carpet and within minutes it disappears beneath a banquet of food. We are served deliciously seasoned chickens with fresh fruit and vegetables and my favourite rice dish, qabli pulao, a local dish of steamed rice with chops of raisins and carrot. They treat us with great respect and try to serve us as much good food as they can provide. The meal seems endless and I am glad when the tea arrives and I can stop eating.

Our hosts are charming, of course, and without the men around, it's easier to relax. The three sisters are aged 14, 16 and 18. The eldest sister, Adela, wears the tinted silver-rimmed glasses. She is betrothed to the young curious man in the deep burgundy salwar kameez. He keeps popping his head through the door. Actually he startles us all each time he bursts open the door to ask if everything is okay. I get the feeling he's worried that we've been either kidnapped or are corrupting his young bride-to-be.

The 14-year-old, Pari, who smiled at me sweetly during the meeting, is interesting and though softly spoken she seems older than a 14-year-old girl, but rather quite a refined young lady. Pari speaks impeccable English and wants to get an education. It seems that she is fortunate compared to other young girls in Afghanistan. Pari talks of marrying for love, having a wonderful wedding and making her father proud. The musical quality of her voice and the way she expresses herself with genuine enthusiasm is delightful. Pari says her father is a good man and that he loves her mother very much. She hopes that her life will be just as wonderful. I wonder if she's ever heard the tale of *Cinderella*.

After learning that Judy is a midwife, Adela wants to ask some medical questions. She's a bit embarrassed at the start and has to rely on Pari to translate because her English is not as good. The burning question on the bride-to-be's lips is the obvious one: 'How do I stop the baby from coming into my body soon after we marry?'

Judy puts on her imaginary registered nurse (RN) hat and delicately explains that both Adela and her partner have to decide whatever is best for them.

'Her husband-to-be wants her to prevent getting pregnant so that they can work together,' blurts Pari.

This is quite a surprise since the husband-to-be seems a more traditional type. Prompted again for information, Judy explains that so long as a woman knows her fertile time, she can avoid pregnancy. A brief exchange takes place between the two girls. Adela lowers her eyes, while Pari boldly asks, 'Can't she just take a pill?'

Judy's eyes widen in surprise. She looks to Diana for guidance. Help! We are completely gobsmacked. I splutter into my tea. Shaking my head as if I'd heard wrong I stare at this young girl who waits patiently waiting for an answer, looking from me to Diana to Judy and back again. Are we supposed to discuss such things? Thinking we had somehow misunderstood the question, Pari repeats herself. 'My sister was told that you can take a pill which can prevent the baby from forming inside you. Is this true?'

'Well, yes ...,' Judy replies carefully.

'Are you allowed to take it in your country?' I want to know.

'Yes, if our father and husband-to-be both agree. They told us to ask you!' Pari says confidently. 'Some mullahs are also quoting the Qur'ān to encourage longer breaks between births.'

'Oh, well,' Diana relaxes, and the atmosphere in the room immediately changes. There is absolutely no fear of us corrupting these modern young ladies. Evidently they are already clued up.

'Adela's husband-to-be wants her to work first before having children,' the young sister presses. 'Most people have many children; particularly male children who will help support the family income, help with the farming and provide protection (against insurgents/ criminals). Others, who are educated or come from urban areas like us, may be permitted to use birth control measures. Her husband-to-be wants her to work with him for a while before children so they can become more successful.'

It sounds positively modern.

'Well, in that case,' says Judy, who goes on to explain the process of contraception while Diana and I sip our tea and listen.

There are so many things still left to discuss but not enough time it seems. The husband-to-be beckons and says we must leave. He allows the girls to drive with us as we make our way back to their village. We happily chat along the way through a series of twists and turns, until we stop outside a narrow dirt laneway that leads to their home. It's a nice part of town. Tall spindly trees line both sides of the road to give it a more up-market appeal. As soon as the mini-van door slides open, I get out and help the three young ladies from the car.

'I wish you can come to have dinner with my family,' says Pari.

'It would be lovely but we must get back to our compound, you understand?'

She nods.

Their menfolk must have concluded that we are trustworthy enough to extend the time we spend in their company because the girls offer to be our language assistants for our prison visit. They excitedly add that they are keen to go to the market and buy us material to have more suitable clothes made for our outings.

'I can make you more beautiful clothes,' says Pari.

'Yes, we can make clothes for you,' Adela smiles.

I have to admit that our salwar kameez clothing is less fashionable than their upmarket styles but for the work we are doing, it's probably not the best idea to look too well off.

'You girls are very kind.' I smile and lean forward to kiss them three times on alternate cheeks, a customary farewell embrace amongst women friends.

'See you soon – *Insha'Allah*,' I wave as the girls head down the laneway. I am looking forward to seeing them again.

In the morning we hit the road early. Diana, Judy, Chris, John and I talk about our families, worry about things that aren't going to go wrong and fuss about our equipment as the mini-van heads back into town. We've all shot so many pictures that our camera batteries are all flat. Diana is the only one with any shots left, and she's running low. So we ask Muslim to organise a battery search, which he does – through the busy marketplace. The street stalls really jam up the traffic. They are merely inches from our mini-van as we drive at a snail's pace up and up the road. Having lived in Southeast Asia I've experienced this sort of thing on many occasions. The sounds of horns honking at each other, the driver's stop/starts are all familiar to me. We are on the far right of the street and traffic is running on both sides of us, manoeuvring both forward and sideways. No-one seems to be taking any notice of the direction in which the traffic is supposed to be travelling. No-one cares.

My visual senses have been so bored by the dusty shades of grey-beige constantly before us that my eyes are instantly drawn to the vivid colours of paprika, cinnamon, chilli and other spices to my right. Rows and rows of big white sacks are brimming with colourful spices. Diana tells Muslim to stop the driver, so she can take pictures.

'Just a couple of pictures, Muslim …' she begs. He taps the driver on the shoulder and we drift to a halt.

A donkey dressed in a bright red coat pulls momentarily alongside our mini-van. He stands patiently waiting, lost beneath the outrageously coloured harness strapped to his tiny frame. He is then 'told' and gently eases forward, effortlessly, under the command of his owner seated behind him on a platform of wooden planks, loaded onto his wooden cart. *Camera batteries please!*

A few minutes later, Muslim finds a store where we can buy the batteries and, after making the purchase, we are back to ploughing our way through the twists and turns of streets that will take us to yesterday's laneway and to our three lovely sisters, who are, of course, waiting in anticipation along with Adela's husband-to-be. The girls greet us warmly with the customary three kisses and the husband-to-be gives us a broad smile of approval. The three girls sit in the back seat next to me and immediately start chattering, enthusiastic to know what we have been up to since yesterday. The husband-to-be sits up front with Muslim and the driver. I tell Pari and her sisters about the spice market, the little donkey in the red coat and the batteries.

'He was so small that donkey with such a heavy load to carry,' we laughed.

'Like some people in Afghanistan,' says Muslim who misses nothing.

Today we are visiting three poultry farms in and around Jalalabad. According to Muslim, the first farm is okay; we won't have any problems with it. Yes, he's right; this poultry farm is in relatively good shape. We meet the farmers, tell them how well they are progressing and move on quickly to the second and third farms. These are having major problems, says Muslim. They don't have chicks. And what's a chicken farm without chicks? Furthermore, the third farm is facing economical problems because after serious difficulties, it doesn't have enough money to re-establish the farm. As we head towards the second farm, crossing a bridge that spans murky dark green water, we drive through an Afghan Army checkpoint. It was once manned by two Taliban tanks. We are not stopped. On our right I notice a tiny school, which doesn't look like a school at all; it looks like a bunch of kids sitting in the dirt under a grass hut.

Further along the road we pass a park and then off we drive, along a section of straight road lined with tall cypresses on each side. Pari explains that the reason the place looks so desolate is because the Taliban cut down all the trees so that people (assuming soldiers) could not use them as camouflage. But since those days, the local people have planted new trees. I try to imagine how it would have looked with lush green gardens and sweet-smelling rose bushes.

I sigh.

Perhaps it will look that way again someday.

We pass through the Farm-I-Hadda area, once the home of the world's most wanted terrorist; it looks like a barren wasteland scattered with high mud wall compounds. Not a single tree in sight. Hardly any sign of life for that matter. Should I be concerned by that? The road, if you could call it that, is almost impassable. I sure hope the tyres don't blow out. There isn't a service station for miles. And so we bump our way along. But as we do, our companions become inquisitive about our personal lives. They want to know how it is that our husbands allow us to travel halfway round the world unaccompanied. How could we leave our children at home? Why we would want to come to Afghanistan at all? After that, it doesn't take Pari long to get into religion. I don't mix religion with humanitarian work. I guess she's just curious like all teenagers. She assumes that I am Christian; I say 'I'm not'. She then becomes even more intrigued, so I tell her, 'I respect everyone's right to believe in whatever they want to believe in.'

Not good enough. Pari wants something more specific. 'Do you believe in God?' she persists. Why do you ask so many questions, Pari?

Oh well, here I go: 'When I was a young girl I believed. But as I grew older I began to question things that seemed scientifically impossible. So now I just try to keep an open mind,' I reply as honestly as I can.

Judging by the expression on her face, she is unimpressed.

'I wish you to believe in Allah. I wish you to become Muslim,' Pari says in all earnestness.

Religious conversations bother me because they are usually sensitive and emotive, especially for the fundamentalists. I'm certain she's not the latter but I think I'll palm her off onto Diana, who has more tact when talking about such things. Muslim says that it is not for her or anyone else to try to convert us. That's not what Muslims do! Many Westerners think that Muslims consider 'those without faith' to be infidels. But I learn that many Islamic scholars discourage the use of this term and regard its use offensive. The Qur'ān commands that people speak kindly to each other. Sadly the term is used by Islamic extremists in reference to all non-Muslims. but this is yet another misinterpretation of the teachings of Islam or so I am told. In fact, the word 'infidel' was traditionally used by the Roman Catholic Church to refer to those who did not believe in the divinity of Jesus. *But don't get me started on the Roman Catholic Church.*

Our conversation is temporarily halted by our arrival at the farm, which again we visit fleetingly. Three visits in one day is rather adventurous, so we stick to the routine of doing an inspection of the compound where the chicks are housed or preparing to be housed, meet the family to discuss the challenges they are facing and then make a list, check it twice and say our farewells. Because of the remoteness of the farms and the dangers that constantly surround us, we are urged to make haste.

Back in the mini-van Pari is back to asking a thousand and one more questions as we head towards the final farm for the day. We pass several tall brick kilns that resemble giant anthills, some standing over five metres high.

'These are the houses where the people make the bricks to build walls and buildings,' says Pari.

They are nothing like the brick factories where thousands of Afghan children reportedly work 12 hours a day, according to a survey conducted by the Child Action Protection Network (CAPN). The report states that up to 90 per cent of 2298 children – boys and girls – who work in 38 brick-making factories in Nangarhar Province, do not go to school and are deprived of other means of education. The tall brick kilns, however, look as if they have not been used in quite a while. Pari says nothing about the factories.

Pari wants me in Islamic Heaven. She takes my hand and repeats, 'I really wish for you to become Muslim, one day.'

What can I say?

'Exactly how does one become a Muslim?' I'm curious.

She knows this topic by heart. 'To become Muslim, you have to believe in one God, Allah, who alone deserves to be worshipped. You also have to believe in Muhammad, peace be upon him, the Messenger of God. You must also accept all God's Prophets, including Jesus. Neither divine nor the Son of God, he too is a messenger of God. Having accepted all that, all that remains to become Muslim is to say the Shahada, believing in it with your heart word for word.'

'What is the Shahada?'

'I bear witness that there is no God except Allah, and I bear witness that Muhammad is the Messenger of Allah. If you do decide then you should say – '*Ash hadu anlla ilaha ilallah, wa ash hadu anna Muhammadan rasul ullah.*''

I try to repeat Pari's words, '*Ash hadu anila* ... what?' because I want her to understand that many Westerners respect the Islamic faith. Plus a tiny part of me also thinks that, in the event of being captured by Taliban, knowing the Shahada by heart might be useful. Content that she has educated me, Pari turns her attention to other things, like my family, where I live, what life is like in Brisbane, what Australians think of Afghanistan and why I want to be in her country amongst so much danger.

By the end of our conversation Pari confides that she is afraid for me. She says that she wants me to leave her country quickly because she does not want me to die. She is concerned that something terrible might happen.

'My country is always with war and killings. No-one can live the way they want,' says Pari.

'*Insha'Allah* we will be safe,' I smile.

'*Insha'Allah*, I hope so,' she replies.

For the next 15 minutes I am engrossed in a dozen or so conversations floating around the mini-van. We must sound like a babble of geese to an outsider, all of us speaking at once in Australian-English, American-English, Afghan-English and Pashtu.

We pull up at our destination. It is the poorest of the farms that we visit. Although it is clean and organised, it is completely empty just as Muslim reported. It is heartbreaking. They have run out of money and there are no chicks. Judy and I stand quietly to one side and watch Diana absorb the details of how this poor family has struggled to make ends meet thus far and are now uncertain about their future. I can't imagine what their lives are like, but I can see the deep furrows on their faces that are obviously caused by months of stress.

I peer out through the windowless pane from the inside of the building that should have been filled with chicks. A little boy about two-years old silently stands in the middle of a sea of orange and gold flowers, a huge garden area covered with marigolds. His clothes are covered in dust. Dressed in an off-white long sleeve shirt that hangs to his knees, he wears no trousers. The boy's attention is focussed on three skinny hens, scourging the ground around him for food. I pull on Judy's sleeve.

'Would you look at that!'

'Oh my ... it looks so beautiful,' she says admiring the garden that is so typical of Afghanistan, to have such beauty and despair in the one place.

As I discover, the marigold flowers are not planted purely to beautify this family's compound. Their petals are edible and often used to add colour to salads. The calendula extract is commonly added to chicken feed to produce darker egg yolks and has been used traditionally for abdominal cramps and constipation. Learn something new every day!

When Diana's meeting with the men concludes, we are invited to meet the women of the household. Again, the men in our group are required to remain outside. Muslim says they'll go wait with the mini-van. A young girl, about 15 years old, with a newborn cradled in her arms, greets us at the doorway of the main house. She lets us in. The three sisters, Judy, Diana and I remove our shoes and the young girl indicates for us to be seated. Behind her is a very dark room, which contrasts with her clothes that are the most beautiful shade of red.

Judy instantly goes into 'registered nurse mode' and asks to examine the baby. Most women love newborns and I am no exception. I beg to hold her too, a decision I almost regret when the baby pees on me. The mother is obviously embarrassed and soon I've got everyone fussing over me.

'It's not a big deal – really,' I smile at their overstated concern. 'I've been peed on many times by my own babies. Please, don't worry ...'

They hand me a wet cloth, which I dab on the wet spot on the front of my salwar kameez.

'Just lucky, I guess!' I laugh, as does everyone else, with relief, I think.

'Can you ask if I can use the bathroom please,' I whisper to Pari. Her delicately shaped eyebrows rise slightly as she makes her enquiry to the oldest woman.

'I can't make the journey back on a full bladder I'm afraid,' I say quietly to Judy.

It wasn't so much the poor road surface I was worried about on our return journey. It was more the dry riverbed crossing. Some of the rocks we hit were enormous and we didn't even have four-wheel drive. It was definitely better to return on an empty bladder, which Judy quickly agreed with. The older woman looks a little alarmed. I recognise the body language even though I can't understand a word she's saying to Pari. Quite obviously she's wondering how I'll cope with peeing in the dirt.

'It's okay, Pari,' I say softly. 'I've peed many times in the dirt.'

Pari giggles just like any other teenager back home. Her hand automatically reaches to cover her mouth. I'm led off to a small mud room that is so dark I have to wait a few minutes for my eyes to adjust. The old lady sets a small pale of water down on the dirt. I see the small hole she's pointing to, obviously the toilet. Judy waits outside.

'It's okay, Judy,' I whisper to her. 'It's nothing you wouldn't have seen in India.'

It's just a hole in the ground. I really am not bothered by the absence of a *proper* toilet, particularly since those in the Laos prison camp are pretty similar; a hole overlooking a stinky sewage pit and a small pail instead of toilet paper. Everywhere I go it seems there will always be small reminders of a time I'd rather forget. When my turn is finished I wait outside for Judy. Pari looks at us rather curiously. I think she's a little stunned that we are not bothered by our surroundings. There's no point telling her that I've been in worse places. I thank the old lady who flashes me her toothless smile. She's adorable.

Diana has completed her list and is ready to depart. We leave the poultry farm after an hour and a half and we head back to Jalalabad, hoping to arrive before dark. It has been a long day but an exciting one and I am thrilled that we are seeing so much of the countryside. I have probably seen more of Afghanistan than most Afghan people. We are very fortunate to have such an excellent guide, Muslim, and the companionship of those in our group, including the three sisters, our three princesses. They are sad when it comes time to say our goodbyes, but for safety's sake they urge us to hurry back to the Taj Guesthouse without delay.

I think of Pari on the way back to the Taj and our final conversation.

'I am so afraid for you,' she says pleading with her giant doleful brown eyes. 'My country is too dangerous ... I don't want you to die here.'

I don't want to die here either. I am quiet for the rest of the journey as I contemplate my situation. No matter how many times I pinch myself, it still feels so surreal that I am actually smack bang in the middle of a war zone. Am I meant to be here?

Back at the Taj, Pari's words are soon forgotten. Muslim says he will see us tomorrow. I'm not sure when because the departure times always change. Muslim says it is better to be unpredictable. Immediately he is gone I don my headscarf and together with Judy, head towards the Bamboo Bar.

'What a day!' I smile at Tim then plant myself firmly on a bar stool.

'Had fun did we?' he smiles back and pours our usual lemonade with just a hint of gin.

'It was amazing!' I reply.

'Hey, Tim ...' the young Japanese engineer calls to him.

Everyone always wants his attention. 'We'll chat later,' I say.

Judy and I strike up a conversation with an American man named Dennis Eaton, who happens to be teaching farming techniques at the Nangarhar University. The program he works for encourages alternative livelihoods and is sponsored by USAID. Dennis teaches farmers how to cultivate food crops instead of illicit opium crops. Like me, he is impressed by the eagerness of local people to be productive. When he admits that he is keen to inspect our sponsored projects, I race inside to drag Diana from her room. After the introductions are made she invites Dennis to visit one of our poultry farms.

'You'll follow us I suppose,' says Diana.

'Sure, we've got a vehicle.'

'A Toyota, I bet!'

'Corolla.'

Well, that'd be right. His small wiry frame would perfectly fit a car like that.

'Can I bring someone for company?' Dennis adds, 'It's okay, he's legit.'

'Sure,' says Diana.

It's just gone after midnight and everyone is in bed. Judy plugs her ears to muffle the sound of my snoring. I told her it wasn't me but rather a wild animal that tore through our room just after midnight the night before.

'You sleep first, Miss Judy, and I'll keep watch,' I tell her as I watch her push the tiny travel plugs into her ears.

She smiles then closes her eyes as I flick off the light. I shouldn't be at all surprised at how quickly she falls asleep. It's been a long day. I wonder what tomorrow will bring. I feel my eyelids getting heavy as I begin to doze … I wonder what Kerry is doing … slowly my eyes close … I wonder …

Sleep.

The night creeps on. Outside the soldiers are hunting down insurgents who bring their terror to the villages. The night raids are an unavoidable consequence of modern counter-insurgency warfare. The insurgents attack the soldiers during the day, as they pass through villages, then retreat to the fields nearby. The soldiers return at night unexpectedly. Some villagers are killed (collateral damage) while others are taken away blindfolded to be interrogated. Children are screaming and women are wailing. The night is filled with terror. I don't hear their screams. I am miles away and sleeping soundly. To me the night is uneventful.

The early morning sunrays creep into our darkened room through the slit of the heavy fabric that drapes our window. I deliberately left them slightly open at night, since Judy's alarm clock has decided not to work. I slept all through the night without a single thought of the insurgents. I bet our US marine host, Tim, probably thought about them, along with his vigilant taskforce of armed guards along the outer perimeter of the fortified compound. I feel safe with Tim around.

It is unbelievably quiet for a country ravished by war. I expect at least a stray dog, a bird or even a cricket to be heard from the surrounding bushes, but I am wrong. Assuming I am still asleep, Judy tiptoes to the bathroom. I lay silently thinking about Kerry and the kids, wondering if they are worrying about me. I hope not. I hear the shower running. It is so wonderful to have hot water. Not everyone has it in these parts. I wonder if today will be as uneventful as last night. Every time we go outside the compound we risk our lives. Every road we travel we risked being ambushed by insurgents. But I am optimistic that we will be safe. If Muslim says we should not go out then we won't. If he says we should leave early we'll leave early. If he says to leave later, we'll leave later. Muslim makes certain we never keep to any routine. He's being careful to leave no clues as to what we are doing or where exactly we are going.

By 9 am we hit the road with a small Toyota Corolla somewhere behind us. We've got two Americans on our tail; they want to check out the chickens too.

'Is that them?' says Judy, pointing out the back window.

'Yes,' their little Toyota Corolla looks so funny bumping along behind us.

We are going to Surkh Rud District of Nangarhar Province where there are about 1200 families in the village we are visiting. On average, each family comprises eight members, of which five are usually children or teenagers. Women comprise half the population of the village. There are primitive mud schools in the village both for girls and boys though they are terribly under resourced. For higher levels of education students need to travel vast distances to adjacent villages or the district centre. Very few can afford such travel. There is no medical clinic in the village, but there is a small clinic in the neighbouring village where people have access to limited medical facilities. For serious cases, people approach the hospitals in Jalalabad City.

Pregnant women have been known to walk hours in the hot sun to seek medical help. Others perch precariously on the back of a donkey if their family is lucky enough to own one. For some the journey is too long. Many barely make it to hospital and some never do. The people in such rural places have few options when it comes to accessing emergency medical care. Most either travel days to get help or die waiting for help to reach them.

The road is horrendous and all that surrounds us is wasteland. We pass by two men changing a tyre on their broken down vehicle laden with giant watermelons. *There's no RACQ breakdown emergency service out here!*

Our vehicle isn't made for off-road driving but when our driver suddenly leaves the gravel road, it is obvious that's what we are about to do! *Clang! Clang! Clang!* Then back. Our host, a lovely Afghan man with raisin brown eyes, apologises for the sudden discomfort. The fact that he escorted us from the Taj Mahal Guesthouse assures us that despite the isolation of his farm, we will be safe. I note that he has lost a limb. What's his story? I'm not nosey enough to ask. Muslim will tell me later. So instead, I turn my attention to the landscape. It is indeed desolate. We bump along the riverbed of Surkh Rud (Surkh

= Red and Rud = River), which is completely dry. The reddish brown water that usually flows in the spring and rainy season of each year isn't there for us. There is barely a single tree in the entire village. I remember again Kerry's words: 'don't go anywhere remote'.

'Is this remote, Miss Judy?' I ask while peering through my camcorder's LCD screen.

'Oh, I think it's pretty remote,' she says then adds ... 'Kerry.'

We laugh. I told her last night that he would worry about me. Why wouldn't he? Kerry had been in plenty of real life action in Oruzgan Province, where Australian Special Forces are based. Smack bang in the centre of some of the heaviest fighting in the country, supported by enough military fire power to obliterate whole villages, and yet to me, it was he who was more at risk than us bumming around in a dusty Toyota mini-van. Were we mad? Probably!

According to our poultry farming host, the drought has created problems for everyone. There are no crops to farm because there is no water to sustain them. No water. Most of the menfolk have been forced to head to neighbouring towns or Jalalabad City in search of work. No electricity either. If they could secure power for the area, they might create industries and establish local employment opportunities. Securing electricity for the area is virtually impossible without significant financial resources and the people are unable to excavate the deep wells on their land because they don't have the equipment to do so. The entire region looks as if it's been destroyed by bombs. Most of the housing compounds we pass along the way are primitively constructed out of rocks and mud. Muslim says the villagers are very poor, and the villages are in a constant state of rebuilding. This is hampered by limited water sources (an essential ingredient to housing construction). That's why most houses seem half-reconstructed. The people in these parts are Pashtun and they've been through a lot. Some are still missing, buried beneath the ruins of their mud houses or buried in the caves to which they ran for protection against the bombings.

Muslim tells me that our host lost his arm in a Soviet air strike during the Jihad (the Holy War). The people in the village still haven't recovered from those days of the Soviets, or the air strikes that followed 9/11. I look out the window up at the sky. It's a beautiful clear day. Not a single cloud or bird for that matter. I know there are at least three dozen unmanned aerial planes scanning the landscape from about 20,000 feet up. They have no way of knowing if our vehicle is carrying friendlies or foes. Unlike our soldiers, we aren't wearing any GPS tracking devices. It's not a pleasant thought that we could be vaporised at any time, however, at least we wouldn't be pre-warned. We'd just be dead. *Beats a slow chop with a blunt machete any day!*

Our poultry farm host smiles but says nothing. I wonder if he can read the apprehension on my face. His own reflects quiet reassurance. *What would my mother say if she could see me now?* He is dressed in a sky blue salwar kameez. It is clean and pressed. I don't know how he manages to look so immaculately groomed but he obviously takes pride in his appearance. We are fortunate to be travelling this road today with him. Few foreigners get to venture out this far from town.

I dare say, rarely would they do what we are doing. I can't help but think; wouldn't it be wonderful if more people could see what we are seeing and visit the places we are visiting? Particularly if those people were Red Cross or Doctors Without Borders. So many Afghan people would have access to essential services. *Damn those insurgents!*

The next hour's driving passes in relative silence. Everyone is hoping that nothing bad happens. There's nowhere to hide and nowhere to run. Some would say we're mad and perhaps they're right, but I still have faith in our host. He has after all survived the Soviets, the Taliban and so far, the Americans! Another ten minutes and Muslim informs us that we have reached the safety of his farm. Anyone who's been to the Australia's Red Centre knows how the red dust gets into everything. Same thing here, different colour. Grey-beige dust covers everything, from the rocks at our feet to the ground to our left and right. The mud walls of the family compound are dusty grey-beige, and suddenly our Toyota mini-van and everything else is too, even my shoes. There is no point cleaning them. Nobody here notices such trivialities. Before getting out of the mini-van I take a few moments to adjust my bright green and gold lace headscarf, a gift from one of the families we'd visited.

Then Dennis Eaton's Corolla arrives. He peels himself out, stares at the dustscape, puts his hands on his hips and says, 'I've been in some remote places but never this far out of Nangarhar.'

'Don't worry, you're safe here,' Muslim replies, though Dennis doesn't look reassured.

Without delay we are led inside the compound to where they house the chicks. Our ears fill to the orchestral sound of about a hundred or so tiny yellow chicks cheeping. It's a very good sign. Cheeping chicks mean income, which in turn means food for the family. Diana is smiling as we walk closer to inspect the building that, at some point, was probably the family's accommodation, now converted to a giant chicken coup. The walls are whitewashed and the window frames are covered with hessian bags, pulled tight to keep the dust and prevailing winds from coming in. The floor is covered in the finest wood shavings and everything smells clean. The chickens scurry across the ground, frequently stopping to drink from little plastic feeders positioned around a brick column in the centre of the room. Our poultry farm host and another Afghan man who helps run the farm watch as Diana bends down and scoops up one of the chicks. I carefully step around the room and film the three of them with my video camera. Diana explains to them that we will show the footage to encourage donors back home, in the States. They indicate their approval.

Following our inspection of the chicks, the men are asked to wait with the vehicles while Diana, Judy and I are invited to meet the women of the village. One is the female community leader representing several hundred women in the district. We are asked to sit together on a wonderfully clean Afghan rug that covers the entire floor area. Diana, is this the carpet you donated? We are served chai tea (to which

I am fast becoming addicted). We talk about the poultry farm and how it is benefiting the family and for a while it is easy to forget how isolated we are and the risks we have taken in order to meet with these families. We talk of dangers, isolation and chickens. Judy invites the women to our Healthy Families Seminar in Nangarhar. We have no idea if they will be permitted to attend. It becomes a side-conversation amongst themselves.

We enjoy about an hour with the women and are thrilled when both assure us that they and the women of the district will attend our seminar in Jalalabad. They are wonderful women. I can imagine my mother sitting and talking with them for hours, about all the things that mothers talk about. I so enjoyed being in their company. It is kind of sad when Muslim summons us, worrying about the amount of time we are taking, talking.

When our meeting concludes, we walk back to the vehicles only to find that Dennis and his colleague are gone.

'They were getting pretty nervous,' says Chris. 'So they decided to leave.'

Diana adds that they are on a tight schedule like us. Although I understand their concern, because it isn't wise to stay in any one place for long, I am a little worried that they have risked the return journey without an escort. Diana adds they have to get back to Jalalabad for other reasons. They are going to try and establish training support for all four poultry farms.

This is wonderful news!

Time to go. To my surprise, our poultry farm host announces that he will escort us back to Jalalabad to see us safely through each of the checkpoints along the way. If anything goes wrong, I have no idea how he can prevent anything from happening to us. I just hope he can. I sit in the back seat of the mini-van with Judy and Diana. Chris sits in front of us, with John. Boys' talk/girls' talk.

'We are the last of the intrepid travellers,' Judy jokes, noting that we are leaving the place where Americans are too afraid to stay.

Black flags flap gently in the breeze on the rooftops of most of the compounds that we pass. I find it slightly unsettling since being told the flags are a Taliban symbol, but there are no telltale Arabic writings on any of them, so far as I can see. I mostly keep my eyes on the road ahead, though I occasionally look behind. I try to do some filming but we bounce all over the road and it is difficult to keep the camera steady.

Reassurances echo in my ears. 'No-one will harm you while you are guests in our district.'

'Insha'Allah,' I pray.

We drive back through the main part of the Jalalabad township about an hour later. The streets are packed with cars, pedestrians, horse-drawn carts, goat herders, goats, stray dogs, rickshaws, barrow-pushing farmers, jingle trucks and honking horns. It's difficult to breathe. On the streets, pale blue burqa women walk in pairs. Pedestrians don't seem to mind mingling in and out of the maze of traffic. Turning a corner we make our way through a maze of turns as we bump along to the beat of an up-tempo Afghan song playing on the radio. I notice two men having a casual conversation, standing on the road, on a corner while the traffic carefully edges around them. They don't think to take a couple of steps to their left and stand on the pavement. More men … a group having an argument across the road; some sort of domestic dispute, maybe? They don't appear violent.

Our conversation is subdued in the mini-van. The dust and the exhaust fumes grate on my throat and my voice has gone too husky to speak much. John is coughing; he can't talk either. We are either tired or all pacing ourselves. Chris tells John that he isn't particularly impressed with Kabul, compared to Jalalabad. Diana agrees; so do I. I continue filming through the side window and most of what I see is covered with a film of soft grey mist. Exhaust fumes? Dust? Or smoke from the roadside shops? Probably a mixture of all three.

A little girl, about 11 years old, stands on the street, still amongst the chaos. She is dressed in a dark green kameez with a bright red scarf around her neck, hanging down to her knees. She has brown short-cropped hair and deep olive skin. I stare at this little icon. Her face turns, her dark eyes stare into mine as our vehicle momentarily stops to give way to an oncoming vehicle. She holds a baby in her arms. There is no sign of an older sister or mother. There she stands in the dirty street saying nothing, a snapshot memory. There are more like her everywhere we turn.

Further down the road, two cars overtake us. They are decorated with flowers; inside we see a bride and groom. Whoosh. Whatever next! It is the last thing I'd expect, a car wash! Afghanistan is one giant dust bowl! Why would anyone wash their car knowing it will be covered in dust again within moments?

The afternoon sun is beginning to set across the distant mountains.

It isn't the most glorious sunset I've ever seen but the golden rays are transforming the grey-beige that has engulfed us all day. We turn into a roundabout. Judy snaps it anyway.

Chapter 12
Nangarhar Women's Prison

My name is Humaira and I am a prison officer at a female prison in central Afghanistan. I was born in 1956 and grew up in a bright-minded family. I finished at the top of my class in secondary school (year nine). I am lucky to have been educated since most of the schools were completely destroyed during the war. By sixteen I was married and through the course of my marriage, gave birth to ten children. I had a medium-class life with my husband. I was satisfied with my children and with my life but everything changed after my husbands' death, after the defeat of the Russians. Those were the worst moments of my life.

Conditions in Afghanistan were terrible. With the war we were forced to move constantly from one area to another area in the hope of being safe. As a result, I lost my eldest son, who was 13 years old. Even now I have no information about him. I have no idea where he is or whatever became of him. This is hard for me to accept but I must for the sake of my other children.

I have faced a lot of problems in my life, many struggles, but I have never completely lost patience. I try my best to be as brave as I can be. I have my job. Even now we are faced with war and the situation is critical but my life is a little easier than some of those I know. I have worked hard and I am rewarded by my superiors. I would love to spend my whole life providing service to my country, my family and my people. Perhaps one day my son will find me. Insha'Allah. Now I have nine children, four sons and five daughters. My hopes are with them surviving the hardships that are yet to come. I hope they will see the example of my life. I hope they will see that we can never give up, despite the difficulties we face.

Nangarhar is a long way from Kabul, not only in distance but in social development. For me it is very much like going from the city where I live (Brisbane) to some outback Australian town where life is harder, there are fewer resources and the people are less sophisticated. According to Diana, *Outback Australia* is a perfect analogy for what we are about to face.

'Whenever I come here, it just makes me sad.'

We are about to go into the Nangarhar women's prison to meet those who are the outcasts of society. Unlike Diana, I have no idea what to expect apart from what I've read in the media. I bite my lip nervously as we wait for permission to take our mini-van inside the heavily fortified mud brick compound. I'm told that few Western women have ever stepped into this place. My insides are mildly churning. Do the women on the other side of the mud wall, just metres away, have access to clean drinking water, proper sanitation and education? Are medical or rehabilitative programs provided? Is there anything we need to do to help them?

The streets are lined on both sides with Afghans, mostly dark surly-eyed bearded men. I shy away from their cold hard stares. Not all of them are visiting prisoners. Some have other reasons for being nearby. They are watching to see who comes and goes. Among them are insurgents planning their next violent attack against the Americans who support the prison. Previous attempts to penetrate the perimeter security have thus far failed. But today they may succeed. No-one knows. I'd say if you let off a firecracker in the middle of the street, most everyone would die of shock. It's that volatile. I can almost hear the time bomb ticking as I watch the ebb and flow of traffic passing by. The donkey pulls the rickety wooden cart piled high with hay, an old hunched-back lady crosses the road in a dirty pale blue burqa. She could be wearing a suicide vest underneath. This one woman has the potential to kill dozens if she believes it's her destiny to become a martyr. The number of female suicide bombers is increasing.

It is a busy street and we are parked on the side of the road waiting like everyone else. Except that we are waiting to go to prison. A row of razor wire separates us from scores of men carrying food and clothing into the men's prison located next door. The security is tight and understandably so. Muslim says that the men's prison houses high level criminals, usually insurgents or those suspected to be insurgents.

Among the detainees are young boys, aged between 14 and 20, captured in failed suicide bombing attempts. Muslim tells me they are ignorant and uneducated. Most he says are trained in Pakistan, which is something the US and Afghanistan's military agree on. They also say that Pakistan is not doing enough to deal with this problem. The suicide bombers, who have failed in their attempts and have been caught, all keep to a common reasoning. They believe that they will be protected by Allah and only the infidels in Afghanistan will be killed or that Allah will grant *paradise* to them for their service to him.

One young orphan boy is only 11 years old. He was caught wearing a suicide bombers vest, almost twice his size, filled with explosives. He told the police that if he doesn't take part in the Holy War then hundreds of non-Muslims will come to their homes and kill them. He said that being a suicide bomber and being blown to pieces is the fast way to get to Heaven. He even laughed during this interview. This is what he learnt in the religious school he attended in Pakistan. Such a sweet-faced child whose mind has been muddled with such destructive notions. He is only 11 years old, but he hopes that when he grows up he can fulfil his dream to rid the world of all non-Muslims! These cowardly acts are abhorrent to Afghan people. Islam does not preach hatred or violence to others. These are gross misinterpretations as I am told. And the majority of those who are killed by these suicide bombers are not infidels and foreigners. They are mostly civilians of Islamic faith.

As a mother of a teenage boy, I find it difficult to imagine how anyone so young can be made to do something so terrible. But there are many young boys just like the 11-year-old imprisoned, who are brainwashed at such a young age. They cannot see just how illogical it is to think that one boy's death will change anything, let alone a dozen young boys' deaths. Or that the people they are hurting are in fact their own. It's so completely pointless and more than a little depressing when you think about it. I decide not to dwell on this.

After waiting a further 10 minutes, our driver finally gets the signal from the group leader in charge of several straight faced Afghan soldiers to proceed through to the *choke point* entry of the compound. (A choke point is a narrow controlled entry used to minimise the threat from attack.) The dirt crunches beneath our tyres as we drive slowly down the narrow laneway until we come face to face with a formidable figure dressed in combat fatigues. Despite the fact that he's wearing dark ballistic sunglasses, I know instantly that he is Nepalese. I worked with many Gurkha soldiers from Nepal in Southeast Asia. They are often used in the security industry as the majority of them speak fairly good English, are well trained in all aspects of security service, and are well disciplined, trustworthy and very committed to the tasks entrusted to them. His black-gloved hand signals our driver to a halt while his other hand remains on his primary weapon, a black M4 assault rifle. Seconds pass as we observe him speak into the small radio mounted in a pouch on the top left of his ballistic vest. The occupants of our vehicle sit very still knowing that any sudden movement at this point could be significant. Another minute passes. The Nepalese guard looks to his right momentarily and then back to our driver with a curt signal for us to proceed to the turning point further down the alleyway and to our left.

On reaching the turning point we are met by another Nepalese guard dressed in similar combat fatigues and told to exit the vehicle. It is at this point we meet Richard Boyed, an American Advisor of the Correction System Support Program (CSSP). His giant athletic frame strides towards us in comfortable beige cargo pants and dark blue polo shirt. He's wearing a beige baseball cap with an American flag just above the visor.

'Welcome,' he says. 'It's a pleasure to have y'all visit us today.'

I note the midwestern accent and then my hand disappears beneath two of his in a firm handshake. *Wow, what a grip!*

My first impression of Richard beyond his professional persona is that he's a family man. He just has an air about him that he is a loving husband and caring father. I feel very secure in his presence.

'*Australia?*' he repeats when I tell him where I'm from. 'My goodness ... well, you sure are a long way from home then too,' he smiles.

We stop for a few minutes so that he can brief us before we head into the main compound. We will probably stay here an hour at the most, just to introduce ourselves to the women and to see if there's anything they need from us. Then we will reschedule for a subsequent visit.

'Come on then.' He waves at us to follow. 'Let's go say hello.'

The sun's light shines down on us as we enter the compound, and are greeted by curious dark-eyed children, all with matted hair. They shamelessly encircle Richard, who reaches into his pocket and pulls out a handful of brightly coloured lollipops. I suspect it is a routine with which they have become familiar and I jokingly scold him for contaminating their tiny teeth with sugar. Their smiles, however, are no doubt worth every ounce of tooth decay in their little mouths. I ponder their existence. Richard is wonderful with the children, who are clearly completely at ease with him. They are instantly excitable and fuss around him, begging to have their picture taken. It's a joy to watch and such a stark contrast to those other little kids, not much older than these, who are detained nearby, like the 11-year-old would-be suicide bomber. The mind boggles.

'You know these poor kids have seen so much violence in their short lives. Some of them have seen their fathers beat their mothers to death, others have seen their mothers shoot their fathers point blank,' he explains, shaking his head at the tragedy of how they came to be in Nangarhar prison.

'Most of the women here are victims of domestic violence, although the state views their actions of self-preservation as premeditated wilful violence.'

I notice the women slowly making their way from the veranda, down the concrete steps and curiously edging closer towards us. They range from about 14 years to their mid-forties and are dressed in bright coloured salwar kameez clothing, shawls wrapped neatly around their heads. One by one we are introduced to the women through our language assistants. We learn about their tragic lives. Most all of them have endured horrific domestic violence. Among them a woman who had been tied to her bed for days and has the scars to prove her lifetime of abuse, but no-one cared. In an act of desperation, after her husband beat her within an inch of her life, she picked up the AK 47 assault rifle he had left by the door, pushed the barrel square against his chest and pulled the trigger. He died almost instantly. She and her children live inside the Nangarhar women's prison. She stands quietly by a prison wall, her children beside her: a little girl with scraggy dark hair and a piece of dark string threaded through the piercing in her nostril, and a cute little boy, with lovely brown eyes and a brilliant smile, who asked me to take his picture. What sort of man will he grow up to be? Will he continue the cycle of violence that has consumed his life? Or will he say, 'Enough'!

I smile at the woman, who shyly smiles back. Many of the women appear to be very young. As Richard informs us, almost all have been abused. Some have been detained for a decade, others less, some more. There are many reasons why women are jailed and some of those reasons are challenging to agree with when taken on face value.

Children as young as 12 can be jailed for refusing to be exchanged for property, or are sold by their male relatives to men old enough to be their grandfathers. They are often forced to work as slaves to the household and in the marriage bed. Some risk everything and run away. But running away is not accepted by law and the punishment is jail, usually regardless of the reason. In most parts of Afghanistan, women and young girls who run away from home or leave the home without permission are typically suspected of having taken a lover and can be prosecuted for adultery, even if they are raped.

According to the law of Afghanistan, if they cannot prove that they were raped then they must be punished. The penalties are harsh. Generally they are jailed, which makes them far luckier than some women who, in the past, were stoned to death under such allegations. These days stoning has ended as an official court ruling but still occurs unofficially. Nowadays women are usually just lashed then jailed. I wonder if Hillary Clinton would have contemplated taking her husband Bill Clinton to task with a big stick after she and the rest of the world found out he was cheating on her with his White House intern, Monica Lewinsky. But all jokes aside, Afghanistan is not an easy place and women are its most vulnerable. Some mothers risk their lives trying to save their daughters and end up in prison or if they are lucky, a secret refuge centre. But refuge centres are scarce. Many women disappear and are never heard of again. Those who might know of their fate, say nothing. To them silence is their best protection.

A large proportion of Afghan women are jailed for drug smuggling. Millions of Afghans are heroin addicts. It's a lucrative business. Many women resort to smuggling the drug to make money. Because of the extreme dangers they face getting across inhospitable terrain, weapons and drugs are usually smuggled by men but women are desperate enough to do it too. Most become smugglers in order to survive.

'We don't have any other income ... nor do we have any other jobs' is the common justification for drug smuggling in Afghanistan. 'Also the government doesn't provide any other options'.

One woman I speak to during our visit is widowed and has three children. She had no means of supporting herself and feeding her family. If she smuggled drugs, she stood to make enough money to save her children from starvation. She had made several successful trips across the border at Torkham and then into Pakistan, but she was eventually caught. In Nangarhar prison, she is safe for the time being. She no longer needs to worry about her children starving, being caught by authorities or raped by criminals. These women smugglers are not thinking of anything beyond their own immediate desperate situation. They cannot relate their actions to the effect on some young Australian who sits on death row in Bali, having been arrested with 1.3 kilograms of heroin strapped to his legs. Nor can she relate to the anguish of his family who live in a world she doesn't even know exists.

Afghan women do whatever they have to do in order to survive. They are no different to any of us, except that they live life more in the extreme.

In Nangarhar prison children at least have some protection in their informative years. Some arrive here at an early age, others are born inside. Then they are released when they turn 16. But what sort of life awaits them? Some may be lucky to return to family. Some, however, may find life in an unfamiliar world more of a struggle. Psychologically damaged and vulnerable, most are illiterate, most have no social skills, no knowledge of the law nor how to interact with people other than with other prisoners. They have learned frustration but not how to deal with it. They have learnt anger but not how to manage it. They have learned hatred but not compassion. They will seek acceptance from anyone who might show them some kindness, even Taliban extremists. This is a real danger.

What hope do they have of living normal lives when their version of *normal* is hardly that? Our visit certainly isn't going to make much of an impact on their lives because in order to do that we would have to remain in the country and help these children on a daily basis. But our visit will achieve something like *the starfish story ... An old man was walking along a beach where he came upon thousands of starfish that had washed ashore. Further on he saw a young woman picking them up and tossing them back into the ocean. Laughing at the hopelessness of her task he said she'd never save all the starfish, there were far too many. The girl replied, 'But I can save this one,' as she tossed another back into the ocean, 'and this one, and ...'*

We can only apply that same logic to the Nangarhar women's prison and hope that our efforts may encourage others in the future to assist the projects we establish. Today we will simply assess the needs of those detained. We will make a list of requirements and tomorrow we will go to the markets and purchase the additional supplies that we haven't brought.

'We can only do the best we can,' says Richard. We follow him as he continues to explain the reality of their situation.

We soon discover their needs are far greater than we anticipated. One baby suffers malnutrition; Judy doesn't think she will survive long. The prison commander agrees to call a doctor. He adds that he would be grateful for any assistance to secure the services of a doctor on a more regular basis. It's not that the doctors don't care; it's simply that their resources are extremely limited. The prison itself is relatively clean and spacious, and the cells are like big open dormitory blocks (3 x 6 metres). At least they are carpeted and the windows have glass, although the rooms must freeze in winter and boil in summer because there doesn't appear to be any heating or cooling systems in place.

'In the summer they bring their mats out during the day and rest on the veranda,' says our language assistant. 'It's a little cooler for them.'

We visit their new learning centre. I'd seen photographs of it before the renovations when it had a dirt floor. It is now carpeted, painted bright blue and it looks quite cheerful. I am amazed at the transformation. I feel really happy that the donation Kerry and I made some months ago has gone towards creating something so positive. It is still pretty bare; it needs to be furnished, but it is definitely a start. Six sewing machines sit in a row on the floor. No-one can tell us if they work properly because they haven't yet been tested. Diana gets busy making her list and says that it won't take much to fit the room with desks and chairs, a reading corner here, a sewing corner there and in between a crèche, a place where women and children can begin to have some quality of life. A young Afghan girl follows me everywhere. Her name is Nadia. She is wearing the brightest pink headscarf I'd ever seen.

'I see you've made a friend,' says Richard.

'*Salam.*' Nadia speaks in almost a whisper.

'*Salam.*' I reply and reach for her hands that I notice are completely orange.

'What is it?' I ask Richard.

'Oh that ... it's henna,' he laughs. 'They love that stuff'.

Our language assistant explains that hennaing the hands in middle-eastern culture is most popular. Usually it's done on the day before a wedding or some other special occasions such as Ramadan. Women will have their hands and feet hennaed with intricate patterns and symbols. I comment on how interesting Nadia's hands are because they lack the typical intricate pattern. They look as though she has dipped her whole hand in henna instead. She laughs and says something to one of the young girls who runs away.

'I will do for you,' says Nadia.

The thought of walking around with an orange hand is not very appealing to me and I try to tell Nadia that it's okay, but she insists that I must experience many things in Afghanistan and hennaing is one of those things.

'Oh great,' I smile and thank her as graciously as I can. *How long does it last?*

Our tour of the prison continues for about an hour and a half in which time we learn a great deal. They have practically nothing. Diana's list is long and she's a little anxious that the women and children have very little to do all day.

'They can't just sit all day long. They need to be busy.' The female warden agrees.

Diana tells Richard that we'll go do some shopping and when we return we'll bring back something special for the women. As we prepare to leave the prison Nadia tugs on my sleeve. She is sad because I didn't get my hand hennaed.

'Next time,' I reassure her. 'When we have more time.'

'Okay,' she smiles and nods her head.

We walk towards the exit gate with Richard shooing away little outstretched hands begging for more candy. The scraggy children run away, turn and wave to us and smile. For some reason they remind me of naughty Christmas elves. I laugh and wave back to them.

'Bye bye!' The image of several Afghan women huddled together on a dusty, dirty would-be courtyard is burned deep into my memory.

Chapter 13

Teaching in Afghanistan

There is no better investment in time or money than in that of a child ... for they are our future. Alma Powell

Today we are driving through Jalalabad, en route to a girls school. We have kept our destination a secret for fear of creating problems for those we intend to visit. Attacks on girls schools are increasing at an alarming rate. According to the Ministry of Education over 670 attacks were carried out this year alone, including arson and the murder of teachers and students. Young militants drop leaflets on doorsteps at night. During the day they watch and wait for young girls daring to walk to school. They warn them to stay away. Sometimes their warnings evoke life-threatening consequences. Sometimes they throw acid bombs. Many headmasters too have received warnings: '*Stop teaching and running the girls' school, otherwise you will be slaughtered.*' There's nothing like a beheading to put the fear of education in you. We risk our lives going to visit the school but our risk is small by comparison to what Afghan students and teachers face on a daily basis.

The livestock marketplace only opens on Saturdays. It is primarily for the sale and purchase of livestock. We drive by thousands of cattle, donkeys, goats, hens, dogs and equally as many Afghan men, covering an area the size of several football fields, metres below the roadside. Along the edge of the embankment, looking down upon the congregated mass, are several hundred more Afghan men quietly observing the goings-on. Their multicoloured wheelbarrows and rickety bicycles are scattered on the edge of the road, occupying every available space. We cross a wide and rather murky river with grassy banks that continue under the road. I note rows of date palms stretching into the blue sky above. Date palms are commonplace and they create a stark contrast to the goings-on on the opposite bank.

Diana wants to stop and take pictures of the men conducting their business. She thinks it will be an interesting sight for people back home, and indeed it would be. The marketplace is chaotic, Muslim thinks she should stay put. As the only blonde in a sea of dark-haired people, Diana's presence would certainly create a fuss. It is just as well we have Muslim wisely keeping the car doors locked, and Diana safe inside. Dressed in her creamy yellow salwar kameez, I chuckle at the thought of Diana struggling through that ruckus. If she could, she would.

'You've been a little cheated this morning with your photo opportunities haven't you, Diana?' I quip.

We all laugh when she says a little wickedly, 'I'm definitely gonna get me some though!'

I have to agree with her logic when she says, 'You don't come all this way, zip by at 60 miles an hour and there it all goes! The people back home, who can't see it, need to have the opportunity to enjoy it with you, at least in a photograph.'

A picture is worth a thousand words and unless the people back home see the visual evidence, how can we ever expect them to understand how things really are over here? I contemplate what my family's reaction will be to the pictures I'll bring back, as we pass the sparse remains of olive groves previously established by the Soviets. All that is left are dirt fields surrounded by a very large cemetery: martyr's graves.

On arriving at the girls school we are invited into the compound to meet the headmaster, Mr Saddaquat. As we walk towards him, he smiles. His kind face is wrinkled with age, and his grey facial hair wisps into a long, thin beard, matching the fine grey hair that peeks out from underneath his camel-coloured *pakol* (Afghan hat). Mr Saddaquat's tall, thin frame is covered by the baggy cotton folds of his once-white salwar kameez. He almost doesn't fit into the dilapidated, rusty, blue-framed homemade-style wheelchair in which he sits. His arms grip the wooden armrests, fastened to the steel tubular frame with several bits of string. His bare feet dangle, limp over the dusty silver footrests.

Mr Saddaquat's chair must hinder his movements greatly. I wonder how he manages to manoeuvre over the clumps of rocks that litter the area. There is no 'all-wheel-terrain' around here! My heart goes out to Mr Saddaquat as I gaze down at him, smiling as if he hasn't a care in the world. I want to rush right out and buy him a brand new, motorised wheelchair that can go four-wheel driving if need be. It would cost less than AUD$200 dollars but on his modest salary, mostly paid for through donations, he will never, ever afford anything so sophisticated. One by one Diana introduces our little group to Mr Saddaquat, who invites us into the freshly painted computer room. It is a wonderful facility, albeit a little bare. At a cost of AUD$5000, the construction of the 4 x 6 metre building has been undertaken by a Dutch group called School Support 4 Afghanistan, John Langerak and a group called the Ladies' Circle of Holland. The room is furnished with pale grey desks and matching brand new computer chairs.

A beautiful red and cream persian style rug covers the entire floor and clean glass windows, edged by silky pale green curtains, keep the cold out. Rotary too has provided much-needed resources, a computer, printer and textbooks. Several heavy, wooden bookcases line the far wall to our right. They are empty.

My video camera follows my gaze to the ceiling above. It is incredibly ornate. The white plaster, supported by grey steel trusses, reminds me of icing on a wedding cake. It is beautiful and for several moments I stand beside Diana, listening to her describing the changes since her last visit: shiny new ceiling fans with delicate gold trim, fluorescent tube lighting on the walls and the freshly painted door. Diana is proud of what has been accomplished with so few resources. Mr Saddaquat tells her that the money from donations was spent wisely; they only purchased the best materials so the workmanship would last longer. He is proud to have such a wonderful facility and is grateful for Diana's support. Her fundraising efforts have assisted in providing notebooks, pens, children's storybooks, and cookbooks. Now, all they need — he says — is a generator to power up the computer ... and some training.

'We'll work on that,' Diana says reassuringly. 'We're certainly a lot further along than we were!'

Diana is a selfless giver, determined to make a difference in the lives of others regardless of how big or how small her contribution. I watch her making mental notes as she scans the room. Here stands a woman who intends to stretch herself beyond her roles as wife, mother and grandmother. Diana can never be accused of perpetuating the 'it's all about me' philosophy. Her intentions are as pure as her heart is gold. She is someone I deeply admire.

Mr Saddaquat is eager to show us the rest of the school and shuffling his wheelchair into place, he carefully manoeuvres his way outside. Curious pupils stop to see what is going on. Their Afghan teachers duck in and out of sight, drawing their veils over their faces when the men in our group approach. Mr Saddaquat says that, on a daily basis, his school provides education and literacy to over 200 girls. They are learning to read and write Pashto and the Qur'ān, as well as studying other subjects such as mathematics, science, home economics and sewing skills (Kandahari embroidery, the finest there is). They also learn practical things like how to use a sewing machine.

Diana tells me that five art workshops were conducted on her previous visits between 2004 and 2007 by Rahraw Omarzad, Executive Director of the Afghan Centre for Contemporary Arts, Kabul, and Rotarian and Artist LaRue Skinner of the Centerville Utah Rotary Club.

'They love arts and crafts,' she explains.

Mr Saddaquat nods and smiles in agreement.

On this trip, Diana, Judy and I will split into three groups to conduct the 2008 art workshops. The men have to wait outside.

'That's okay,' says Chris. 'I'm not into beading.'

John and Muslim laugh.

Fortunately we have our language assistants with us. Pari goes with Diana to help set up her session, which will have the older girls make wooden jewellery boxes. Judy will be assisted by Adela and her other sister, who speaks English. They're going to paint in watercolours. As for me, I don't have a language assistant but that's okay. I'm sure I'll get by with my splattering of Pashto.

I head to the two mud brick classrooms across from the new computer lab. As I expect, there are no tables and chairs. Although they're pretty lucky to have a big blackboard and carpet covering the dirt floor.

'*As-Salaam Alaykum,*' I say as I remove my shoes and dip my head to enter the classroom.

Dozens of little brown eyes stare back at me curiously. For some it will be the first time they have seen a foreign woman. The brave ones touch my salwar kameez as I brush by them. I am eager to make a lasting positive impression, but as I walk to the front of the classroom it suddenly dawns on me that I am not a schoolteacher. Sure in my early twenties I used to teach flute classes in a local primary school but that's hardly anything to rave about. No use explaining. I'm guessing most of these kids wouldn't even know what a flute is. For the life of me I never imagined standing in an Afghan classroom about to do my best impersonation of a teacher. How difficult can it be?

'Difficult,' I hear my neighbour Liz Law whisper into my subconscious. Liz teaches at a local primary school back home and says that it has got to be the most challenging job in the world. 'Challenging but also rewarding.'

'And terrifying, Liz ... don't forget terrifying!' I pause before I turn to face the students. 'Well, here goes ... to all those teachers at Manly West Primary ... I salute you!'

I take a deep breath and smile. 'Today, kids, we are going to do some beading.'

They look puzzled.

Then I hold out the packets of brightly coloured beads and one by one their little faces light up with anticipation of 'play time.'

'Way to go, Kay,' I imagine Liz saying.

I stand in my red salwar kameez looking every bit like I belong, or so Judy tells me when she enters my classroom 20 minutes later. Her tiny silver camera is keeping record of the occasion.

What a lovely experience. Language really is no barrier. We manage to communicate using the universal hand signals and body language. It's amazing how interactive you can be without needing to know precisely what the other person is saying. I show them a picture book and as I turn each page I express myself with sounds, not words.

'*Oooooohhh,*' I express.

They repeat, '*Oooooohhh*' and giggle. Turn the page ... '*Oo-Ahhh* ...!'

'*Oo-Ahhh,*' they repeat.

I'm sure my speech is very strange to them. Obviously it is because every time I speak someone giggles. Then I find myself doing the same thing when a little girl babbles something to me in Pashto, forgetting that I don't understand a word she's saying. I giggle. They giggle. In the end, the teacher has to click her tongue at all of us. Mr Saddaquat laughs at us from his vantage point just beyond the window.

Pari soon joins us and tells me that the teacher says my lesson has been most enjoyable. I laugh thinking how ridiculous I must have sounded. Graciously I thank her and while the children are beading we take a few moments to chat. Apparently the teacher works on a voluntary capacity and has done for several years. There isn't enough money to pay her a salary. She has four children of her own and her husband works as a labourer. He barely makes enough to buy food, which is naan bread and rice. Although extremely poor, this teacher sells chickens and eggs to cover her travel costs. She persists in teaching because she understands the importance that education will make to the girls' lives. She knows nothing of 'teacher's strikes'. In fact, if I were to tell her that teachers in Australia walk off the job for better pay, she wouldn't believe it! She would not understand how they could have so much, by comparison, yet want so much more! It's all relative though. Teaching in Afghanistan gives a new meaning to 'work health and safety' or 'hazardous working conditions'.

The teacher from next door comes into the classroom. She is studying at the university in her spare time. She hopes to improve her own education so that she can be of greater value to the school. Getting an education is important to this young woman on a number of levels: *Education is the knowledge of putting one's potentials to maximum use.'* (Maulana Wahiduddin Khan, spiritual leader of Islamic literature.)

The challenges they face every day have taught them that to succeed in life, you have to see each difficulty as a challenge and not a problem. You have to persist. You have to be focussed and you have to believe in yourself that you must endure despite your fears. Thinking of the acid-throwing motorcyclists, I think they have to be incredibly brave!

Being female in Afghanistan is not easy. Being a female teacher is doubly difficult. It takes courage to walk several kilometres to the school, over rough terrain, through the heat of summer and the frost of winter, not knowing if you'll actually get there. Hoping you aren't accidently shot by soldiers or insurgents, caught in a bomb blast, kidnapped or worse. It takes a lot to face a classroom filled to capacity with students eager to learn, but not knowing if your classroom might be suddenly overrun by men with guns. The vision of a bloodied massacre of your students may be the last thing you see, as you yourself, fall to the ground to die. It takes determination to teach knowing there are not enough learning resources for everybody, or chairs for every student to sit on, or desks to write at. And knowing that the hours spent in that classroom may not yield a salary, a school excursion, let alone a juicy red apple from a favourite pupil.

Pari explains that a few years ago, Taliban entered a male teacher's house. They dragged him into the street, disembowelled him, tied his arms and legs to motorbikes and tore him apart. His entrails were put on display to warn others against educating girls. Many young girls, too, fill the burns ward at a hospital nearby. Defiantly they say they will continue their education after their wounds have healed and despite the fact that they will carry the scars of their ordeal forever.

The smile leaves my face and is replaced with a look of deep concern. The teacher's dark brown eyes mirror that concern.

Hard line extremists lurk in every shadow. Wishful thinking has me hoping they don't see us as a threat. All we want to do is help women learn how to take better care of their families and themselves. We are not political and we certainly do not want to convert anyone to another religion.

'Those bad people do not understand this,' says the teacher. 'Islam encourages me to become a teacher. But some people do not understand these teachings because they are not educated.'

'Clearly,' I respond.

In fact, as Pari explains, Islam encourages women to pursue higher studies, provided they attend local institutions. Many fathers agree that their daughters may be educated in other countries, but of course this takes money and usually it's money that most don't have. So for those who don't have much, but understand the importance of education, they do whatever they can to ensure their daughters have access to some form of education. Even if it is only from within the safety of their own households they are determined to win the battle against ignorance.

Education, for women and girls in particular, has been one of the biggest achievements for Afghan society in the last decade. But the struggle to keep these schools open is constant. The people are frequently rebuilding after every attack, after every drive-by shooting, after every bomb thrown through their compound door. Most know that education will bring economic progress to their community and improve quality of life for everyone. But it comes at a cost and sometimes that cost is life of a teacher or several of her students or an entire school. The extremists know that in order to control the people you have to keep them ignorant and in fear. 'An uneducated *people* is *easy* to deceive.' (Ernesto Ché Guevara.)

'I think it is I who has learnt a lot today' I tell Pari. She quickly translates and the teachers smile and lean forward to gently embrace me. 'Thank you.'

'No ... *thank you*,' says the teacher, '... for being brave enough to come to my country and for sharing this day with us.'

Fortunately, our day has not been marked by tragedy so we can call it a good day. I only wish we could spend more time with the girls, but our presence alone serves to heighten the danger for them. Perhaps we can return soon? I walk towards Diana, who is packing up and saying last minute farewells. I sure hope nothing bad happens to Mr Saddaquat and his school. How on earth he manages to do what he does under such conditions is completely beyond me. I know some people back home who won't get out of bed for less than AUD$45,000 a year. They certainly don't have the worries that he has. Yet he smiles and bravely faces his world in a dilapidated blue wheelchair!

We wave goodbye with our promises to help still lingering in the air. These are promises we intend to keep. This is a day I will never forget.

Our driver steers the mini-van once more back onto the dusty road and within a short time we return to the Taj Mahal Guesthouse where I study my henna hand, courtesy of the young students from Mr Saddaquat's school. They decide, like Nadia, that I need to experience *everything* in Afghanistan. At least their work is artistic. The delicate deep red ornate flowers begin on my left hand, at the wrist and branch all the way up, across my palm to the tip of my index finger. Nadia will be impressed! The students said that it is my gift for being their teacher for the day. But in my heart I know that their smiling faces are all the payment I need. It renews my belief that we are all capable of overcoming seemingly insurmountable hardships, some more than others. They remind me that we should all face challenges with a positive attitude, understanding that in overcoming adversity, we will become better able to deal with new challenges and help others along the way. They remind me that nothing in my world will ever be as difficult as everything in their world. They remind me that I have nothing to complain about and that every day I am alive is a day worth celebrating!

I also think back to a conversation I had with Dr Dave Warner on the rooftop of the Taj Mahal Guesthouse: 'Cyber Pass meets the Khyber Pass ... we can use communications and information technology as an empowerment for people to make informed decisions to choose a better quality of life. Instead of fighting the war with soldiers and guns, it would be better to link humans to humans through modern technology, giving people access to internet support, to schools and hospitals, to assist them in new ways with new methods, enhancing their current skills to help create greater sustainability.'

I think there are many practical ways that we can help Mr Saddaquat and the students in his care. Diana for one has set up a PayPal account on the Childlight Foundation website so that people can donate directly to his school. I've seen firsthand all the amazing achievements she has helped create, so I'm definitely going to continue putting my money into these programs. And this is all it takes ... to drop a pebble in a pond and watch to see how far it ripples. One child's life is surely worth the effort.

In Nangarhar Province alone, the Provincial Reconstruction Team (PRT) is working hard to bring even more new schools to the seven districts in Nangarhar. They have proposed approximately 40 new school buildings to be built in 2010. This year alone, some 50,000 students have been enrolled in higher education. It is estimated that there will be 100,000 high school graduates by 2010 and one million by 2014. The Afghanistan National Development Strategy (ANDS) is addressing the needs of the higher education sector, with a focus on skills development. Surprisingly I learn that according to the constitution, general education and higher education (university) are free for students. Of course, some students may still need to purchase additional study books and manuals or require private tuition (for those who can afford it) to bring their grades up or participate in external sporting activities. And of course, students must also undertake a university entrance exam. Only those who score higher grades go on to study medicine, engineering, etc. The government provides free on campus accommodation to students from distant provinces, which is very costly for the government, but shows the level of commitment to combating illiteracy that has gripped the nation.

One Pashtun man said that becoming educated is a new way to carry on the tradition of being a warrior. He said it was better to fight with knowledge and skills than with guns and bombs.

In the afternoon, Muslim takes us to the bazaar in Jalalabad. He tells us we must be careful because we will most likely be the only Westerners at the bazaar.

'You must follow my instruction carefully,' he cautions.

Our driver makes a roadside stop where he thinks we will best be able to slip unnoticed into one of the less crowded alleyways. It's dirty and crowded. The sound of military helicopters flying overhead does nothing to ease my nerves. Stay alert.

The fabric stores don't really look like stores. They are rows upon rows of stall type boxes with no windows, closed in on three sides with the short side opening as the entrance. They remind me of the morning market stalls in Laos. Although the feeling here is more unsettling. We cannot escape the dozens of dark male eyes watching us as we quickly climb onto the planks of wood, makeshift steps, leading to a 3 x 6 metre box stall.

'I'll be right next door,' says Muslim. John and Chris follow him to the tailor's shop.

Diana and Judy enter first as I follow discreetly behind. The stall owner's assistant quietly hands me back my dusty shoes that I'd kicked off at the shop's opening.

'They might be stolen,' he says cautiously.

'Thank you,' I respond in Pashto.

'Please sit,' he instructs. A young boy scurries quickly from the rear of the stall bringing three piping hot glasses of tea.

We sit on the dark coloured persian style carpets that cover the floor. The walls look a mosaic of colours because the store owner has covered the walls with his samples. It's an amazing feeling being in this ancient world and I almost forget the dangers, except for the curious dark eyes passing by and peering in. The shopkeepers are all men because trade is thought of as a man's job. I think the name bazaar is apt for where we are; I think it's extremely *bizarre* to go to a fabric market where there are no women at all. As discreet as we have tried to be it is obvious after a mere 10 minutes that we have created a stir of curiosity. The all-male crowd gathers quickly.

Muslim returns and says we must get the hell out of here. 'There's no time to waste,' he insists.

'We'll take all these' Diana says quickly to the store owner.

'And these.' I throw dozens of bundles of material, pre-wrapped in clear plastic bags, on the floor that Judy and I have literally grabbed from the shelves. 'A quick shop's a good shop.'

This makes Diana laugh.

My eyes dart to Muslim when one man raises his voice at him. I have no idea what he is saying but the sweat is forming on Muslim's worried brow. I notice other men talking amongst themselves while pointing at us. Young boys with coal black eyes move to the opening of our fabric shop. Soon dozens more join them. Where did they all come from? Why aren't they smiling?

'Quickly, Diana,' Muslim insists.

He either really doesn't like shopping or he's worried we're about to start a riot. I'll put my money on the latter and throw a fistful of rupees at Diana. She quickly counts the notes and hands them to the shop owner. Why he wants rupees and not Afghanis is anyone's guess. Luckily I have both. His assistant suddenly notices the crowd forming outside and stops momentarily in his tracks. Then springs into action when the shop owner barks something unintelligible at him, like, 'Get them the hell out of here before we're over-run!'

'They want to know where your husbands are and why you are here,' says Muslim as we quickly put our shoes back on and grab our packages. It is scandalous that we should travel without them. We leave the fabric shop swiftly. I make sure my purple headscarf is firmly secure. Muslim strides ahead of us like our older brother, but we are not Afghan women. To the crowd, we have no right to even be here. Diana wants to take a few photos because it's so amazing to see so many people crammed into one tiny alleyway. But her suggestion nearly gives Muslim a heart attack. Any minute now I expect him to faint, but patiently as ever he quietly urges us to hurry. No photo today.

Thankfully we make it back in one piece. The mini-van is parked a short 50 metres away with the engine running. As soon as we are inside, Muslim slams the heavy side door closed and locks it. He then races back around to the passenger's side and climbs in. His door is shut with a thud and for a few moments he peels back several dirty grimy hands holding onto his door. Beggar boys. Within minutes our driver merges into the traffic and we are once again on our way.

The next morning after a light breakfast of cereal and toast, courtesy of the Taj Guesthouse, we grab our ice-cold bottled water and begin to load the mini-van with books, toys, art supplies, sewing supplies and the bright-coloured fabrics we'd bought at the bazaar the day before. We drive to pick up Pari and her sisters and then make our way to the Nangarhar prison.

It's a glorious day. The sun is shining and the sky is clear. It's a wonderful day to visit a prison.

Within half an hour we arrive at the prison compound where we go through all the usual security procedures. We park in the exact same spot, greet Richard as before and walk through the heavy steel gate that is locked firmly behind us. The only real difference this time are the familiar smiles. The women and children probably didn't expect us to return so soon, if at all. The children all come running up to Richard, waiting for his candy. Behind us, John and Chris help the men carry the supplies into the prison but they are not allowed to stay. They go off with Muslim to purchase a generator for the Jalalabad girls' school and I picture the smiling face of the headmaster, Mr Saddaquat, sitting in his dilapidated blue wheelchair. He will be pleasantly surprised by John and Chris' visit. In these parts, little things mean so much.

Then Diana, Judy and I organise the day's activities, before inviting the women and children back into the bright blue room of the renovated learning centre. There we separate into three groups. Judy, being a registered nurse, takes the older women into one corner where she talks to them about health and hygiene. She shows them how to care for their newborn babies, and why it is so important to keep them as germ-free as possible.

Diana takes her group of teeny-tots into another corner with Pari acting as her language assistant. I take the teenage girls into the middle of the room where we sit in a circle, paired up, and we begin beading from the supplies we bought at the bazaar. I have an amazing time with the teenagers and make sure I hug them all individually at least once. At first they are a little shy but I am a very affectionate person. Everyone needs a hug from time to time. I show them my hennaed hand and judging by their squeals they are delighted. The ice is broken. Nadia is impressed.

'Ah,' she says. Her dark brown eyes light up. Her delicate eyebrows arch.

'Good hey?' I smile back at her proudly.

She nods and then says we must trade headscarves. Mine is pure white with tiny sequins sewn into the fabric. Nadia's is hot pink and she says it looks very beautiful on me. We do a 'best friends' pose as one of the other girls takes our picture on Richard's camera. Nadia loves photography and says she is quite good at it, though I doubt she's ever owned a camera. So I hand her Richard's very expensive looking Canon camera and my Panasonic camcorder and tell her to have fun with them while we're here. She has no idea that what she's holding in her hands is about AUD$5000 dollars' worth of equipment. They're just cameras.

Nadia becomes an instant 'Ms CNN'. The prison commander just looks on. He doesn't mind if we shoot film. In fact, he hopes that it will show the world how things have changed for the better. We are encouraged to learn about their lives. The commander is completely different to what I expected him to be. Sure he's tall and brooding but he's actually quite friendly. He appears to genuinely care about the women and their children. He makes several suggestions to us, as requests, for small improvements that could be made which would be meaningful to the women. Is this the influence of Richard and his team? The prison is different too. Back home, I'd read so many internet reports about how badly women prisoners are treated, the squalor in which they live and that they wept day-in day-out at the tragedy of their lives. But looking around me, I see that the prison is far more comfortable than the dirty old tents we saw on the roadside coming in from Sorubi and it's certainly more comfortable than most local accommodation. Despite not having their freedom, these women are safe. But what is freedom when most of them were prisoners in their own homes anyway? We are free to walk around and talk to whomever we want, in private if we wish.

For a moment I think of when I was in the Laos prison and make mental comparisons. We never had visitors except when new prisoners came in, or when the brutal interrogators decided to torture us or the other prisoners. I crouched by the fishpond holding my hands over my ears trying to block out the screams of the young African boy. They were burning his genitals in the interrogation room just metres away. I can still hear him screaming. I can still see Mr Kylie, the young Sri Lankan, who died for not paying his friend's AUD$200 dollar telephone bill. The old Chinese woman cries over and over, begging to go home. She's lost her mind they say. Here in Nangarhar women's prison the women are kept separate to the men; whereas in Phonthong prison in Laos, the men and women were detained in the same compound. In Laos, no-one had a camera that's for sure and the presence of the commander was enough to make your throat go dry with fear. His steely gaze was terrifying even to me.

This prison is nothing like a Laotian prison, of course, where dozens of prisoners are crammed into sauna-like 3 x 3 metre cells, but all the same, I feel claustrophobic despite standing in the middle of this open dirt compound.

I want to ask these Afghan women a hundred questions but at the same time, I don't want to pry. When you are a prisoner it often feels like you are living under a microscope. You have such little privacy. In the Laos prison everything we did was watched. Every conversation recorded and then reported. It was stifling. At times I wanted to stand in the middle of the compound and just scream my head off. I constantly felt the rage building in me but there was no release. Not yet. Someone was always watching and waiting for you to lose control. I didn't. I knew from the other prisoners that that kind of behaviour would only get me locked in solitary, in the dark room, and possibly shackled in heavy wooden leg blocks. Sharing each other's stories in the Laos prison was difficult too because you never knew who you could trust or what information you'd share that would be twisted and then used against you. But these women didn't seem to face those same restrictions. They didn't appear to face those kinds of fears and they didn't appear to mind sharing their stories. As the minutes ticked by, I was shown a rare but precious glimpse into their existence.

One young woman escaped from a neighbouring country to Afghanistan with her infant son. She was then kidnapped by her neighbour and given to an Afghan man who decided to make her his wife.

A bunker at Kabul Airport. Photo Kay Danes

The brilliant colour of Kabul street stalls are a stark contrast to the dust covering everything else. Photo Diana Tacey

There is a constant presence of the pale blue burqa women in Kabul.
Photo Kay Danes

A picture is often worth a thousand words. Photo Richard Boyed

Afghan village destroyed by the Soviets. Photo Todd Huffman

A woman begs in the burnt asphalt of a previous explosion. Photo Todd Huffman

The most dangerous stretch of road between Kabul and Jalalabad.
Photo Todd Huffman

Tankers explode under insurgent fire on the road from Jalalabad to Kabul.
Photo Logan Lynch

Taliban are 100 metres left of this photo. Photo Kay Danes

Tim Lynch scans the horizon for any threats. Photo Logan Lynch

Tourist spot and a place to sell knockoff watches. Photo Todd Huffman

Road-side messages from Kabul to Jalalabad on what not to touch.
Photo Todd Huffman

Lovely valley between Kabul and Jalalabad. Photo Todd Huffman

Buddhist caves in Jalalabad. Photo Dave Warner

Heading through a beautiful valley into Jalalabad. Photo Kay Danes

Opening day of Rotary Club School in Jalalabad. Photo Stephen Brown

Some are born to carry the heaviest loads. Photo Diana Tacey

Sultan Hamidy (or Ahmad) and his family have been making famous Herati blue glass for generations. Photo Kay Danes

Poppy eradication billboard. Photo Todd Huffman

Anti-poppy poster telling people that poppies are the crop of death. Grow wheat and make bread instead. Photo Todd Huffman

Down the first tunnel that leads to a village. A more secure way of moving between compounds. Photo Kay Danes

Chris Dickinson follows Dr Katiby through a catacomb compound system. Photo Kay Danes

The only water source for an entire district, which freezes in winter.
Photo Kay Danes

Diana Tacey and I meet the community leader of a remote village.
Photo Kay Danes

Travellers of the famous Silk Road from Kabul to Nangarhar. Photo Kay Danes

The 800-year-old Masjid-I-Jami Mosque is noted for its most beautiful Islamic architecture. Photo Kay Danes

Visiting Masjid-I-Jami Mosque moments before 3000 men come to pray.
Photo Diana Tacey

A remote village in Herat where we provide vital aid supplies. Photo Kay Danes

Judy Hutcherson meets one of Herat hospital's senior female doctors.
Photo Kay Danes

Judy Hutcherson, Mr Nazir, Dr Katiby, Kay Danes, Mayor Mujaddadi, Chris Dickinson, Diana Tacey, John Dell. Photo Kay Danes

The rebuild of Herat University after being completely destroyed by bombs.
Photo Kay Danes

Former Mujahadeen fighter Ali was shot in the spine when fighting the Soviets.
He is optimistic for the future. Photo Kay Danes

Exquisite craftsmanship on the pillars that adorn the main hall inside the Governor of Herat's office building. Photo Kay Danes

Herat's Masjid-I-Jami or Friday mosque is an important pilgrimage centre for Afghans. Photo Kay Danes

Mayor of Herat Haji Mohammad Rafiq Mujaddadi and Kay Danes take tea at the Governor's Guesthouse. Photo Kay Danes

Mayor of Herat Haji Mohammad Rafiq Mujaddadi proudly presents a magazine showing the Way of Reconstruction. Photo Judy Hutcherson

A typical village compound in Nangarhar. Photo Logan Lynch

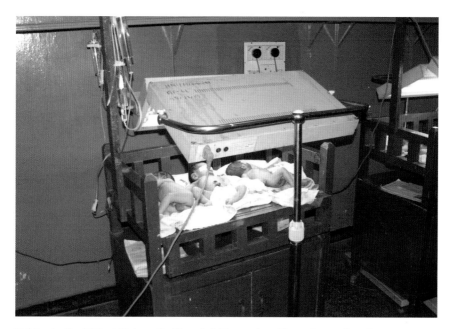

Babies in the ICU at University Hospital, Nangarhar. Photo Logan Lynch

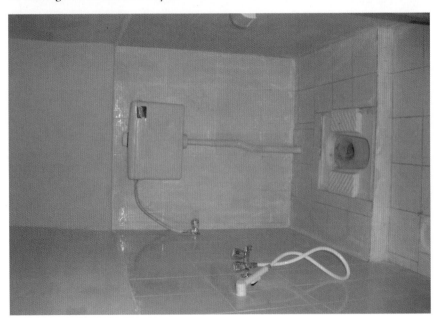

Original toilet for Nangarhar female prisoners. Nothing more than a dirt floor and no drainage. Photo Richard Boyed

Thanks to US Department funding the women of Nangarhar Prison now have clean, servicable toilets and shower blocks. Photo Richard Boyed

Original dormitory-style accomodation for female prisoners in Nangarhar prison.
Photo Richard Boyed

Renovated dormitory-style accomodation for female prisoners in Nangarhar prison.
Photo Richard Boyed

Original veranda of Nangarhar women's prison. Photo Richard Boyed

Renovated veranda of Nangarhar women's prison. Photo Richard Boyed

Original water source for women in Nangarhar prison. Photo Richard Boyed

Renovated water filtration system for women in Nangarhar prison.
Photo Richard Boyed

US troops deliver swing set to children at Nangarhar prison. Photo Rita Thomas

These US troops haven't seen their own families for 12 months or more.
Photo Rita Thomas

Teaching high-five to young boy at Nangarhar prison. Photo Kay Danes

A malnourished baby and her mother, who smiles after we arrange to get milk delivered. Photo Kay Danes

Richard Boyed gains trust of children who have only known violence.
Photo Richard Boyed.

Showing the girls at Nangarhar prison that someone cares. Photo Richard Boyed

Security at Nangarhar prison is understandably serious but for a second they agree to show a softer side. Photo Kay Danes

View from the Taj Mahal Guesthouse, Nangarhar. Photo Todd Huffman

Tim Lynch keeps us safe at the Taj Mahal Guesthouse, Nangarhar. Photo Tim Lynch

Ester with one of the Turquoise Mountain potters. Photo Judy Hutcherson

UNHCR tents have become popular with the Kuchis, a large nomadic tribe that forms the backbone of goat trade. Photo Todd Huffman

Ester contemplates the disappearance of the French National in Kabul. Photo Judy Hutcherson

Over the coming months he raped her repeatedly. Then he made a deal with another Afghan man to sell her. The young woman ran away because her son was not part of the deal. She feared losing him. Her husband tracked her down, and brutally beat her and the infant.

'When I lifted the blanket that covered him, my son looked into my eyes, took his last breaths and then died,' she cried.

Her husband was arrested after she reported the incident to the police and the judge sentenced him 20 years for the murder. The prosecutor acknowledged that the young woman was raped by her husband but that she shared a portion of the blame. He sentenced her to four years for adultery and escaping her house. The chief prosecutor suggested she got off lightly. I had read about this young girl's plight before coming here. I never thought I'd actually get to meet her.

'I'm innocent,' she said.

Most likely she is.

Nadia calls out to me. She has Richard's camera strapped around her neck. She clicks my image and then laughs. She is so beautiful. I can't help but smile back. Momentarily I am distracted as Diana begins handing out puzzles, books and toys to the youngest children. They immediately go into a frenzy of excitement. Their little brown hands thrash out to grab as many of the items as they can. Diana eventually calms them down long enough to explain that these items are not going to be taken away when we depart.

Most all of the children have never been in a positive learning environment before. They don't know how to act, how to share or how to interact. Diana shows them how one child can hold a puzzle while the other child removes the pieces and places them on the carpeted floor. She shows them how to take turns, how to work together to complete the simple task and when they succeed, she invites the other children to applaud their accomplishments. The smiles that light up their faces is worth every dollar we spent getting those puzzles across several countries and into their little hands. I watch Diana's story-time reading activity. She is so intuitive because she is a grandmother and has the patience of a saint. I follow her lead and just enjoy being there in the moment.

The big colourful book she holds is filled with amazing scenes, animals and plants from every country of the world. She shows the children where Afghanistan is on the map in relation to the rest of the world. They fall completely silent under her spell. She slowly turns each page to reveal another magical scene. At her request, I take over the storytelling session so she can spend time with the older mothers and their babies. I turn to the centre of the book which reveals a giant cartoon-style world map. I teach the children how to say *hello* in the language of each country I point to. It becomes really fun when I point to various animals and make the sound of humpback whales, farmyard roosters and squawking crows. The children fall into laughter when they repeat the sounds themselves. An image flashes from my past. In the communist Laos prison my cellmates laughed in hysterics when I mimicked the crazy cats that roam the prison. 'Meooow meooow … *I want to go home*!' Perhaps these children, like me, will one day hear sounds that remind them of this very day and the things we shared. Perhaps, like me, they will be reminded that even in the most despairing situations there can still be enjoyment, laughter and complete abandonment of our fears, even for a moment. It's those moments that count towards us surviving all the others.

It is lunchtime and in traditional Afghan style, it's time for us to take tea. The women don't have much but the plate of red apples look delicious. I hear Diana ask where we can wash our hands. Several of the women and children seem unsure of what she is talking about.

'You do wash your hands with soap and water before meals, don't you?' Diana enquires.

Several of the children jump up and say, 'Oh, yes, let's go wash!'

Picking up one of the bars of soap we brought, Diana goes to the outside water pump and a large group follow her, as if this is something unusual. I grab my video camera and film her leaning over and pumping the water. Diana sets the example and washes her own hands before handing the bar of soap to a boy about age 10, who washes his hands, face, then feet! One by one each of the children get into line and do the same, the women follow suit. Diana could have achieved the same by taking them all to the shower block, but it was more fun watching her outside, surrounded by kids, all eager to see what new thing this crazy Western lady has in store for them. Nadia is standing behind me.

'Nadia, wash your hands too.'

My white headscarf she's wearing flashes before the viewfinder and we both laugh as I sidestep to get her in shot washing her hands. I zoom in on the cleanest little children I've seen since coming to Afghanistan. Meanwhile, Diana is bent over, lathering the sea of hands coming her way.

'More, more … much more soap,' she instructs. 'Scrub, scrub … like this …'

Diana tells them about bacteria as she plunges another cake of soap into the next dirty hand.

'On the next trip we need to bring more combs and some shampoo,' she concludes.

Most of them can't understand a word Diana says, but that doesn't matter. They understand what she wants them to do and they do it with great enthusiasm. A cute little boy comes up next, washes his hands twice and then his face. His little matted-haired sister with the string through her nose-piercing follows his lead and her face soon becomes a lather of white soap. They smell so good now. It is amazing that the simple act of washing can give so much pleasure.

'Diana, what's going through your heart right now?' I ask as I watch her scrub one dirty hand after another.

'I just want to cry,' she says looking up at me and then at the sweet children before her.

She's too emotional to say anything more but later confides, 'I just wish these simple things in life were not so difficult to provide.'

Not wanting the children to see how affected she is, Diana lowers her head, wipes her eyes, bites her bottom lip and gets back to scrubbing those tiny little hands. We are all mothers together and we all feel protective and helpless. All of us are brimming with emotion but we each hold it all inside. None of these children even has toothpaste or a toothbrush. All have cavities. None of the girls has a pretty little clip to put in their hair or pink satin ribbons. None have baby dolls to play with or little toy cars. The children have nothing because they are nothing to society. As a mother I feel like packing them all up in our mini-van and taking them back to Brisbane. Diana says she feels like taking them home every time she comes to Afghanistan.

Our language assistants, the three sisters, don't understand why we would want to help such unclean women and children, especially prisoners. The 'princesses' are sweet girls who have lived a very sheltered life. I know they would have preferred us to expend our limited resources in other ways, but I explain, 'We must do what we can to help those who have far less. You are lucky Pari. You have a good father and mother to take care of you. These women have only known a lifetime of misery.'

Pari and her sisters are getting an unexpected lesson in social needs, which they receive graciously. I go outside to join Judy and Diana. Judy talks to an English-speaking woman who tells her that they get given very little.

'They said that they would certainly use combs and brushes if they had them but they just don't have anything,' said Judy. 'They get one bar of soap every 15 days to last them all.'

'That's the one bar for the whole prison?' I exclaim. 'Oh my God!'

'Yeah,' says Judy. 'Food is not their problem, but they need more than that.'

And then we twig to the obvious! The reason all the children have matted hair is because they don't have comb or brushes. Judy, Diana and I are sad to hear that.

'I wish I had brought more,' says Diana.

I am quite surprised when Judy says none of them has head lice. When I loaned Nadia my headscarf I half expected to see little black mites jumping all over the place. I couldn't stop scratching my head after that.

'I just had to loan her my scarf, Judy. I had to do the girlie thing.'

'Of course,' she smiles, 'Just rid them later if you get lice.'

Video camera in action, Nadia follows me and Judy around the prison while the women go off to eat lunch. She shows us the showers, followed by the medical facility that is merely a standard room fitted with a bookcase and examination table. There are no medicine cabinets or medical instruments or even a set of baby scales to monitor the weights of the newborns. There are no baby bottles, no baby formula, no nappies, and no sanitary items for women. They have nothing. A doctor from the US military base pays occasional visits to Nangarhar Women's Prison. When he does, he vaccinates the children. This is a voluntary service, not done on a regular basis, however.

'We need to find the funds to hire a nurse,' says Judy. 'We need to get these kids immunised.'

'We'd need to find the salary for a fully trained Afghan female nurse,' says Richard.

Diana makes a mental note of that along with all the other priorities. Their needs are so great. There is very little treatment available. There is no dentist. The women rarely smile but when they do they have beautiful smiles, except most of their teeth are chipped, broken or missing. The cost of supporting a woman in the Nangarhar prison is approximately AUD$1.50 per day. That's less than sponsoring an orphan in Africa, yet these women get no international attention. Bob Geldof is not writing songs about their struggles.

After taking tea and some slices of the juicy red apples, we return to the learning centre. I cross the lovely carpeted floor area to find Richard and his staff busy affixing two whiteboards to the bright blue walls. I film them hammering in nails.

'Is the whiteboard straight?' asks Richard.

I respond, 'I think the whole building is crooked.'

Richard doubles over laughing.

We pile a stack of coloured markers into plastic holders and set them down beside the learning resources and toys kindly donated by Jacqueline Elstein on behalf of Mosman Library, Sydney. We make a list of all the things they still need, like a wall locker for each woman and child, because the only space they have to store personal items is under their individual bunk beds. We know it's going to take time to see the impact of our efforts but we are optimistic. We have to be.

When it's time to say our goodbyes, we gather the women and children around us and thank them for their kind hospitality. We take turns saying goodbye and hugging each of the women with a promise to return someday in the future, *Insha'Allah*. We will never forget them. Nadia and I once again exchange headscarfs. As she adjusts the white fabric around my face she looks a little sad. I'm sad too. Even though our time together was short, it feels like Nadia and I have a special connection. I wish she could go home with me. It would do no good to say this out loud. Nadia smiles sweetly. It's a smile I shall always remember.

Silently the past intrudes on my farewell with Nadia and I am reminded of another time, when I left the Laos prison. It should have been the happiest day of my life but it was an incredibly sad time. I was no longer a hostage. My government had secured my freedom. But I was forced to let go of friendships with people who had taught me to survive the torture, the endless days and nights without my children and the horrors of seeing prisoners beaten, burned and brutalised. That day the tears fell down my cheeks unashamedly. As I hug Nadia one last time, I think of my Thai sister Mon and how it felt to leave her behind in the Lao jail. I feel a twinge of pain pierce my heart then push those thoughts from my mind. I squeeze my eyes shut and wish Nadia a good life, good health and to meet someone with a kind and generous heart. I hope that we will meet again but if we don't, I will content myself with thinking that she is happy. To think anything other than that would surely break my heart. In the dirt clearing she stands with the rest of the women waving goodbye. The scraggy children wave too. The heavy door is closed and locked behind us.

Outside the prison compound, John, Chris and Muslim have returned from the Jalalabad girls' school.

'How did you go?' Diana asks.

'It was great,' says Chris.

'You should have seen Mr Saddaquat's face when we delivered the brand new generator,' says John. 'He was tickled pink when Muslim fired up the computer!'

'Yes, he was very happy indeed,' said Muslim proudly.

'Ooh, that's wonderful!'

The young Nepalese security officer named Niranjan, standing by, asks when I plan to return to the prison.

'Hopefully next year,' I reply. 'It is difficult to know, because I don't have the money to come often.'

'Then I would hope that you will have a safe journey home,' Niranjan adds, prayerfully.

'Thank you,' I smile and place my palms together in the customary prayer-like greeting and add, '*Namaste*.'

'*Namaste*, madam,' the young man replies.

Namaste is used as a greeting or upon parting, by putting the palms of the hands together in prayer position. It means, 'I honour the Spirit in you which is also in me'. This, of course, is also a way of saying, 'I recognise that we are all equal' (Deepak Chopra.)

Richard comes over and expresses heartfelt appreciation for the joy we have brought to the women and children in our two visits. He encourages us to share our experiences with people back home in the hope that they too might understand the harsh reality that he and his co-workers face. I feel privileged to know him. Standing with the mud-walled prison behind him Richard graciously says a few words into my video camera. His honesty and sincerity humbles us.

I just want you to know just how much of a blessing it's been for me working here. When I first came to Afghanistan, it was for the money. That was until I started to realise just how needful these people truly are. They need somebody to care for them and to show them that there is a different way, a better way, for their country and for themselves. My whole outlook has changed. I was going to only be here for a year. I'm on my third year now. So I want to thank y'all for coming. It's been a blessing for me. Thank y'all from the bottom of my heart.

I almost weep as I hug Richard goodbye but instead, in the last second, I decide to leave him with my most brilliant smile. I hope that when his duty here is up that he makes it safely home to his family and that he won't suffer any ill effects, in the years to come, when he remembers all the chaos and despair that engulfed him. I hope this day is one memory he will treasure.

'Y'all take care,' he says.

I think a great deal about the women and children behind the mud brick wall, as we climb into the mini-van and wave goodbye to Richard and his team. Their lives will never be as easy as mine. Diana is right about so many things. Our journey through Afghanistan was never going to be some fancy tour like those that you would normally book through a travel agent. It is going to be hard work, emotionally challenging and physically draining. It is shaping up to be an experience of a lifetime.

Good governance is impossible without a strong legal framework and unfortunately the rule of law in Afghanistan is fragile. Organisations like the United Nations Office on Drugs and Crime (UNODC) partner with others to monitor the prisons. They are now endeavouring to improve the legal process and the conditions and to work with the government of Afghanistan to develop alternatives to imprisonment. From what I learn today, the system is far from perfect, but it is improving. Time, money and effort will make things better, as Afghanistan currently endeavours to grasp modern thinking. Many countries will not allow anyone to enter their prisons, let alone foreigners who film detainees. That Afghanistan should be so transparent is a positive step, showing real intent to improve their standing in the international community.

Two female prison officers stand quietly to one side and smile ever so briefly as our mini-van passes them by. I press my palm to the window. Who will ever hear their story? Who would ever want to know their hardships?

I am a 3rd Lieutenant and have worked in the prison system for many years. I have a son who is disabled and a daughter who has mental health problems. My husband is aged and jobless and we are homeless. We rent a house and I pay the rent from the salary I make as a prison guard. Life is incredibly difficult but what else can I do?' (Anisa, Prison Officer.)

There are hundreds of Afghan women in the same tragic situation as prison officer Anisa. Most are single-parent, female prison officers on a salary somewhere between AUD$90 to AUD$140 per month. This is far below a living wage, as it costs a minimum of AUD$75 a month for rent, and AUD$50 a month for food for a family of six. Many prison staff struggle financially but courageously endure hardships in order to survive.

'Thank you,' they whisper when I quietly shove a few US dollars into their hands before hugging them goodbye.

It isn't nearly enough cash to change their lives but perhaps it'll solve a few short-term problems. Maybe they'll buy food for their children or a new pair of shoes. A dust cloud obscures their faces and then they are gone.

In Afghanistan, there are around 34 prisons at the provincial level and at least one detention centre in each of 376 districts. The total number of prisoners is estimated at around 4500. When the Taliban government seized power in Afghanistan in the early 1990s, the Pol-e-Charkhi Prison in Kabul experienced a sudden intake of prisoners, particularly females. According to the many reports coming out of Afghanistan at that time, they were crammed into cells, tortured, raped and beaten on a daily basis. Most were detained without sentence. Some died and there were even reports that some were buried alive in the prison basements. Some disappeared and were never heard of again. Those who were lucky enough to walk beyond the prison walls of Pol-e-Charkhi carry, even today, bitter memories of all manner of atrocities. Some witnessed mass shootings. One time, 60 prisoners were made to stand in line and then executed by firing squad. Their bodies were dumped into mass graves outside the prison.

After the fall of the Taliban government in 2001, Pol-e-Charkhi was taken over by the Northern Alliance forces. Fortunately, the incoming administration treated the prisons as a priority and made them more serviceable. Even so, prison conditions did not improve much by Western standards. Prison populations did not decrease because many of the records of prisoners under the Taliban system were destroyed. It has received some improvements but, in general, the conditions are poor. The Ministry of Justice, however, is seeking to improve the general standards of prisons across Afghanistan, starting with those in Kabul.

In January 2008, the new Kabul women's prison, named Badam Bagh, which means Almond Orchard, was officially handed over to the Afghan Justice Ministry. The prison is surrounded by towering snow-capped mountains. With help from the Italian Government, it was built by the UN Office of Drugs and Crime (UNODC). According to the UN, it is built to international standards and is probably the best prison in Afghanistan. All of the 119 women prisoners and 57 children were transferred from Pol-e-Charki Prison to Badam Bagh in April 2008. Pol-e-Charki Prison is currently an all-male prison. At least 1300 inmates are kept there, including a number of insurgents. The Corrections System Support Program (CSSP), a State Department program, has worked hard to develop positive relationships with the prison staff and key personnel to assist with training and mentoring. The women prisoners are actively involved in education programs.

The Afghan Women's Education Centre (AWEC) in Kabul is also providing a literacy teacher for the women and older girls so that they can become fluent in Dari and English. They also provide a vocational and sewing instructor, a computer trainer and a children's teacher for the 27 children aged between 5 and 12 years, who attend lessons daily. The kindergarten, or young child day care, teacher is a female inmate. She is very sweet and she smiles a lot. Her children love the puzzles, coloured paper and felt markers provided by the Childlight Foundation. There are about five little children's beds/cribs in the classrooms and the younger children watch the older children in class and also those who sleep in this room. It's not ideal but it's not draconian either. There are no cells in the prison. There are four to six bunk beds in each room, some curtained off for privacy. The rooms are painted white, although the whole place needs repainting because paint quickly deteriorates with such heavy wear and tear. Small children play in a fully enclosed balcony overlooking the compound where there is plenty of light. In the same room, two infants in their cribs watch everything that is going on.

Many of the women are serving time for crimes committed by their husbands; husbands who ran away to evade justice. Some are jailed for committing crimes like drug trafficking, theft and murder. But the majority are jailed for moral crimes. As an outsider, I struggle to understand this concept. It's all hearsay evidence. My Western mind asks: is adultery a crime when your neighbour gossips about you to your husband? Or if your husband thinks you are looking at someone the wrong way? Or maybe you spoke too loudly? Or maybe someone said you were promiscuous? There are lots of things I don't understand. Is smuggling really a crime when you are trying to get your children to safety? Is conspiracy a crime when you are escaping forced marriage? Is murder what it seems when you shoot the man who raped you just like he raped you the day before and the day before that?

Questions of morality and law are easy to separate in a Western mind but here it's all so complex. Here there appears to be a great deal of inconsistency throughout the country as to how women should be treated. The judicial system and many of its municipal and provincial authorities rely, in theory, on some interpretation of Islamic law and traditional tribal codes of justice, but the system is far from perfect. It doesn't even live up to its own standards because the law in Afghanistan, and various international treaties signed by Afghanistan, guarantees equal rights for women!

Article 22, Chapter 2, and Article 1 of the Constitution of Afghanistan states: 'Any kind of discrimination and privilege between the citizens of Afghanistan are prohibited. The citizens of Afghanistan — whether man or woman — have equal rights and duties before the law'. It seems that the biggest problem for women in Afghanistan stems from ignorance of the law. This is why it is so important for the people to be educated.

Chapter 14

Explosions

International news: A young man greets the morning with a smile. Today he will be married. His bride and his relatives and friends have gathered to form a procession. He is about to step outside to meet his betrothed but without warning, an explosion shakes the ground beneath his feet. He falls on the road, quickly picks himself up and runs outside. The screams of women and children assault his ears, then a second explosion hits. The flashpoint, the smoke, the smell of burnt flesh, bits of buildings flying everywhere; he sees it all, then falls to his knees sobbing. His bride and many of his family members have just been blown to bits.

He looks up to Heaven and howls, 'Allah!'

The International Coalition Forces certainly don't target civilians deliberately. They go to great lengths to avoid killing innocent people but, sadly in war, innocent people die. We have all heard of the term 'collateral damage', which is damage that is unintended or incidental to the outcome. I cannot imagine this young man's grief. His family and his future are wiped out in an instant. The International Coalition Forces will pay a mere AUD$2000 compensation for each dead member of his family.

Every time we go 'outside the wire' we too risk becoming collateral damage. It is impossible to outrun a 225 kg bomb. Inside the Taj Mahal Guesthouse we are as safe as one can be in a war zone. Even so, none of us can afford to become complacent. Kerry says, 'Complacency is your worst enemy'.

The night is still.

The last of the non-government organisation (NGO) workers say their farewells and wave to Tim from their vehicles.

'G'night, Tim,' they call, before driving through the heavy steel gates, turning left, then along the Silk Road that will return them to their neighbouring compounds. Tim waves back.

'I think we'll turn in now too, Tim.' says Judy, 'Goodnight.'

'Nighty-night, ladies,' he replies cheerfully.

'It was a great day wasn't it, Judy?' I say, as we walk to our room.

'It was wonderful,' she sighs. 'Oh, my Lord, what those poor women go through it just breaks my heart.'

A look of reflection washes over Judy's face. Her expression says it all. Here, we are surrounded by incredible poverty, but everyone we meet is determined to find that something that makes life tolerable.

We enter our room, I close the door and immediately kick off my shoes, Judy heads for the shower and I lay out tomorrow's clothes. It has been a lovely evening with the visiting NGOs and it was nice to be in the company of people who didn't have to get drunk to have a good time. Tomorrow and the next day we are visiting the poultry farms and after that there's the Women's Healthy Families Seminar at the Nangarhar University. My topic is 'Taking Care of Ourselves as Women: the journey towards emotional health and personal happiness'. I'm looking forward to it. I find my presentation notes and place them on the chair by my bed.

'Shower's all yours,' says Judy bursting out, and wearing a giant fluffy lavender towel.

'Great. I'm exhausted.' Off I go, to the bathroom.

It is glorious to feel the hot water on the back of my neck, cascading over my aching shoulders. It has been such a long day. My head slumps forward as I rest both arms against the wall tiles and close my eyes. The water is soothing. How fortunate am I to have been born into 'privilege'? In actual fact, I've worked hard for everything I have, but where I come from, I am privileged to have that option! I'm privileged to own a video-camera, privileged to have had an education, privileged to enjoy this shower. I am so lucky. Yet my life has not been without its moments of desperation. Momentarily I allow my mind to drift back to memories of 2001, to a place where I once stood, alone in a bathroom, despairing.

I cried silently wishing for help to come but it didn't and the darkness enveloped me. The once pale blue tiles stank of urine and shit. I almost choked on its foul aroma. The thought of putting my bare feet on those tiles made the bile rise in my throat. 'My God,' I cried and covered my mouth with my hands to stop myself from dry-retching. My heart pounded. My hands shook. I reached down for the tiny pail and plunged it into the dirty cement trough full of water. I showered quickly but afterwards had nothing to dry myself with, so I just patted my skin dry as best I could ...

The memory of that night, the beginning of Kerry's and my horrendous ordeal, when we were held captive by ruthless communist police, still has the power to haunt me. Funnily enough, it isn't today's prison visit that has reminded me of those dark days when I was a prisoner in Laos. It is the fact that I am in a bathroom. Bathrooms trigger memories in me that remind me of my deepest despair.

My whole body ached with an incredible pain beyond all sorrow and when I thought of my children waving me goodbye, I cried even more. I had no idea how long I stood in the 'bathroom' praying this was all just a dream and that I would soon wake up.

I turn off the taps and force those memories firmly back into the abyss of my mind where they are locked away, until I get another flashback. I am used to forgetting. I am good at it now. I dry my hair vigorously, run the thick towel over my body, get dry and into my pyjamas.

Judy is already asleep. I creep across the carpet, flick off the light and wait for my eyes to adjust to the darkness. Quietly I make my way back to my side of the room. I crawl into my single bed, sink into the soft mattress with a sigh, thinking of nothing but how good sleep will feel. Silence fills the room. Then ...

Boom!

A thunderous explosion crashes through the night. At first, I freeze. Then my head angles towards the heavy drapes covering the windows. My ears strain to hear what might follow; a rapid burst of machine-gun fire? Incoming rockets? Or mortars perhaps?

I hear footsteps scurrying around outside. Judy sleeps on. I can't believe she hasn't heard any of this.

'Come on!' I hear a voice. Then running footsteps.

I'll find out what's going on and then alert Judy. No need to wake her; it might be nothing. I race to the door, feeling around in the dark for my shoes. Everything has gone quiet. I step into the hallway; still silence. Within seconds I am through the main door.

Outside the night air envelopes me. I crouch low. My eyes dart from left to right, adjusting.

'Tim!'

I run quickly down the concrete steps, turn a sharp left and dash across the pathway before turning towards the accommodation building. Tim will be there; at least, I hope he is. I mount the stairs two at a time. One of the Special Forces guys is now beside me.

'Stick with me,' he whispers.

Together we run up three flights to the rooftop. I stay with my back to the wall. We pass Dr Dave's private quarters. The bathroom light is on.

'Get down,' Tim whispers, beckoning.

I crouch, hiding behind the rooftop wall as Tim whispers to Dr Dave. Both are armed with US military-issued M4 carbines; a shorter and lighter version of the M16 assault rifle, which I know about, in some detail, because of Kerry's SAS training.

'Over there,' I hear Tim say, his hands steadily shifting his rifle to the left. He stares down the Picatinny rail and into the attached telescopic night vision sight. 'There! Near the orange light!'

My eyes immediately home in on him. A figure scurrying along the pathway and into an open door of a house 100 metres away.

'There's another one,' I whisper to Tim.

'Where?'

'There!' I point, 'Fifty metres from that that blue light!' He shifts his M4 in that direction.

'Got him!' Tim says, pointing.

'Got him too,' Dr Dave confirms. 'Now what?'

For the next 10 minutes we search the darkness for shadowy figures. There is a calmness that suggests this is not an attack. Tim and Dr Dave keep their eyes peeled and their rifles pointed. This is definitely not an attack; there is no excitement and panic. The explosion must have been caused by a gas cylinder somewhere in the township on the other side of the Silk Road. Cylinders have a tendency to leak and explode around here. Apparently it is not uncommon to see screaming neighbours with singed hair, running frantically from their burning kitchens. It is a poignant reminder of the precarious situation in Afghanistan, the need to be kept up to date with news and to have a realistic understanding of the risks, in order to make informed decisions. Phew.

'Well, that's about it folks,' Tim declares, slapping his hands together conclusively. 'I'll get the boys to double up on the perimeter just in case.'

I follow Tim who, always the gentlemen, says 'ladies first' as he slings his heavy assault rifle over his shoulder and points to the stairs.

'Thanks, Tim,' I flash a smile. 'Lucky I didn't wait for you to come drag me from my bed ... otherwise I would have missed all the action!'

'I was just about to come drag you from your bed,' Dr Dave quips.

I laugh and make my way back down the stairs with Tim and Dr Dave behind me. Like true gentlemen, they walk me back to my accommodation building where I bid them goodnight.

'Have a good night's sleep and don't worry about a thing,' says Tim 'We'll be right outside.'

I creep back inside the main building, through the hall and to my room. I slip off my shoes and put them along the wall. I don't need the light now; my eyes are fully adjusted to the darkness. Judy sleeps peacefully.

I'll tell her the news over breakfast.

I'll laugh at her for sleeping like a baby, while we were scurrying about like a make-believe crackpot commando team on some secret surveillance operation.

I wonder what Kerry would make of all this?

Is there trouble afoot? Or are we just scaredy-cats?

I tiptoe to my side of the room, slip into the sack and again sink into the soft mattress. I am sound asleep within minutes.

Chapter 15
White Ribbon Day in Nangarhar

When you are a mother,
you are never really alone in your thoughts.

A mother always has to think twice,
once for herself and once for her child.

Charlotte Gray

On the morning of 27 October 2008, Judy and I are deciding what to wear. We are also going over our notes for the Women's Health Seminar at which we are speakers. The seminar is due to start in an hour or so. I have been so careful in preparing my talk. I've thought long and hard on this for many weeks. I even consulted a friend who is trained in psychology. She told me to follow my heart. So I decided to think of some inspirational verses related to difficulties I have faced. It's too easy to Google wisdom quotes and use them. I want my contribution to be more personal than copying someone else's work. I prepared a slideshow too and made some simple bookmarks as gifts. Each bookmark has on it my inspirational verses in English and Pashtu. Of course, many of the women could be illiterate so I have pasted felt flowers and fake gemstones on each of the pretty coloured bookmarkers and sprinkled them with glitter. I'm not the most artistic person, but I want them each to have a gift made by my own hand. I think this means more when they know it comes from your heart.

Then there are the white ribbons. Mustn't forget the white ribbons. In a way, they're the main thing.

Judy decides to dress in a sea-green swirl-patterned tunic with dark trousers. She also wears a white cotton headscarf, a gift from one of the schools. She looks so lovely. I sit on the edge of my bed, impressed with what I'm wearing; it is a beautiful raw silk, earthy red salwar kameez made by Muslim's sister-in-law two nights ago. She hand-sewed every stitch and her detailed work impresses us all. There are many talented women in Afghanistan who could easily compete with the high fashion couturiers in Paris and Milan. Sadly the world has only ever heard the worst of Afghanistan — the bloodshed, the suffering — and not the beauty that we are seeing every day. No-one seems to care about the good news; certainly not foreign journalists with whom we share our stories. They are focused only on the war. All they ever ask is, 'Did you see anyone killed today?' or 'Did you see Taliban?' They don't care that we are about to participate in the first ever Healthy Families Seminar in this area. That should have made the news!

Judy smiles and says the colour of my salwar kameez perfectly complements my dark hair. I like that. Red is, of course, a rather bold colour to wear in Afghanistan, but ever since childhood, it has been my favourite colour. Many women wear even bolder colours. I gaze quietly at my notes, wondering how much will be lost in translation. Judy reassures me that everything will be fine and that we can only do our best.

Over the years I've spoken to many people who have experienced traumas and personal tragedies. One family in my community back home lost their son one night, after a teenager hit him with a single punch. The young boy fell to the ground dead. My mind goes back to my own experiences — those terrifying nights I endured as a hostage. In my mind, that was nowhere near as traumatic as watching your 15-year-old son lying dead on the street. There is always someone worse off than the next person. Many people have had it worse than me, some of whom have told me that they've known people who've had it worse than them!

As the saying goes, 'I cried because I had no shoes. Then I met a man who had no feet.'

Those profound words put everything about pain and suffering into perspective. Too often we fail to consider those worse off than us and even if we don't have the resources others may have, we still have the potential to give. So in preparing my presentation for the women of Nangarhar, I decide to follow my friend's advice and simply share from my heart and let the rest take care of itself.

Nangarhar University is the second-largest university in Afghanistan built on 160 hectares of land, 11 kilometres from Jalalabad City. Most of its students are male but there is a growing culture of female students, not counting the eight female faculty members on staff. We park as close to the International Learning Centre (ILC) as we can. The ILC has only just opened and we are among the first to use it. We are greeted at the door by a fellow Rotarian and ILC administrator, Mohammad. He has a warm smile and dark intelligent eyes. Mohammad is witty and capable; he ensures we have everything we need to run a successful seminar. He informs us that he has arranged two female translators fluent in Pashto and English to assist us. (To my relief, they *really* are fluent in English.) Mohammad is pleased to show us around and proud of what has been achieved.

We will be talking in a large room with ceiling fans, a wall-to-wall whiteboard, overhead projector, laptop and many other mod cons. The smell of freshly laid carpet is in the air.

In attendance are two nurse midwives from Surkh Rud area, and a field health worker and trainer from Heserak. Also in attendance are several women who represent large numbers of women from their communities; they are scheduled as speakers in the latter part of the program.

At 9 am precisely our guests arrive. It's like a sea of pale blue burqas. We invite them to enter the room and sit in rows. They put their burqas to one side, keeping their heads respectfully covered with headscarves. Some draw their scarves across their faces, as Mohammad, Chris and a couple of other men are present in the room. We greet the women from the remote poultry farm with open arms. We are so excited to see them again. Fifteen minutes later we begin. Diana welcomes the women and states the purpose of our visit. Then she introduces the first speaker, Mohammad, whose opening address touches on the history and purpose of the ILC. Coming to this university is the first time most of the women have ventured beyond their village. That these women have lived in such remote circumstances for all their lives doesn't shock me as much as some, because Australians are familiar with outback stations where the residents live in areas so remote that they sometimes drive half an hour to reach their nearest neighbour. There are many similarities between outback Australia and Afghanistan.

Next, the Minister from the Ministry of Health welcomes the midwives, the field health worker and trainer, and the women who represent their communities. He explains the importance of attending this seminar and says that it will be as much about learning from us, as us learning about them.

Judy is speaking next. Her language assistant is a little nervous.

Judy's subject is, The Role of Mothers and Women in Establishing a Foundation for a Healthy Society. I set up my camera near the front, in a quiet corner of the room, so as not to make anyone feel uncomfortable.

Judy begins.

What is a healthy society? It is healthy communities.

What is a healthy community? It is healthy families.

What is a healthy family? It is healthy fathers and mothers and children.

What is a healthy father? He is a loving, caring, responsible and respectful human being.

What is a healthy mother? She is a loving, caring, responsible and respectful human being. What is a healthy child? He/she is loving, happy, growing human being.

How do we, as mothers and women, promote a healthy society? We have to start with ourselves. How do we take care of ourselves? We need the support of our families. Our husbands, our mothers, our fathers, our sisters and other close relatives. We need the help of our whole communities. We need to help our whole communities. We don't live in isolation. We live with our families and in communities. In most societies of the world, the work of the family and house falls on women's shoulders. That is our primary job, to care for our families. To care for their health, physically, emotionally and spiritually is the greatest privilege anyone person can have. I can hear you thinking, 'How can she say that? It is hard work to be responsible for everyone in my family. I have to cook, clean, wash all the clothes, get the food and water, bathe the children, change the diapers, discipline them, and what if I don't have family to help me? How can I do all that?' It seems overwhelming. But we do have resources within ourselves. We have friends we can talk to. And we have spiritual help.

Judy shares her life with the group. She tells how she grew up in a loving home with her mother, father and older sister near Dallas, Texas. Judy acknowledges that her parents had expectations of her, just as many parents of young Afghan children have expectations of their daughters. Her audience understands all this because the concept, structure and order of the family is equally respected in the West, as it is in the East.

In Judy's family, education is highly valued. Her older sister attended medical school. On graduating from high school, Judy was also expected to go to college, which she did. But after attending college for a year, Judy had other ideas. She wanted to get married more than go to school. Her parents were not exactly thrilled about this. They wanted more for her. At 19, Judy married fellow student Ray Boykin. He was two weeks shy of 21.

Ray became a loving father to their two daughters and worked hard to support his family. He was diabetic. Diabetes is a life-threatening disease, which he'd had since high school. As he got older the diabetes became harder to control. In his 30s he had pain in his feet and legs. He became blind a few years after that. He had surgery but lost the sight of his left eye and had it removed. In 1985, he lost the function of his kidneys and had to go on a dialysis machine. In May 1987, he had a kidney transplant after which he lived another five weeks and died aged 41. That he died so young strikes a chord with Judy's audience, as the average life expectancy of Afghan males is only 46 years. It is at this point that Judy has everyone's complete attention. She is such a quietly spoken woman, so unassuming. I quietly observe her through the lens of my video camera.

During our 21 years of marriage, I did go back to school and become a nurse. I knew that I would have to take care of him during his illness. He was a very brave man. Everyone in our town looked up to him for spiritual and emotional strength. We had a very strong faith in God. The people in town were looking at us to see how we would handle this crisis. It was not easy after he died. I did not have much money. My children were 14 and 18. It was very hard for them to realise that their father was not coming home any more, that we would have to survive without him. What would we do? Where would we go? We did not own our home. We had to move out. I felt so alone. No-one else in my family had lost a husband that young. I knew that I could get a job but I was in shock! I could not really function mentally for about three months. All my routines would have to change. My friends from one town could not go with me to another town. But my family was steadfast. My close friends and my sister came and helped me pack and move all my belongings to another town where my daughter was in school. I could not work yet, but in a few weeks I did find a job and was able to clear my thoughts and plan for the future. What else was there to help me? My faith in God was all I had.

Many of the older ladies are quietly nodding. Clearly they are relating to Judy's experiences. Her life journey poses many questions.

How do you deal with difficulties in your life?

Do you ask your friends, family and God to help you?

Where can you go when there seems no place to go?

What resources do you have?

Do you have a doctor or other medically-qualified person to go to if you are ill?

What if you have problems within your family?

Do you have some other trusted friend to share your problems with?

Do you know someone that you can rely on for wise advice?

These questions put into perspective that no matter where we are, or what culture we are from, we all share fundamental concerns. Building a healthy community begins with helping one person at a time. It's about caring.

> *When I do something good for someone else, I feel good. It helps to think about someone else and not myself, not my difficulties. There is always someone who has a worse problem than I do. If you can walk down the street, there is always someone who cannot. What can you do for that person? Can you be their friend? Can you pray for them? Can you help them in some way? Challenge yourself to help someone today.*

Each of us has a miracle story in our lives. Each of us has something to share with someone else, to show they are not alone in their struggle, whatever that struggle may be. Judy concludes with a message of encouragement:

> *Our families need us to be sane and whole. They rely on our wisdom and our resourcefulness to help them survive in this challenging world. Your children are watching you and will repeat what they see. Make that a positive and loving person they see. May God bless you in everything you do.*

The women show their appreciation by clapping and I smile at Judy to give some reassurance that hers has been the most amazing presentation. Her language assistant stands smiling beside her.

I was supposed to speak after lunch but for some reason they change the schedule and Diana tells me that I am up next.

'Next?'

'Yes.'

I check the slideshow is ready, and then ask my language assistant to hand out the bookmarks on which I quoted a few inspirational verses. These are actually the headings of my presentation. It is a simple gesture that is meant as an expression that we can, if we have the will, do something special for someone else, even a stranger.

I also give each woman a white ribbon attached with a gold pin that I'd received from Katrina Brooks, Marketing Manager of the White Ribbon Campaign (Australia) — Making violence against women a thing of the past (www.whiteribbonday.org.au). The women pin their white ribbons to their burqas; or for those who have discarded their burqa pin them elsewhere on their dresses.

I explain the meaning behind the white ribbon. It's a visible sign that the wearer will not condone violence against women, and together we will reinforce our commitment to ending such violence. White Ribbon Day was created by a handful of Canadian men in 1991 on the second anniversary of the massacre of 14 women in Montreal. For 45 minutes on 6 December 1989 an enraged gunman, Marc Lepine, aged 25, roamed the corridors of Montreal's École Polytechnique and killed 14 women. He separated the men from the women and then opened fire on the classroom of female engineering students. As he did so, he screamed, 'I hate feminists'. One student tried pleading with Lepine that the women students were not feminists. They were just students taking engineering. But Lepine didn't listen. He killed those 14 young girls and then himself. Since then, and with the formation of the White Ribbon Campaign, men are urged to speak out against violence against women. The women seated before me are incredulous the campaign was devised by men.

Everyone has a bookmark and a white ribbon, the slideshow has been checked, I am about to begin my presentation. The room falls silent. I begin by telling the women that Kerry and I were kidnapped by the communist police. I was taken against my will and put in an ugly prison. There I was forced to watch Kerry being tortured and other prisoners too. Some of them died, others went crazy; then came my turn to suffer. The women in the room silently nod. This is an all too familiar story for them but perhaps they are surprised that something so terrible could happen to a Westerner.

Some people find it difficult to share their inner feelings with complete strangers, but I've never felt embarrassed going public with my pain. I've bared my soul more times than I can count. I do so to ensure that what I endured in that communist prison was not in vain. I also think that we endure hardships for a reason. Perhaps it is to light a path for someone else. Perhaps it is to put us on a platform where we can have relevance, like today.

As I relate these experiences I also share that it was difficult for me to believe how cruel human beings can be to each other. I lived every day in utter despair and, as the months passed, I felt increasingly afraid that I would never see my three children — Jessica, Sahra and Nathan — again. In that place, at that time, there was no-one to help me physically survive those hardships; they were too preoccupied trying to survive their own ordeals. So it was up to me to find a way to do everything that I could to endure the seemingly impossible. I click the laptop key to reveal my first slide. It reads: 'Life is not easy and requires a great deal of patience, but I can endure!'

That's what I told myself every morning after waking up and finding myself trapped in the same nightmare that I had endured the day before, and the day before that. I tell my audience that I looked for the simple things to focus on: blue sky above, white clouds, distant palm trees; and I forced myself to remember that there was life beyond the prison walls and one day, if I did not give up, I would be free. I counted my blessings every day: I was healthy, I was fit, I was mentally strong and I was determined to live. We always have something to be thankful for. Often we cannot understand why we must endure hardships. Sometimes there is no apparent reason why bad things should come our way. A friend of mine once told me that we may feel we are walking alone, but we seldom are.

I click the key to reveal slide two: 'I am a good person who just happens to be traveling a difficult journey. I will survive!'

I share that there were times when I felt my strength failing, along with my health and emotional wellbeing. But through those times, other women prisoners gave me courage and reminded me that we are all in life's struggle together. Life is meant to be lived, which means it will have its ups and downs. In that prison, I learned to simplify my life into minutes and to tell myself that I can endure one minute, then the next and the next. Even amidst so much pain and anguish, not knowing when or if I would see my children again, I forced myself to see the happiness that could have been easily overlooked; to share a smile with a friend, to light up an otherwise darkened day, to exchange a knowing look that can express more than words, to sit with other women and sew tiny flowers on a faded piece of cloth, to draw comfort in not being alone.

I click slide three: 'In the world there are others I may never meet – but I take comfort knowing they CARE about me'.

I share that lots of people care about the plight of Afghanistan. Many are women they may never meet and who may never come to this place, but they care nonetheless. I remind them that their lives have meaning and purpose. That each of our lives may differ in experiences, environments, struggles and beliefs, but what we all share in common is our desire to take care of ourselves as women and to continue the journey towards emotional health and personal happiness. One of the many valuable lessons that I have learned as I continue my life's journey, is that we can be happy even in despair. Even when we lack freedom or material wealth, we can have abundance in so many other ways. We must learn to embrace all that we are and to remind ourselves daily that every moment in our life is valuable and worthwhile. We are the culmination of every moment we have experienced, both good and bad.

We must learn to appreciate ourselves, and all we have been through, and to release the pain of past hurts.

We must learn to love the person that we are.

We must learn to be positive and look on the bright side of life. Inside each and every one of us, there is an energy that is directly linked to our emotions. If we look deeply into our selves, we can often discover the things that make us feel emotionally heavy. Negative thoughts drain our inner energy and block us from finding our true happiness. Of course we are all different, so we need to examine ourselves to find out what specifically brings us down emotionally.

I tell them, 'Most of my negative energy was fuelled by the feelings of anger because of the injustices I had been subjected to, fear of losing control of my life and resentment towards those who had caused me so much pain. If left to their own devices these emotions would have prevented me from becoming whole again.'

My fourth slide reveals: 'I am amazing — designed to endure the seemingly impossible.'

I share how I have finally accepted that there are some things I cannot and probably will never change. I had to learn how to let go of all the negativity that was keeping me down.

'Life will continue to be challenging and I don't expect all my journeys to be easy. I am alive and I will never walk alone so long as I continue to remain upbeat. I surround myself with women who are amazing, who remain positive even during hard times, women who never give up their hopes and dreams, women who truly believe that they can overcome the seemingly impossible.'

My fifth slide: 'If I can force myself to smile while tears are flowing — then I will endure another day!'

I explain how I had searched for a long time to find the key to unlock my heart to happiness. That key was my smile. Of course, I know that Afghan women aren't supposed to smile but in the safety of other women, why not? One by one, I make eye contact with every woman in the room and one by one, we share the most beautiful thing: a smile. This is our secret. This is something that no-one can take from us. The smiles fill the room and prompt one lady to ask boldly through the language assistants, 'What will be the most memorable thing about my country that you will take back to yours?'

I look at every face smiling back at me. I don't even need to pause to think of my response.

'Oh, that's an easy one,' I say, smiling. 'The smiles on each of your beautiful faces will be my everlasting memory of Afghanistan.' I gently clench my hand into a fist and place it over my heart and softly utter '*Manana,*' which is Pashto for 'thank you'.

The room erupts into applause.

My language assistant beams her most brilliant smile beside me. Her lovely dark brown eyes assure me that my presentation was a success.

After my presentation we break for lunch. Take-away chicken packs with salad, traditional naan bread and rice are handed out to each woman, along with a can of ice-cold soda. It sparks an immediate feeding frenzy as their hands grab at the food; obviously they fear missing out. Judy, Diana and I tell them there is plenty of food for everyone, which does little to stem the frantic snatching of each item placed before them and the desperate tearing of the plastic coverings. And then it dawns on us that these women have not eaten all morning. For the next half an hour everyone sits quietly and eats. We notice afterwards that the women seem less anxious and certainly more content. Perhaps we should have fed them sooner, but none of us knew how hungry they were. Next time we'll know better. Afghan people are proud, they would prefer to watch their guests eat to their fill than let it be known that they have gone without. Graciously, the women in the room overlook our poor planning because they know our intentions are good. But next time we will begin with the food.

A sudden commotion catches my eye. 'Oh my God, Judy!' is all I have time to exclaim. A US marine bursts through the doorway of the learning centre and he walks towards us; there are others behind. I hold my breath. There is complete silence. The barrel of a gun points slowly at me, the marine looks me over and then passes onto someone else. He has mistaken me for an Afghan woman, I can tell. My dark eyes cautiously follow his movements. His face is unsmiling. Carefully I adjust my headscarf to tuck my dark hair back underneath the raw silk.

I avert my eyes, lower my head and whisper, '*Salam Al-aye kum.*' (Greetings).

It is the first thing that comes to mind. He does not respond. His eyes turned to Judy and soften. She remains silent. Where's Muslim?

One by one, the US marines file in until the room is completely surrounded. All are dressed in camouflage uniforms with ballistic helmets and flak jackets. They are also carrying a full range of weapons, including grenades. It's war alright. Next, the colonel is given the nod that the building is secured, after which he formally addresses our group.

'Greetings, ladies,' he smiles. He *smiles*!

The colonel tells us that our event will make an excellent addition to their documentary on positive military interaction within community. Is that what it's all about? The Home Box Office (HBO) cameraman doesn't look like he's from HBO, although he explains to Judy that he is required to dress like the marines, for safety reasons. Here they all are in full combat gear, ten giant men escorting one single HBO cameraman/reporter. The women have experienced genuine fear. I feel like we have betrayed them, but none of us had any idea this intrusion would occur. I wonder how we are going to show our faces when the marines leave? Granted that their intentions were good but the women in the room didn't know that. We are easily forgiven when it is explained that we were just as startled as them.

'Especially me,' I laugh. 'They thought I was an Afghan woman!'

The women break into a cackle of laughter. The presence of the marines is soon forgotten because we are all determined not to let anything spoil our time together. In the back of mind I think momentarily about the insurgents, wondering if they are aware of our little get-together.

I also think how brave these women and their husbands are to agree to such assemblies. I hope there won't be repercussions. I think about Muslim and the reality that, as an Afghan, he could easily be mistaken for the enemy. He could be whisked off to secret detention, like Guantanamo Bay prison, or shot by insurgents as a spy for the Americans even though he is not. It's more horrible to think of these things becoming reality when it is someone you know. As Muslim waits patiently in the next room, I try to push such thoughts and fears from my mind. In Afghanistan, uncertainty is an existential reality!

When we reconvene, the head of Obstetrics and Gynaecology gives a presentation on 'Understanding the Basic Principles of Maternal Health'. The doctor graduated from Kabul University Medical School where she specialised in pregnancy, wellness, and positive labour and delivery outcomes. This presentation is followed by a panel discussion with four community healthcare professionals, which Judy facilitates.

For three-quarters of an hour they talk about basic nutrition and hygiene techniques that can be used in the home, for disease reduction, reduced mortality, increased longevity and improved health. At one point the question is asked, 'How many women in this room have had home births, without the assistance of a doctor, nurse or midwife?' About 20 women stand up. One describes how she dug a ditch during labour where she would deliver her baby. She had previously used this birthing method for three of her children. I visualise this woman scratching around in the dirt in some isolated area, outside the sanctity of her community's compound, preparing her version of what we might call a delivery room. Her fingernails are broken and splintered. She is unwashed and bloody. My heart skips a beat as I listen to her describing those painfully lonely hours of uncertainty. Did she know that she could easily die if things did not proceed right? What if the baby had gotten stuck or the cord wrapped around its neck, or if she lost too much blood?

I had my first child at 18. I found the experience extremely traumatic, lying flat on my back on a old cast iron bed with no place to put my feet to push when I needed to, and grouchy Catholic nuns shouting at me to not make such a fuss. What the hell did they know about birthing anyway? I didn't have any idea about what was about to happen. At the time I thought that was the worst experience ever, until I came here and heard these accounts.

One young woman told me how she had watched her mother suffer in labour for 16 hours before dying. Their village was remote — no clinic, no doctor, no way of getting to a hospital or having a doctor get to them. I learned from one of the midwives that almost every 26 minutes, an Afghan woman dies giving birth. One in nine dies during pregnancy. Most are under the age of 18. In one Afghan province (Badakshan) there are 6500 reported deaths per 100,000 reported births. The leading causes of maternal death in these remote areas are mostly haemorrhaging and complications resulting from prolonged or obstructed labour. As explained to me, there are no hospitals in 20 of the 31 provinces of Afghanistan. The Red Cross has mobile clinics of which the majority remain in the cities and seldom, if ever, venture out to where they are urgently needed. Who can blame them? After all, after Somalia, Afghanistan is the second most dangerous place in the world for aid workers, with a reported 33 aid workers killed in 2008 and 141 security incidents recorded against aid workers. Iraq comes in as the third most dangerous, and Israel fourth.

In winter, the difficulties escalate tenfold. The heavy snowfalls make most roads impassable. During these times, and in these remote provinces, millions of Afghans go hungry. Thousands of babies risk starvation in the first month of life. The hardships these women face are incredible. This is the reality of their existence. Most of them have none of the luxuries that even our Australian colonial ancestors had, like hot water, a clean cloth to wrap baby in, a clean sheet to lie on during delivery, and a friend to see them through the experience in case something should go wrong.

Despite all the tragedies Afghan women have faced over the past decades, they have proven to be among the most resilient women in the world. Being able to share these intimate details bonds us, despite our obvious cultural differences. We share ideas about basic nutrition and hygiene techniques. We talk about disease reduction, reducing mortality, increased longevity and improved health. The questions and answers flow back and forth. Our conversations have nothing to do with Western ideals or politics. Nothing we say will change the power play going on around us. We are simply learning, from each other, ways of taking care of each other as women. Nothing more and certainly nothing for the men to ever feel threatened by!

I learn that my language assistant's 24-year-old sister has already had five kids to her cousin. She was married to him at the age of 13 when he was 20 years old. It was all arranged by their parents. Apparently, too, he is very abusive and she can do nothing because it will bring shame on her and her family. So she just bears it as many abused wives do! My language assistant tells me that her family home was firebombed by the Taliban and that her father has received threatening letters from the Taliban, who question why he sends his daughters to the university. It was so bad at one point she had to leave the province for several months. She wants me to understand that no matter how difficult life may seem, Afghan women just get on with it.

I amm of course, impressed.

At the end of our seminar, we draw the names of the lucky door prize winners and distribute health literature packets and hygiene packs for every woman who attended. Judy presents the midwives with a special midwifery magazine and several newborn kits to distribute to the pregnant women. Everyone gets something and everyone is happy that they came.

As the women are getting ready to leave some are already putting on their burqas. I ask the younger girls close by if I can try one on. They find it funny to see me walking around the room dressed like that, mostly bumping into everything. I grab two girls and throw them under the burqa too, 'Hey, we could have a party under here!' I laugh, as they do too. When I release them, all the other women are laughing. I am glad our day ends like this and not with that awful memory of the invading marines.

Muslim enters the room, so I slip back under the burqa, slowly walk outside and then double back to stand near him, '*As-Salaam Alaykum*,' I say softly.

'What are you doing, Kay? Are you trying to trick me?' he laughs.

I throw back the burqa and reveal my surprised face, 'How did you know it was me?' I ask.

'You are the only woman in Afghanistan to wear a red salwar kameez!'

'Oh, and I thought I was invisible,' I respond, flashing a smile.

He shakes his head and probably thinks I'm crazy while the women clearly find our little exchange intriguing.

With our seminar at its conclusion, I have a tremendous feeling of admiration for these women. In typical female fashion, we hug and I wish all the women a safe journey home. We thank them for attending the conference, for sharing their stories and for listening so attentively to ours. We ask them to pass on our sincerest appreciation to their husbands, brothers and fathers, for allowing them to visit with us, and for those who have driven them from afar, from the remote communities of Farm Hadda, Surkh Rud and Heserak. We acknowledge the difficulties of them making such a journey and we express our gratitude.

Wearing their white ribbons, the blue burqa women file out of the room one after another as silently as they arrived hours before.

'It was simply incredible!' I sigh as we survey the mess we'd made of Mohammad's beautiful room.

'Next time we should give them lunch outside,' Diana replies and shakes her head. 'It was incredible wasn't it?'

'Indeed it was,' said Judy.

All three of us know that we are fortunate to have been allowed such an interaction with the women of Nangarhar province. It isn't often that foreigners are invited to share an intimate glimpse into their secluded world. Most of it depends upon the will of the men — folk, whether they think there will be complications by introducing strange Western women to their wives and daughters, versus their interest and excitement at being able to visit with foreigners. Our intention is always to respect their culture and their traditions. We simply want to be women among women.

On Monday evening of 27 October 2008, we prepare for our departure from the guesthouse in Jalalabad and to return to Kabul. We have only six days left of our eastern adventure. Chris, John, Judy and I sit at the far end of the giant dining table that seats 14 and quietly listen as Diana shares a few final ideas with Muslim; ideas that are designed to provide further assistance to the poultry farmers whom we visited during the course of our Jalalabad tour. Muslim nods his head and occasionally interjects with sound advice. It is decided we will leave at 9 am the next morning.

'If we are not departed by 10 am then I cannot go back to Kabul because after that time it is too dangerous,' says Muslim.

'We'll be ready,' says Diana.

I am sad to be leaving Jalalabad when there is still so much more to be done. I think of the children in the prison and I wish we could have bought some dolls for the little girls, toy racing cars for the little boys and colourful building blocks for both. All children like to play and have fun. It is what they should be doing, not reliving the constant nightmare of Daddy coming home and beating Mummy, or the sound of machine gunfire, or the image of bullets ripping into people, or seeing blood in the dirt. Children shouldn't have to see such ugly images but that is all they know, most of them anyway. Thinking of the children living in Nangarhar prison, I feel sorry that there is nothing much else for them to occupy their minds. There are no toys. There are no tall oak trees or a swing attached that might take them soaring above all their fears. Theirs is just an endless routine existence filled with memories that would haunt an average human being to despair.

We promised the children we would return some other time, perhaps in a year or so, or sooner if we can raise the funds. We promised the women that we would make a difference to their lives and not forget our time spent together in the dusty prison grounds. We promised to keep them in our hearts and we will. Diana said it best when she quoted Richard L. Evans (one of the most senior leaders in her Mormon Church): 'Children will not remember you for the material things you provided but for the feeling that you cherished them.'

I hope they felt cherished. Every moment we spent with them has been precious.

Tomorrow we will farewell the Taj Mahal Guesthouse. We'll take two mini-vans and drive as inconspicuously as we can through the treacherous hairpin turns, along roads and into dark tunnels, through the township of Sorubi and beyond the mountains. We will stop at military checkpoints and wait nervously while Muslim explains what we are doing in a war zone. At times, we will wonder if the cars that speed past us are carrying suicide bombers. Other times we will wonder why Diana's vehicle has fallen way behind or why they take longer to get through various military checkpoints. This time we will not stop for the delicious red pomegranates. Following Muslim's instructions, we will drive as safely and as quickly as possible to Kabul and we pray to Allah that nothing will hinder our journey.

Chapter 16

Herat Today, Gone Tomorrow

If we could have flown from Jalalabad directly to Herat province, and bypassed Kabul altogether, then we would have. Unfortunately, the war has hampered all commercial air travel so there are no direct flights. We had to drive but we arrived in Kabul safely, much to our relief. From here we will take a Kam Air flight north. Hopefully our plane won't be shot down!

Although he has to get back to his job, I tell Muslim, 'I wish you could come with us.'

He smiles.

We stand together beside the rusty cannon in the garden of the Gandamack Lodge. He was ever so patient when I bombarded him with questions earlier in the trip. 'You've been a real blessing, Muslim.'

Click. Judy snaps our picture.

'*Insha'Allah*,' we will meet again soon,' Muslim replies.

We all feel incredibly sad to be saying farewell. None of us really acknowledged, until that moment, just how much we have depended on him. It was Muslim who showed us the heart and soul of ordinary Afghan people. He made sure that we had everything we needed, especially safe travel. In his care, not once did we ever feel that we were in serious danger. He was constantly vigilant. He opened our eyes to so many new experiences and places that we would never have seen without him as our guide. He told us stories of ancient times, of Islam, and of the hardships and the triumphs of the people. There is still so much for me to learn about his homeland, its people and its customs but I feel that I am less ignorant than I was before. I feel that I have grown a great deal as a person, as has my empathy for the Afghan people.

There is a lot to be said for having someone like Muslim as your guide in Afghanistan, particularly when you must rely on local sources for intelligence. It can be the difference between life and death, and for many NGO workers, it has been that exactly. I don't know what will happen in Herat. I just wish that Muslim was coming with us.

'You will be fine,' he smiles as we climb into the mini-van that will take us to the airport.

'*Insha'Allah*!' I call out just before the door slams shut.

Muslim smiles as he waves. None of us are entirely certain that we will see him again.

It is raining when we reach the airport. Our Kam Air flight is due to depart at 10 am and we are expected to arrive in Herat an hour after takeoff. Diana's contact, Dr Katiby, will be there to meet us. Everyone is wearing warm jackets in preparation for the cold, everyone except me of course. I only packed light cotton clothing. So typical of a Queenslander, living in a state where it's beautiful one day and perfect the next. I'm always the one who, despite the weather forecast, wears T-shirts to Sydney in winter because I can't imagine anything colder than 13 degrees celsius. John pulls his wool jumper snugly over his sturdy frame. *Brrr*. I wrap my salwar kameez around me, hoping I won't freeze to death.

'It's not *that* cold,' says Judy.

Actually she's right. It's not that cold but with the wind blowing it does feel colder.

Judy and I sit together on the flight, wondering if some smelly man who is yet to fully bathe for Friday prayers will sit beside me. On a practical level, there isn't enough water in Afghanistan to enable its 32 million citizens to fully bathe five times a day for prayer time. In any case, we will only have to endure an hour of flying before reaching Herat.

Take-off.

I gaze at the landscape below. It is a series of interconnecting brown squares and mud brick compounds, much the same as any other place in this arid country with little vegetation, surrounded by vast desert plains and formidable mountains. I wonder if the insurgents are watching as the wings tip and the plane banks hard to the right. An eerie silence fills the cabin. I suspect everyone else is praying we don't die today. Do the Taliban even have surface to air missiles? I recall reading that one was used by Iraqi insurgents to shoot down a Lynx helicopter over Basra in May 2006. It could have been one of those belonging to the United States.

During the Soviet War in Afghanistan, the Central Intelligence Agency supplied 500 FIM-92 Stingers (surface to air missiles) to the Mujahedeen. Some sources claim it was more like 1500 to 2000. After the Soviet withdrawal the United States attempted to buy back the Stingers without much success. Some of them found their way into Iran, Qatar and North Korea. It's quite possible the Taliban acquired some too and if they did, would they waste them on a civilian airline when they have so many more military targets to choose from?

Does Kam Air have any defensive systems to deflect an attempted strike? I doubt it. Ten minutes into our flight and we are still alive. I re-read my tourist guide looking for something pleasant to distract me from the thought of suddenly becoming a pile of ashes. According to the section on Herat, it is one of the oldest cities in Afghanistan and one that has been repeatedly destroyed by foreign invaders. It is also one of the country's most favoured tourist destinations. Fantastic! I hope I live to see the citadel Qala-e Ikhtiyaruddin that, according to the book, stands in the centre of the city with its 18 towers and huge battlements.

'Inside tourists may marvel at its ancient Persian tile-work and centuries-old Islamic calligraphy,' I read aloud to Judy.

'Sounds wonderful,' she responds.

Chris leans closer to the back of our seat and says he wants to see the 'Old Fort'. I flick to the page on it and read aloud: 'Alexander the Great occupied the Old Fort during his reign over Afghanistan (330 BCE). It is now occupied by the Afghan Army, having been restored with help from UNESCO. The Old Fort sits on top of a mound at the northern edge of the Old City (Shahr-e Kuhna) and is home to an ethnographic museum, a military museum, handicraft workshops and an archaeological museum … now that does sound interesting.'

All of us agree that we are keen to visit the Old Fort and the Great Mosque (Masjid-I-Jami) that features Ghorid and Timurid tiling and is arguably the most stunning mosque in the world.

'It says the tile factory is a 'must-see.' I show Judy the page.

Being a lover of history, I am excited that I will be walking in the footsteps of the ancient tribes of the Barlas, the original Mongol army of the great Genghis Khan. My interest in Genghis Khan and Soviet history was sparked long ago through my friendship with Stuart Bromley, an international museum curator who once arranged for the Kremlin to loan him their Fabergé pieces so that he could tour the world with them to mark the 150th anniversary of Fabergé. It was an amazing collection. In fact, because of Stuart, the very first Western film crew was allowed access to the Kremlin for a special Fabergé preview. I would listen for hours as Stuart described all the amazing adventures of Mongol kings and ancient civilisations and all these battles on the very ground that I will soon be walking.

Another side to Herat is less pleasant to think about. Like many other places in Afghanistan, Herat did not escape the Taliban's reign of terror or the mass killings of innocent people found in mass graves. Heinous acts of genocide were committed on thousands of innocent people, not just war prisoners and not just those hated because of their ethnicity. The Taliban threw the tortured, charred dead bodies of their victims onto the streets of Herat City. No-one was allowed to bury them. No-one was allowed to mourn them. Innocent eyes of Afghan children were forced to witness such atrocities. Their minds cannot ever hope to escape these images that surely must haunt them. Having seen the reports, the photographs and eye-witness accounts of such atrocities, I cannot help but wonder if these people will ever truly recover from the nightmare of those days.

A history of suffering awaits us, just like everywhere else we go in this formidable country. *Sorrow. Pain. Despair.* These three words come to mind as I look out the cabin window.

The plane touches down and skids to a halt. The air is a crisp 13 degrees Celsius. The wind has picked up. We exit the aircraft and walk across the black asphalt of the tarmac to a silvery chain wire fence. None of us has any idea where to collect our luggage but we follow the crowd of turbans and tribal hats. The familiar grey uniformed Afghan Border Police observe the passengers. They're looking for anyone who looks remotely suspicious. They point to the silvery chain wire fence. I guess that's where we're meant to wait. They shut the gate behind us.

Diana and the others are distracted by a swarm of young boys, all offering to collect our bags from the other side of the fence. From the corner of my eye, I suddenly notice a truck tearing across the black asphalt tarmac. Where it came from is anyone's guess. I slowly take several steps back without even realising, until I find myself actually standing alone and at least several metres from Diana and the others.

The Afghan Border Police seem unconcerned. I look at the faces on those around me for a sign of distress. They too are not bothered by the commotion. The truck pulls up to a rather primitive looking loading area. The driver gets out and starts throwing all the bags onto the wooden dock in a pile. The swarm of young boys become frenzied. It's like watching a pack of dogs fighting over a bone. Somewhere in amongst them are Diana, Judy and Chris; with John, like me, is watching from a safe distance away. Several men gather in a group behind me, chattering like most do, when they've been away from friends. I imagine they have returned from holiday. I look briefly at the large white sign suspended from the building behind me: 'Welcome to the Historical City of Herat'. I pull my scarf around my body for warmth and slowly gaze about me, taking in the parking lot several metres away.

An Afghan man approaches me, smiling and shaking his head. I return his smile and politely say hello. Although I have no idea who he is, it seems a natural thing to do. Dressed in a dark blue business suit and matching pale blue shirt, he obviously has some social standing. He speaks quickly, assuming I can follow his conversation. After several moments he pauses, puzzled.

'I'm sorry. I'm Australian. Do you speak English?' I say.

He laughs, 'Oh, my goodness, I thought you were the language assistant for the Americans who I have come to meet,' he says pointing to Diana.

'Dr Katiby, how are you?' she smiles with recognition and waves from the centre of the pack.

Dr Katiby will be our guide for the duration of our stay.

'Please forgive me,' he bows, 'But you look like a lady from Kazakhstan and your Pashtu greeting is perfect.'

'I've been practising,' I reply, and shake his outstretched hand, thinking Muslim would be proud.

'Oh you are cold,' he exclaims. 'Please sit in the car straightaway'. He indicates to the driver to open the door of a nearby Toyota mini-van and says, 'Come.' Never mind its plush burgundy interior, I want the heater.

'That's much better for you, please wait here, rest.' And then he is gone. The door slides shut behind him and I watch him trudge over to Diana and the others who have accumulated quite a collection of young baggage boys. Dr Katiby waves half a dozen of them away and instructs the others to load the bags in the rear of the mini-van.

'He thought I was a local,' I joke to Diana and Judy as they climb in beside me.

'So did the US marines!' Judy exclaims.

After a round of introductions, Dr Katiby tells the driver to get going. We are 15 minutes south of the city and heading towards the Marco Polo Hotel on Jad-e Badmurghan Road, Herat.

'It is the most popular Western-standard hotel in the city,' says Dr Katiby. 'The rooms aren't elaborate but they do boast 24-hour hot water and free internet.'

'And breakfast?' asks Chris.

'Breakfast is also included — a huge spread of bread, cheese, yoghurt, eggs and fruit. At AUD$45 per night that is quite reasonable. I know the manager and he is more than willing to give you a special rate since you are staying several nights.'

Since the fall of the Taliban, Herat is considered one of the safer cities in Afghanistan but Dr Katiby advises that we should not venture out alone. We are still in a war zone, even though it *seems* quite peaceful. Iran is only 80 kilometres away, which explains the strong Iranian cultural influence. I get the impression that things are just as troubled here as elsewhere in the country but perhaps less obvious. We mustn't become complacent.

After checking in at reception and depositing our bags upstairs, we quickly freshen up before heading back downstairs to the main lounge to await the Herat Rotarians. At Diana's request, Dr Katiby arranged the meeting. I learn that he is the club's president and one of its founders. Brad Hanson, from the United States State Department, also joins us, as do members of the Herat University. We are keen to find out how far the Rotary Club of Herat has progressed since forming in June 2004.

'We do many good works with the support of our international Rotarians. It is really new for us and we are trying to make strong our Rotary contribution,' says Dr Katiby in his opening address to our small group assembled. 'We cordially invite you to support our Rotary endeavours and wish that you will help bring a difference to the lives of our vulnerable people. Hopefully one day we will stand on our own feet.'

It is wonderful to discover that the principle motto of Rotary (Service Above Self) is alive and well in Herat, and although the club is small in membership, each has pledged to support the broader aims of Rotary: combating hunger, improving health and sanitation, finding ways to provide education and job training, promoting peace, and eradicating polio. Rotarians of Herat are certainly among those who, throughout the world, value human life.

As night begins to fall, Dr Katiby invites us for a street tour of our outside surroundings.

'Is it safe?' I wonder.

'You are with me,' Dr Katiby says.

The people of Herat know him well and we will not experience any difficulty. It seems strange walking on the sidewalk in Afghanistan without having to worry about being seen. In fact, everyone we pass smiles in greeting. Diana instantly spots many photo opportunities and begins, though rather discreetly at first, engaging stall owners along the way. They are only too happy to comply. I wonder what Muslim would think if he saw us now? He would always tell us that it is not safe to draw attention to ourselves, though that was in Jalalabad where things are more intense. Here in Herat it feels a lot safer. The people seem very hospitable; some even offer us free cookies from their stores.

'I feel more at ease here than elsewhere,' I admit to Judy, adding Kerry's words, 'but I know it is unwise to become complacent.'

'I know what you mean, Kay; it feels so odd to be so exposed like this,' she says quietly.

'It's wonderful!' I reply.

We tell Dr Katiby how different things are on the eastern side of his country. He says, 'Herat is more peaceful than anywhere else, but life is still difficult for many people. While you are here, you will see that many people have the wrong impression about Afghanistan due to a lot of media propaganda. It has given people a negative impression.'

We listen as we walk.

'The ordinary people are tired of war. Most of our problems come from internal corruptions and neighbouring countries like Pakistan. Because the people are not politically aware, some politicians misuse their trust. Fortunately the people now realise what is going on and the young generation, both male and female, are trying to improve their knowledge through education. This will bring hope for a prosperous future.'

'I hope so,' I reply. 'Surely it must with the support of the international community?'

'We can only hope this is so,' he responds. 'If I compare the past to now then I can say that there has been great change, which is still very new but will grow gradually. We feel more optimistic than before and although the economy is not good, we are all hoping that it will improve as our country moves more and more towards democracy. Afghanistan has lost its middle class and now only has two classes, the very rich and the very poor. Eighty per cent of the people live in poverty. We are all trying to make life better,' he concludes.

Born in Herat, Dr Katiby is one of the lucky ones who received a scholarship under the American Field Service (AFS) program in 1967. The following year he was sent to high school in Chelmsford, Massachusetts, USA.

'I lived with an Irish family for one year and learned a great deal from them and other people in the community. It was an incredible experience and my life would probably be very different now if I had not had that opportunity. I returned to Herat with many good ideas, eager to share my experiences with my fellow students. After completing my degree at the Kabul University, I became a doctor, a gynaecologist actually. I have never forgotten the struggle to get where I am today. Even now, though I am a doctor, I am still a very poor man but I am rich in helping others.'

'You have seen many changes in your country?' I asked.

'Yes indeed. When President Muhammad Dauod Khan came to power it was believed that he wanted to bring changes and progress. He made plans that the Government would no longer have any personal relationships with the Soviet Union and try to make Afghanistan closer to the West, especially with other oil rich Middle East nations. He also made a development plan for 25 years for the whole country which would include rights of women. Unfortunately, the Soviets were unhappy with him. He and his whole family were shot to death in the Presidential Palace.'

'What about your own family?' I ask.

'Yes, I have a very loving family,' he smiles. 'Many years ago when the war broke out, I sent them to a neighbouring country. I stayed here working in the hospital. I sent my salary to my family every three months. Life was difficult for them and for me. There were few doctors and nurses working at that time. We were under pressure from the Mujahedeen and the communist party. Both sides wanted our help. In fact, I visited clinics on both sides to provide vaccines, nutritional biscuits, milk and training of medical staff. I was one of the very few doctors secretly supporting the mothers and children in terms of vaccinations, food, and other basic needs. There was no electricity so I would conduct operations by torchlight. This was very dangerous of course.'

'Did you make house calls?' I enquire.

'Yes, I did. When there was a VIP patient they would pick up me from my house in a tank,' Dr Katiby laughs. 'Other times I had to travel to villages in outer provinces. I had to go by donkey or horse because there was no other way of getting there. One time the communists caught me providing first aid to the Mujahedeen, so they put me in jail for one month. They beat me severely, then the war ended and I was set free. When the Taliban came to take power, I was working with the International Federation of Red Cross and Red Crescent Society. I was a health officer working for two regions, Kandahar and Herat. Frequently I had to visit Kandahar clinics to do supervision and monitoring of their work. At that time, Mullah Muhammad Omar, the Taliban Supreme Leader, was at Kandahar.'

Mullah Muhammad Omar is the man who, according to one legend, had a dream in which a woman told him: 'We need your help; you must rise. You must end the chaos. God will help you,' and thus formed the Taliban.

'In those days, I had to wear a very long beard. Life was certainly dangerous,' Dr Katiby continued. 'I always tried to work for the people. The politics did not interest me but like everyone else, I wished the fighting would end,' he sighs.

'Watch your step' says Judy as I almost trip over a sleeping dog.

'Yes, be careful,' Dr Katiby says and then continues with his story. 'Now I am working in Herat as a gynaecologist. We support three other districts too, which I frequently visit to conduct refresher training courses for the staff. I also do general surgery and obstetrics and gynaecology in very remote areas.'

'Being a gynaecologist I imagine you must face great difficulties when examining women. How do the husbands react to what you must do?'

'Oh, they believe in the doctor and there is no restriction for me because in this position it commands respect and trust. It is quite necessary for a male gynaecologist to have a good reputation with positive results in the community. Fortunately I have their confidence and they see my work as valuable.'

'Are you happy? What I mean to say is that you must see some horrific things ...'

'Of course ... life here is difficult. We have had more than 30 years of internal war and it's still ongoing. Absolutely it has affected the entire nation. So many people have no hope and no clear future for the new generation, the poverty, the immigration, the lack of education and no systems. Then there is the problem that everybody has war trauma and even I am affected this way. It means that most of the people have psychiatric problems.'

This is especially true of the younger generation of Afghans.

'Besides that we have many cultural problems in terms of engagement, selection of a wife and husband by the parents without any consultation with couples because maybe there is no-one left in the family to represent the young girl to be married. There is difficultly between people who live in the cities and those who live in rural areas. But fortunately now is much better than before. But still we are too far from being intellectual. We are not ready to digest all the good facts of civilisation. It takes time,' he says.

Dr Katiby shows me that the real battle is not just one fought with guns and bombs. The true devastation that has affected the entire population, save none, is one where scars are invisible and wounds lay open, still festering.

'It must feel so hopeless at times.'

'Mmmmm ... but my days are filled with the service to our poor and vulnerable people and that gives my life purpose,' he says with the genuineness of a doctor.

Diana is taking a picture of four decapitated goats. Their heads are all bloodied on the small wooden bench.

'*Aw,* that's just gross!' I think out loud and remember the meat markets in Laos.

'I am also a member of Rotary,' says Dr Katiby. He's oblivious to the goats guts tossed into the gutter. 'We are able to do many good things for people.'

'I am honoured to know you, Dr Katiby,' I say as we forget about the goats to cross the street and head back towards the hotel. 'You are an amazing man and a wonderful Rotarian.'

'Thank you,' he says. 'But sometimes, even now, I go to very remote places and I still have to ride the donkey.'

I laugh at the thought of Dr Katiby straddling a donkey in his nice blue suit, although the actual reality of this is far from funny.

The next morning, I sit clicking away at the keyboard hoping the internet at the Marco Polo Hotel won't cut out, as it frequently did at Gandamack Lodge. We are in the internet lounge, waiting for Diana and John to join us. Chris reads and Judy talks, while typing her email home.

'Have you told your mother where we are?' she asks.

'Hell no!' I exclaim.

As far as my sister Karen and Mum are concerned, I am still in Sydney, doing media interviews for the publisher of my last book, *Standing Ground*. They have no idea that I am in the middle of a war zone (that's usually Kerry's department!). It is better that way. Better for their blood pressure and easier than me having to explain my actions. I email that I am 'doing the usual' and will give them a full update upon my return. I wasn't exactly lying. Chris sits behind me, checking the news reports.

'Obama looks like he's leading in the US election polls,' says Chris, 'This report claims that McCain had said that Obama's real objective is to redistribute the wealth from the rich to the poor.'

'What's McCain's definition of poor, Chris?' I ask, while typing emails.

'Yeah, I'm poor,' says Judy, 'He can give me some money!'

The US presidential election is a popular topic in Afghanistan. To them, and many others in the world, George W Bush will leave behind a legacy of the most catastrophic collapse in America's reputation since World War II In fact, the main danger I face travelling in Afghanistan is that I am with Americans.

I take a sip of hot tea handed to me by a young Afghan man who works at the hotel.

'Tashakur,' I smile.

'Wow, you speak Dari?'

'Not really,' I reply.

Now that we are in Herat, I am trying to speak what little Dari I know. Muslim taught me a few words of greeting and I learned to say 'thank you' from the young Arab man who stamped my passport at Dubai Airport.

Forty per cent of the population speak Dari, particularly in provinces north-west of Kabul. In Herat, most are Persian-speaking Tajiks, a generalisation for a wide range of people of Iranian origin with traditional homelands in present-day Afghanistan, Tajikistan and southern Uzbekistan. The rest are Pashtu (10 per cent), Hazaras (2 per cent), Uzbeks (2 per cent) and Turkmens (1 per cent).

In recent years, the Hazara population has increased in Herat City, making around 12 per cent of the province's total population. In the times of the Taliban, however, the policy was to 'exterminate the Hazaras' or so proclaimed Maulawi Mohammed Hanif, Taliban Commander to a crowd of 300 people summoned to a mosque. This was after his Taliban had killed 15,000 Hazaras in one day. The then Governor of Mazar-e-Sharif, Mullah Manon Niazi, shared a similar view and announced that 'Hazaras are not Muslim. You can kill them. It is not a sin.'

My first exposure to the Hazaras was on 26 August 2001 when I and everyone else in the world witnessed an event that is now referred to as 'The Tampa Incident'. The Norwegian freighter, the MV *Tampa*, was responding to an Australian Coastal Surveillance alert that a 20 metre wooden fishing boat, the *Palapa 1*, was sinking 140 kilometres north of Australia's west coast. On board were 438 people (369 men, 26 women and 43 children), mostly all of were Afghans who boarded the *Palapa 1* in Indonesia and then attempted to gain illegal entry to Australia. The Australian Government deployed Australian Special Forces soldiers, led by squadron commander Major Vance Khan, acting under orders of Colonel Gus Gilmore, to have the SASR troops board the *Tampa* and prevent it from entering Australian waters. This would stop the asylum seekers from applying for asylum, which they could legally do as soon as they stepped foot on Australian territory.

Apart from the 5 people smugglers on the boat, the people rescued by Tampa *comprised for the most part terrified Hazaras from Afghanistan, men, women and children. They were fleeing the Taliban. We knew all this. We also knew that the Taliban were a brutal and repressive regime. We knew that Hazaras, one of the three ethnic groups in Afghanistan, had been persecuted for centuries, but that the persecution had become increasingly harsh under the Taliban who come from the Pashtun ethnic group.*

The captain of Tampa *asked for medical help. Many of the women and children were ill or injured. When* Tampa *entered Australian territorial waters at Christmas Island, Australia sent the SAS and took control of the ship, to prevent the 438 refugees from coming ashore.*

The arrival of the Tampa *in Australian waters was misrepresented to the public as a threat to our national sovereignty. The notion that 438 terrified, persecuted men, women and children constituted a threat to national sovereignty is so bizarre that it defies discussion.*

Julian Burnside QC
Monday, August 28, 2006

Article: In the Tampa confusion, we lost our moral bearings.

Afghans: Terrorists, Boat People — these words came to the minds of most Australians whenever there was talk about the people of Afghanistan. The events of 9/11 had opened the floodgates to fear. Many thought the Afghan Hazaras were all terrorists en route to destroy our way of life.

My thoughts are pleasantly interrupted by the young tea boy who quietly refills my cup. He looks all of 17. Judy tells him he looks and sounds exactly like Tom Cruise. I call him 'Tom' after that. He obviously has no idea who Tom Cruise is, but Judy and I assure him that it is a good thing.

'He is very handsome ...' I laugh. '...And famous.'

The young man blushes and shakes his head.

'Hey, you even have his smile too!' I say, noting his perfect white teeth.

'Thank you,' he bows slightly, removes the empty tray and informs us politely that if we need any more tea to just signal.

'Diana was right ... Afghan men are so good-looking,' I smile to Judy, typing away on the keyboard.

My attention returns to an email from Kerry. He continues to write with advice about being careful, avoid setting routines and above all, to come home safely. It makes me homesick. I write back that everything is okay and I tell him a little of what we've been doing, including the part about meeting Tom Cruise, then I sign off 'I love you always'. I press 'send', shut down my web mail, sigh and smile at Judy. 'I'm done!'

'I'm done too,' she replies in her Texas drawl.

Diana and John come into view right at that moment with Dr Katiby walking alongside them. Dr Katiby always looks comfortable despite the fact that as a doctor in a war zone he must witness some pretty horrendous things. Today he is dressed in a dark blue winter jacket that sure looks warm.

'*As-Salaam Alaykum*,' he smiles sincerely.

'*Wa Alaykum As-Salaam*,' I respond (and upon you be peace).

'Very good,' he replies. 'You are more familiar with our language than many foreigners, I think.'

'Oh, I have a good teacher,' I shrug, thinking of Muslim. I wonder if he's okay.

Over the coming days Dr Katiby plans to take us to the remote village in the Karokh District, 80 kilometres from the Iran-Afghanistan border. He describes it as one of the poorest villages in Afghanistan.

'Because of the failed harvests, the people there have very little. There are thousands of people in need of food throughout the entire province. In the households they cannot work to support themselves because they are mostly widowed, elderly, disabled or chronically ill,' he explains.

Winter is also approaching Herat, which means those who live in remote locations, and who have little to no heating may literally freeze to death. 'You will see many graves out there. Many have died not only from conflict but from hypothermia too,' says Dr Katiby.

The village isn't on Diana's itinerary but after hearing how destitute the people are, it is of no surprise to any of us when she agrees that's where we must go. Dr Katiby will take us only if the security is in place. He also agrees to take us on a tour of the Herat Women's Hospital if time permits. Judy, in particular, is thrilled.

On the morning of 31 October 2008, we are scheduled to meet with the Governor of Herat, Haji Sayed Hussain Anwari. He is the former Chief Military Commander of the Harakat-e Islami-yi Afghanistan (Islamic Movement of Afghanistan), one of five factions of Mujahedeen fighters that united under the Northern Alliance. On our way to Governor Anwari's office we pass by the carpet bazaar and again I am tempted to make a few purchases, especially as there are so many intricate red carpets, my favourite.

'I want the one that flies,' I joke with Dr Katiby.

'If you get that one, then I will fly with you back to Australia I think,' he laughs.

I'm sure my government would be thrilled with that. They'd probably rip him right off the rug and send him to Christmas Island or Nauru.

'Is this a nice place?' asks Dr Katiby.

'Not really. It's kind of like Guantanamo but without the torture and water-boarding,' I reply.

Since 'The Tampa Incident' anyone who attempts to circumvent Australia's immigration process (generally boat people) is usually sent to an offshore detention centre on Christmas Island. When the asylum seekers get there, women and children are forcibly removed from their husbands and fathers. It's not pleasant. Most stay in this forced separation for years. Our government tries to convince the women to return to their homeland, hoping their husbands will follow. Children grow up without ever seeing their fathers. It's woeful.'

'Then I should not like to go there,' says Dr Katiby.

The mini-van pulls up at the Governor's compound. His office doesn't look like much from the outside, but after we pass security and step inside, it is like stepping into a grand palace. I half expect the Moghul King to make a grand entrance. The Arrivals Hall is about the half the size of a football stadium. Its floor is adorned with striking persian swirls of marble tiles. Two rows of intricately gold leaf and navy blue columns stretch all the way to the heavily ornate ceiling that is at least 6 metres above us and bordered by even more gold leaf. The walls are covered with exquisite calligraphy of vines; creepers with flowers entwining the impressive century-old tile work of red, blue, pink, cream, green and orange.

Several large crystal chandeliers light the paintings on the wall. Afghan calligraphy is on the walls, capturing proverbs, religious texts and the great poems of the classical Perso-Afghan tradition. Artworks depict the Old Fort, the minarets, the Friday Mosque and not least of all, portraits of President Karzai. The interior is the epitome of perfection and beauty.

Governor Anwari is a delightful man. The first thing I notice about him is that his beard is short and his dress is Western. Dark blue tailored slacks and a grey sports coat. He greets us warmly.

'Welcome to Herat, it is an honour to have you in my country!' he announces. 'I am pleased that you are here and are helping the poor people in Afghanistan.'

I feel a rush of pride to be included in such a heartfelt welcome. Everywhere we go the Afghan people surprise me with their kindness. They are completely different to who I thought they were behind the leathery brown skin and dust covered turbans. Not that Governor Anwari looks like he spends much time in the field. His skin is smooth and his beard well kept. His shoes shine from at least a dozen or so buffs of a soft bristled brush. His smile reveals strong white teeth and a warmth that makes me feel as if I am meeting an old friend.

When we sit all together in his office we talk about the wondrous things we have experienced so far and how impressed we are with the people. Dr Katiby does a fine job translating and he chuckles when Governor Anwari confesses that he initially thought I was the Americans' language assistant.

'He says that you have the mannerisms of a Middle Eastern woman,' says Dr Katiby.

I beam at the Governor and say, 'Tashakor' (thank you).

He snaps his head back and releases a big belly laugh. That's his answer.

A young man brings tea and as he sets the glass down on the table in front of me, Governor Anwari says something to him. Whatever it is, it makes the young man look twice at me in astonishment. I guess they all think it amusing that I don't look Australian. Well, not in these clothes anyway! I don't mind, I feel it is quite the compliment. Then a film crew arrives and little do we know that we will go to air tonight on national television across Afghanistan. Governor Anwari wants everyone to know how impressed we are with Herat and the good work being done for the people. National unity is very important to Afghans.

In my thoughts I hear Muslim say 'Don't draw too much attention to yourselves!' We can't help it Muslim. Everywhere we go the people stare at us and want to know what we are doing and why. Governor Anwari is proud of us and very surprised that much of our journey has been by road.

'You have certainly seen a great deal of my country,' he responds.

'It's so beautiful,' Judy says. 'The people have been most hospitable.'

'Good... that's good to hear.'

When it is time to leave we feel more positive about our time to be spent in Herat. Governor Anwari insists that Dr Katiby will take good care of us and will have the full support of his office in regards to our safety. What an amazing man and what an amazing privilege to meet him.

Next on our busy itinerary we are visiting the Herat University. It is one of 13 universities in the country with 11 faculties (Medical, Agriculture, Language and Literature, Engineering, Law, Shariya, Education, Economy, Science, Computer Science and Art). It also boasts 247 professors, of which 210 are male and 37 female, and well over 6000 students, of which 1723 are female. It's certainly a long way short of the 40,000 that attend Queensland University, but this is a significant number given that education in Herat is recovering from its previous annihilation.

As we are seated in Mr Nazir's office I am surprised to learn that he has previously met a fellow Australian.

'I received this gift,' he says as he points to the object proudly displayed on corner of his brown laminated desk. He then confesses that he's not really sure what the gift is.

'May I?' I lean forward and pick it up thinking this is going to be a little embarrassing for both of us, and half ashamed that my fellow countryman has given Mr Nazir only half a gift.

'Do you know what it is supposed to do?' he asks curiously.

'When did you get this?' I reply.

'A couple of years ago we had an Australian visiting from his university.'

'Mmmmm.' I examine the object wondering why the giver failed to include the other parts. Maybe he forgot to pack them?

'It's a Rolodex ... or at least ... it's half of one,' I confess. 'You're supposed to have a collection of cards that go with it so you can keep a record of your contacts. Sort of like an address book.'

'Oh,' he says intrigued. I place the object back on the edge of his table, grateful that I am able to solve this particular mystery. Mr Nazir chuckles to his assistant. I wonder if he thinks Australians are dim-witted. I'll have to leave a better impression.

We finish our tea as Mr Nazir decides it's time to tour the grounds. We begin outside. In contrast to the brilliant blue sky above, a layer of depressingly grey gravel covers the ground below to hug the several four story buildings that make up the university campus. I expect the gravel is there to keep the dust down. There are no trees, no pathways, and no cypress pine mulch covering landscaped garden beds. There's not a single blade of grass or water feature and there are no signs indicating that this is even a university, let alone a sign for *parking here* or *this way to the toilets.*

Even despite these anomalies, the vision of what will be is simply impressive. Grey brick block buildings instead of compressed mud brick are covered in scaffolding, a clear sign that modernisation is underway. Some of the buildings are finished and have long, rendered feature columns in beautiful shades of lemon and apricot. My eyes are drawn instantly to the glass brick tiles that resemble huge bay windows that curve beautifully above major entrance points. I let my imagination run wild as I picture how lovely it will all look with marble flooring and pure white daisy bushes, sweet smelling jasmine, neatly trimmed garden hedges, stone paving, green grassy areas and tall trees. One would then be forgiven for thinking they were in an Australian university. I am thoroughly impressed with where my imagination is taking me. I see girls and books sitting in courtyards screened by rows and rows of scented rose bushes. Some are painting, some are reading while others are simply enjoying each other's company without fear of being attacked. Young men enjoying a vigorous game of basketball on an outdoor court at the other end of the campus while another completely different group of intellects, challenges their peers to a more taxing game of chess. No-one is coming to hurt them or accuse them of destroying the culture of Islam. The scene is just like any other typically normal university scene in any other typically normal part of the world but in order to complete this vision, as Mr Nazir points out, they need stability coupled with major financial aid.

We walk to a bare area behind the apricot building where Mr Nazir wants to install a greenhouse for the Agricultural department. The students would 'green' the university and thus have a practical aspect to their field of study.

'It would be nice to establish a women's garden too,' says Dr Katiby.

'Most definitely,' says Diana, scribbling the idea on her 'to do list'.

It's all completely doable. It's just finding the people to help. I wonder if I can find someone in Queensland University to partner up with one of the faculties. I make a mental note. After the tour of the grounds, we go back inside to meet with the students of the Arts faculty. Their work is incredible. Many of the artworks depict the war and the brutality of what the Afghan people were forced to endure during the Soviet invasion. A child's face stares back at me from the plain white canvas. He is a boy of about nine years of age carrying his baby sister on his back. A blood-stained pale blue burqa worn by his mother lies in the background, alongside his father. His family have been massacred. What will he do? Where will he go, now that he has no-one? These scenes are confronting, disturbing and graphic but this is the brutality of these people's lives. Who are we to look away? Not every painting, however, characterises Afghanistan with such rawness of reality and to my relief, we are drawn to gaze upon incredible depictions of glorious landscapes, local villagers and the sweet smiles of children laughing. Diana and I each purchase an oil painting from the pile. There are so many to choose from but in the end I settle for a painting of a young Afghan girl writing in a notebook. The bright hot pink colour of her headscarf reminds me of Nadia in Nangarhar prison. We are shown an impressive collection of Islamic calligraphy artwork. I am stunned by the sheer beauty of the intricate coloured ink Arabic script carefully stroked onto the white parchment paper. A single word, 'Allah', is adorned with floral ornamentation in the style of miniature paintings. It's exquisite. I immediately want to buy one until I discover the paintings are selling for $1000. I'm left a little breathless at that.

Next we tour the Computer Science faculty where row upon row of computers are installed and ready for use. Plastic still covers the brand new computer chairs. There's no dust in this room! I can imagine my friend Glenn Irvine, the CEO of Webagility, standing in front of the class and taking the students to a whole new cyber world of cloud technologies and beyond. I remind myself to tell Glenn about this when I go back home. We then head back along the corridor and up the stairs to where the students studying English language are waiting for us. There are at least 40 students, both male and female seated in a single classroom when we arrive. Boys are on one side and girls are on the other side. The girls are understandably shy and leave the questions up to the boys. One boy is particularly eager to show us how well he speaks English. The other boys laugh and the girls giggle like girls do back home. I get the impression these young men and women are no different to young people back home. Even the way they are dressed is at odds with other places we've been. They're wearing blue jeans and trendy jackets and some even have Nike joggers on. I look down at my own dust-covered canvas shoes. They look uninspiringly plain. Damn I wish I had brought something less old-fashioned to wear! I ask their permission to take a photo to show people back home. Most would not believe that girls and boys are being educated together. But here lies the proof that change has come.

'I want to become a doctor,' says one young male student in the back row.

'I would like to become a teacher,' says a female student seated across the invisible line that divides them.

'I would like to become a lawyer,' says another young woman.

It is unanimous that everyone wants to become more than what they are. More educated, more globally aware, more qualified to make a difference in the lives of their countrymen and women. There is no talk of leaving Afghanistan to get on a leaky boat to my country!

Following our visit with the students, John quietly admits to Diana that he's starting to feel quite ill. She alerts Mr Nazir, who agrees we should head back to the hotel. In any case, it's getting late and we don't really want to get caught in the afternoon rush when the final bell sounds. We make our farewell departure quickly and without fuss climbing into the mini-van and waving farewell to Mr Nazir. Inside the mini-van John explains his dilemma. 'I woke up this morning feeling nauseous but I thought it was nothing.'

'You did eat quite a bit of yogurt last night at dinner,' Judy cautions and hands him some bottled water.

Poor John looks washed out and, in fact, green around the gills. Dr Katiby urges our driver to make haste. Then back at the hotel Dr Katiby marches him straight to his room and orders him to bed. After a careful examination it is decided that John has food poisoning. Dr Katiby announces that he will be in no state to travel with us tomorrow.

'I'm fine with that,' says John weakly and on that note we say goodnight.

The next morning John is obviously no better. All he wants to do is sleep. Sleep and vomit.

'I'll be fine here,' John waves us away. 'Go on, guys, go enjoy yourselves, I'll be fine,' John whispers as he sinks back into the pillows.

Dr Katiby is worried that John will become dehydrated so he lectures him on the importance of fluid intake. We're reluctant to leave his bedside but John insists that he doesn't want us there. He just wants to sleep.

'You guys will only keep me awake,' his voice croaks from the soft folds of his pillow.

Dr Katiby is forced to agree that rest is best.

'I will notify the hotel staff to check on him during our absence,' he informs Diana.

Judy leaves a bottle of diluted juice on John's bedside table and reminds him once more of the dangers of becoming dehydrated. Satisfied, we leave him in peace to make our way downstairs and outside.

The mini-van door shuts with a thud and soon we are driving out of the hotel compound, past the armed security guards and onto Bodmurghan Street, which will take us into Herat City and beyond. Diana reminds us to be careful to remember simple rules of hygiene when eating and drinking. 'If you peel the fruit yourself, it's probably okay to eat it but remember; only drink bottled water.'

I know Judy is thinking the same thing I am: since we've got here, we've both eaten and drunk virtually everything put before us.

'If anything can live in my stomach after Laos, then good luck to it,' I say, thinking back to the time I was fed maggot-infested beef.

'I had Delhi belly in India one trip,' Judy confesses.

'*Aggh!*'

All joking aside, Diana raises some very good points on how to avoid travel sickness. Just another example of how seriously she takes the general wellbeing of her travelling companions. A half-hour later we arrive at a disabled rehabilitation centre. It's nothing much to look at from the outside, just another dilapidated building like all the others in town. Dr Katiby says it's important we visit. The dust swirls around the mini-van as the driver brings it to a halt just inside the compound.

'Here is where another real tragedy begins,' he explains as we exit the mini-van and follow him inside to the reception area. 'Much of the population of Afghanistan suffer some form of disability resulting from war injuries, mainly from mines and polio.'

We walk to the entrance of the centre not knowing what to expect and are greeted by some older gentlemen. Clearly they are excited by our visit. Dr Katiby ushers us forward to follow them into a sunlit room at the back of the building. It is here we are introduced to Mr Abdul 'Ali' Barakszai, an impressive young man seated in a steel-framed wheelchair wearing a crisp white salwar kameez and dark navy suit jacket. Ali sits beside white lace curtains in the corner of the room. He invites us to join him and in a few moments an older man brings tea. Dr Katiby explains while we are drinking the surprisingly flavoursome amber liquid that Ali is a quadriplegic, someone who has a loss of sensation and movement in all their limbs and body.

'Ali was recruited as a teenager to fight with the Mujahedeen against the Soviets. He was in the frontline when he got injured in his spine by a bullet. His commander sent him to Tehran for treatment. He was more than two months at the hospital but the doctors could not do much because his injuries were too extensive.'

Ali was still a relatively young man. He looked about 40 but then again, it's difficult to accurately estimate a person's age in Afghanistan. Most I've met are a lot younger than they look. The hardships faced have etched deep furrows in their otherwise youthful skin.

'As you can see he cannot move his body, his arms or legs.'

Ali gently shakes his dark head like it doesn't matter. I look beneath the gold-rimmed spectacles into his coffee-coloured eyes to see if he genuine. His eyes smile back at me. Quietly we listen to him explaining the situation for many in his care. He is the head of the centre.

'Our organisation was founded for the disabled who need support to be rehabilitated. From the beginning we had 400 disabled recognised and around 205 received registration. Besides the rehabilitation they get training in various fields such as literacy, mathematics, English, fine art, sewing, making flowers and so on. We have around 200 girls and ladies who are disabled and deprived each year to receive any training,' he explains.

It is not difficult to imagine that close to a million Afghans are severely disabled, most as a result of war. Afghanistan, like Cambodia, is contaminated with landmines or unexploded ordnance (UXO). Every day throughout the country dozens of people are killed or injured. Almost half of the mine victims are males of working age, generally farmers or young boys tending to their herds or collecting firewood to keep out the bitter cold of an Afghan winter. Most are the sole breadwinners of their family. Ali says that war alone has created thousands of amputees, blindness and paralysis. In most hospitals a damaged limb, resulting from a mine explosion, may be amputated instead of being saved because of the lack of resources. There is insufficient funding to enable mine victims and other persons with disabilities from receiving the care and rehabilitation services they desperately need to survive and reintegrate into Afghan society.

Life for an able-bodied person in Afghanistan is difficult enough, let alone the challenges faced by those who are disabled. The general infrastructure presents immediate barriers to living a normal life. Most of the bustling streets are unpaved and littered with rubble. Some streets are not really streets at all. They're more like windy goat tracks. Some are wide enough for cars, others are not. Many of the mud brick houses are built into steep hillsides and the only way to get to them is by foot. These are inaccessible for an unaided person in a wheelchair, hence why many disabled never leave their homes.

As Ali talks I sit trying to absorb and process the life he is describing. It's one thing to hear how many Afghan people never leave their village or venture beyond their street. It's almost impossible to process the fact that many have never left their house. Even Ali's centre is a little gloomy. Everything is old and in immediate need of repair. There are no freshly painted walls, shiny glass windows or neatly pressed hospital sheets covering clean comfortable mattresses. There are no disabled toilets or showers, or mobile walking frames. I see a man sitting against a paint-chipped cream wall on a dusty concrete floor. His dark clothes are typically dusty and crumpled. He has no legs. He does not even have a wheelchair. They are too expensive, he says. I watch as he drags himself across the room. He looks lonely. How long has he been living like this? Where is his family? Were they killed in a bomb exploding on their compound, leaving him as the sole survivor? I want to ask but I fear being too nosy. Ali invites us to speak to anyone we want. I look back to find the legless man but he's gone. Did he disappear into the shadows? Meanwhile, Ali begins drawing a picture for Diana. His aid carefully places a pencil in his mouth. Impressive!

I wander out of the room into the next where I find another old man quietly observing us. He says, through a language assistant, that when he was a child he contracted the severe, debilitating form of polio (paralytic polio) and blames the inexperienced doctor who vaccinated him. I'm assuming he's bitter but I can't tell for sure because of the language barrier. In any case, he's paralysed. He says he wants to become a properly qualified doctor. His message to others is, 'don't visit unprofessional doctors'. I tell him a little about the Rotary's polio plus program that is on the brink of eradicating this tenacious disease throughout the world. He has no idea what Rotary is, of course, or who Bill Gates is (founder of the Microsoft software company). Nor can he comprehend that the Gates Foundation has awarded The Rotary Foundation a challenge grant of AUD$100 million, which Rotary will attempt to match, dollar for dollar, over the next three years. I wish I could speak Dari so I could properly explain all this.

'I am sorry that I cannot explain everything you say well,' says the young man working at the centre. 'My English is not the best.'

'It's okay,' I reply.

The lines on his crinkled face shift into a smile. I am momentarily reminded of an old Chinese man I once knew. He was a political prisoner in the Laos jail. We could not speak each other's language but we could talk for hours and our conversations always ended with his crinkly face shifting into a toothless tobacco-stained smile. I step back into the room where the others are with that memory haunting my face, just as Ali finishes Diana's drawing, a lovely flower with a beautiful butterfly. He's eyes brim with delight as she admires his work. It's a pleasant distraction.

'That's amazing!' I say, genuinely impressed and ask if he will draw something for me.

'Of course,' he says and calls for a fresh sheet of paper. The older man holds the clipboard steady and places the pencil between Ali's perfectly white teeth.

Carefully he places the pencil on the paper and begins moving it slowly left, then down, up, twisting right. My eyes are riveted to the page watching the image take shape. His skill is incredible. I couldn't even attempt to draw that well with my good hand. His lips tighten and within minutes he begins writing my name.

'Oh, it's so beautiful!' I fall to my knees beside Ali's wheelchair. I take the paper like I am handling the most precious gift, which to me it is.

'What is it?' asks Judy.

'Look!' I turn the page to her. 'It's a beautiful dove.' I smile back at Ali.

'For peace, he says,' explains Dr Katiby.

'Oh, that's so sweet,' says Diana.

'I must get a photo of us together.' I hand Dr Katiby my camera and lean up against Ali. And just for fun, I reach over and gently grab his right arm and wrap it round my shoulder.

Ali and I both laugh at that moment as the camera goes *click*.

Lucky Ali is sitting down because unexpectedly I lean down and give him a sisterly peck on the cheek.

'You are my brother,' I smile at him. He blushes and says thank you.

I don't ask Dr Katiby to translate. It's better not to know what the Afghan men are thinking. By the looks of them they want to trade places with Ali. Steal a kiss perhaps?

'I think you just made his day,' said Chris grinning.

Ali graciously offers to draw for Judy. And after that, we continue with our tour. In a dimly lit room, I sit with a group of children who are all amputees, missing either a leg, an arm or both. They are being taught to make handicrafts for sale at local markets, like tissue boxes, jewellery boxes, photo albums and lampshades. I admire their work displayed on the shelf that runs along the wall behind them. Their paintings are bold and beautiful. Some paint farm animals and bowls of fruit, but most depict other disabled children.

I notice a little girl who wears oversized clothes and a chunky orange knitted hat. It pulls down around her ears and leaves only a little pixie face exposed. I love her smile, because it is so sweet. Not until I ask her to stand with the other children do I notice she has only one leg. Slowly she hobbles over to the gloomy wall, assisted by a wooden crutch. She stands quietly and smiles back at me. Her face is adorable. How long would she last on the streets with the competing beggar boys? I shudder to think about it or what other fate has in store for this beautiful brave heart.

I've heard it said that Afghanistan is the place where God only comes to weep and surely he must weep every day at what he sees. But from what I've seen so far, Afghanistan is also a place where God would be tremendously proud. Proud to see the courage of the people, particularly the children, who for all their hardships, continue to overcome so much of what life throws at them. They are born into war. They are forced to work long before they become teenagers, they starve because they have no food, they freeze in the winter because they have no fire to keep warm, and they see their little friends die because they are worse off and have no place to live. Yet still, despite all these unimaginable hardships, they smile.

It makes me think of children elsewhere who complain when their Xbox breaks down or when Mum won't buy them the latest iPhone so they can be just like their friends. This is a problem within our capitalistic society where we place financial achievement above the importance of living a purposeful life. Sure it is nice to have nice things but some of these children would simply be grateful for a loaf of bread or warm jacket.

Ali offers us all a gift to take back home as a reminder of this day. As if any of us could ever forget the time we have spent here. He selects a lovely beaded peace dove to match the one he drew for me.

'It's so lovely, Ali — thank you.' I smile then waggle my finger at him for offering his cheek. 'You are naughty,' I laugh.

He looks so happy and in that instant I am able to forget where we are. It seems as if I have just gone to visit an old friend and the war outside is forgotten. Ali tells me that if they had a good internet connection, and knew someone who could create a website for them, then they could sell their products online. Then they could buy wheelchairs and walking frames. They might even be able to buy clean sheets to sleep on and a blanket to keep away the cold. But they have no money for such things. He smiles again because there is nothing to do but smile. The need is so great and a little would definitely go a long way! I really want to stay in Afghanistan longer to organise, to plan and to make big differences to their lives. But the reality is that I have to go home to my children and my husband, to my own responsibilities.

'It's okay,' Ali tells me. 'When you go home then you will tell people about us and help may come — *Insha'Allah.*'

Our visit is over before we know it and sadly we say farewell, hoping to return sometime in the near future and promising to tell others that if they can help then they must. We climb back into the mini-van. Ali sits in his chair in the dust outside the disabled centre. The blue sky shines high above his head. A gentle breeze stirs against the giant pine tree. Ali's arms hang limp by his side. His eyes are fixed on our vehicle and as we slowly move towards the roadside, he begins shaking his head from side to side like the blind American singer Stevie Wonder seated at his piano singing 'I just called to say I love you'. I almost cry at the sight of this brave young Afghan man trapped in a body that no longer works, trapped in a country that no longer cares. He smiles as if he hasn't a care in the world.

Chapter 17

Tunnels and Turkeys

John's health is still no better the next day.

'He just needs rest.' says Dr Katiby.

We all agree John will remain at the hotel. There's no way he's well enough to make today's journey. We get no argument from him of course. He says the thought of travelling makes him ill.

Today we intend to drive west to visit a remote village outside of Herat. Our journey will take us through some of the most remote countryside where the situation is very serious. In fact, we will be driving right through an area that is home to Herat's most powerful Taliban commander, Ghullam Yahya Akbari, the former Mayor of Herat and his battalion of Taliban fighters, some of the fiercest in the country. Each one has pledged to spill the very last drop of blood in their bodies to drive out all American forces from Afghanistan. They are currently holding three Afghan policemen hostage.

Several months ago, NGO workers were gunned down on the very road we will be taking, by men armed with kalashnikov assault rifles. Most likely they were Akbari's men. The reports claimed that the aid workers were spies 'not working in the interests of Afghanistan'. The insurgent spokesman said they were from countries that 'took Afghanistan's freedom'. There was no dialogue between the aid workers and the gunmen before the bullets flared into their vehicle. The driver/language assistant was not required to speak. There was no opportunity for them to explain that they were disinterested in the politics of war. They were just caught in the middle. And shot.

I toyed with the idea of even going to this village. Over coffee I shared my concerns with Dr Katiby while the others were upstairs checking on John. Thinking of the NGO workers being gunned down before having time to explain why they were there gave me little comfort. I had planned on having enough time at least to show them I hadn't any US stamps in my passport. But that now seems a rather moot point. Dr Katiby laughed and explained the security procedures in greater detail.

'No-one is ever 100 per cent safe,' he says. 'But we can do certain things to increase our chances of staying alive.'

'How so?' I ask.

'Unlike the aid workers who drove around in flashy, marked NGO vehicles, our transportation is unmarked and discreet. We won't attract attention,' he explains.

And so we sit and discuss the trip and contingencies in great detail. From this conversation alone I learn that Dr Katiby knows what time we should arrive at the remote village, how long we should stay and when we should leave. He knows the area well, its customs and its people. He has an extensive network that will give him eyes and ears from here to the border and back. As he talks, I think of Muslim and how the two men are very different from each other and yet very much the same. Muslim wears a beard whereas Dr Katiby is clean shaven. Muslim's skin is dark whereas Dr Katiby's skin is light-tan. Muslim dresses as a Pashtun, Dr Katiby dresses more like a Westerner. But aside from their physical differences, both are extremely vigilant planners. Both are familiar with the environment and both take security very seriously.

It is good to know that every checkpoint we pass through will be secure before we even attempt to go through. Dr Katiby will phone ahead. But in between there is a lot of territory where anyone — insurgents or bandits — could lay an ambush.

'Please don't worry,' he says, again and again. 'I have someone going ahead of us.'

I sip the last of my coffee.

'I think it is better you not say anything to the others,' he says quietly. 'There's no need to worry them.'

'I think they'd go regardless of anything I said.' I say in agreement.

Dr Katiby is on the phone again to his security police contacts. He's already called them a dozen times, at least. From behind him I see Diana, Chris and Judy walking towards us. 'Ready?' I ask Diana.

'Absolutely,' she smiles just as Dr Katiby gets off the phone.

'Then let's go!' he says.

Driving to the far remote west of the province is like driving through a dead zone. It looks like a nuclear bomb has been dropped on the entire province. There are barely any trees, no flowing rivers and not a bird in sight. There are no cows grazing in lush green fields. There are no lush green fields despite the fact that Afghanistan was once covered with cedar-rich forests. We drive along the desolate sands. At least the road is good, but we are well beyond the safety of the green zone, the wire, and far from UN monitors and US convoys.

After a quarter of an hour we arrive at our destination, a tiny village that's not listed on any map, a mud compound that sits smack bang in the middle of nowhere. Our driver steers the mini-van to stop off the main road and waits. Silence fills the air as I wonder what will happen next. No-one says a thing. We just sit and wait. Then suddenly Dr Katiby opens the door and gets out.

Someone is coming down the road on foot.

'Please wait here,' he says through the window and walks off towards the lone figure. He raises his hand to hail what looks like an old goat herder walking casually up the hill with two younger men followed by a herd of goats and a young boy. I watch the man acknowledge Dr Katiby. Then they stop for a moment and talk, with the doctor pointing at us every now and then, and the old man nodding.

After a few moments, Dr Katiby returns and invites us to accompany him. 'Everything is fine,' he says, 'We have been invited into the compound.'

From the outside of the compound, there doesn't appear to be a living soul in sight. I don't know if that is good or bad. The soldiers back home told me that usually when you see the women and children leaving the village suddenly it is often a sign that trouble is looming. However, I don't see any women and children. Have they already vacated the area? Dr Katiby says to follow him but does he know what lies beyond the mud brick wall or is he just hoping the old goat herder is genuinely pleased to see us? In any case, it's too late to turn back now. We cross the double lane road not bothering to look left or right simply because there is no traffic on it at all, and there clearly hasn't been for some time. The road is surprisingly good, as if newly laid. Doesn't anyone travel this far? The Iranian border is only a few kilometres down the road. I want to venture there but daydreams like that are fanciful and dangerous.

Borders are never safe places to hang around, especially for foreigners and especially in Afghanistan. The goat herder, whom we learn is also the community leader, is not a tall man and is far from intimidating. His eyes are small and dark like raisins set deep into his wrinkled face, weathered by many years of living in extreme conditions. His white hair tucks into a light brown turban, and matches his beard. He wears a typical light-coloured salwar kameez, the long dress-type shirt with comfortable pants, and a dark blue knitted jumper. A dark grey coat falls over his jumper and a tan-coloured wool blanket drapes casually over that. His shoes are black but covered in layers of dust. His eyes wander carefully over each of our faces as we approach, probably assessing whether we are appropriately dressed.

I am invited by Dr Katiby to greet him with my usual '*As-Salaam Alaykum*', not shaking his hand but respectfully raising my closed hand to my heart, according to the customary greeting. Dr Katiby explains that I am Australian, which causes the community leader to look slightly bemused.

'Thank you for allowing us to visit,' I say quietly.

He nods politely, so I ask Dr Katiby if I can shoot his image on video.

The doctor asks. The answer is, 'Yes, of course; it is no problem.'

The community leader is expressionless as he stares into the lens. His face tells a story but I can't fathom what that story might be. I show him his image on the little LCD screen and he suddenly becomes quite animated. The hardened lines of his weathered face soften and he seems more approachable, enough for me to pluck up the courage to ask Dr Katiby if it is all right for me to have my picture taken with him. He says it's fine. We stand together in the dirt posing for a shot as Dr Katiby chatters away. It has been a very long time since any foreigners have visited. Normally people are too afraid to come here, and I suspect with good reason. The little voice inside my head mocks me. *'You are completely mad!'*

Diana swaps places with me and I take her photo. I wonder how many foreigners he's seen in his entire lifetime or if he killed anyone during the war with the Soviets? Maybe he's buried many young men, perhaps even his own brothers. Dr Katiby confirms that there has been a great deal of fighting in Herat, particularly in the towns closest to the border. With so much misery inflicted upon them it is amazing they are still so welcoming to strangers.

I would have thought the last thing they wanted was to see another lot of new foreigners in their lands, but they continue to surprise me with their hospitality. In fact, Dr Katiby tells me that Afghans are taught to show hospitality to all visitors, regardless of whom they are, their ethnic, religious or national background, without hope of remuneration or favour. The little voice in my head echoes something someone I know who once said, *'Don't get sucked in by their hospitality. They are obliged to offer it but then when you leave, that's where the obligation ends. They can kill you if they want to.'*

As we walk and I silently tell myself I will survive today, Dr Katiby explains that the basic needs of the village are simple but they are the poorest of the poor. Virtually all babies and young children are malnourished and only survive on powdered milk with little other nutritional support.

'They need rice or oat cereal, vitamins and nutritional food. Their situation is desperate,' he says. 'The population here is 85 to 90 families and a total of 800 to 1000 in the district. There is only one tube well for the entire village and it needs to be improved. It's too shallow.'

'How many babies do they have here?' Judy asks.

'There are 20 to 25 newborns and infants under the age of two in desperate need of nutritional support and food supplementation. Come, you will meet the community midwife.'

The community leader goes ahead to summon her. We follow behind with Dr Katiby, who takes us into a compound where we inspect the general surrounds. A yak cuts a lonely figure in one of the 'hole in the wall' livestock pens. A few chickens scamper about, a scraggy dog barks and a vegetable patch grows. I can't make out the type of fruit trees in the gardens, but they appear to be doing okay. The compound is like a series of catacombs. Behind every mud wall is another set of walls and tunnel systems that connects one yard to another. A ladder leans against the far end of one wall, leading to the roof, which looks out towards the road. I imagine this is a sort of early warning vantage point. The policeman's motorbike leans against the inside compound wall. We walk carefully around it and follow Dr Katiby up a small rise and then through another mud opening.

The community midwife greets us here. Her dark curly hair is respectfully covered. The woman holding the small child is married to the village policeman. When the little girl starts crying, he suddenly appears on the scene to comfort the child. It is nice to see a man of his obvious social standing rushing to help his wife. So much for the news reports that paint a very different picture of family life in Afghanistan. If not for the obvious external differences, the way the mother and father interacted could have been a scene from back home.

Diana asks Dr Katiby to translate that we are honoured to meet her and appreciate her hospitality. A few pleasantries are exchanged before the community leader urges us to keep moving. We are told to follow him. I am keen to see what lies ahead, and this time I take the lead in our group instead of following a safe distance behind. There is something reassuring about the community leader's manner. I feel completely at ease, ready to embark on the next part of our adventure. I follow him without worrying that something bad might happen. What could I do if it did?

The community leader pauses as I catch him up, then he turns and walks through a dark archway. I flick on my DVD camera and look where I am going through the viewfinder. It really is quite dark. I flick on the camera's light. The pathway dips, taking me deeper and deeper into the tunnel. I faintly hear Diana ask the others if they want to go in, but I am further ahead of them and excited to see where exactly the community leader is going. The tunnel twists left, straightens, twists right, and then dips. It seems like we are going deep underground. Dr Katiby's voice is a little fainter and as I peer into my viewfinder, I suddenly realise that I am alone. *Perhaps this wasn't such a good idea after all*, I think to myself. 'Oh dear,' I whisper faintly.

I turn my head hoping to hear footsteps behind me but the ground is too soft and if the others are coming, they aren't making a sound. Why is that? Have they decided to stay outside the tunnel in the sunlight? Has Dr Katiby stayed with them? Where did the community leader go? Why has he walked so quickly? I keep moving forward. The tunnel grows darker, and I keep putting one foot in front of the other. Why don't I retreat? Then my nerves settle and subside. I realise that I am not afraid. I keep moving forward and after the next turn I see, with much relief, sunlight, another archway and the community leader waving me towards him.

'I'm coming!' I call out behind me, 'It's fantastic!'

As I walk into the sunshine I find myself in the community leader's compound, his home. A little white dog runs towards me, barking. Following him, dressed in a khaki salwar kameez, is the young boy from the goat herd, perhaps 13 years old, with short dark hair and a cheeky smile. He looks amazingly happy and carefree. I smile at him and wave eagerly, then turn to follow the community leader, who is walking alongside a mud wall about a metre high. Then, where the mud wall ends, a screen of chicken wire stretches up to the logs that support a roof. The community leader smiles widely as he points to the caged birds behind the wire.

'Oh my, they're spectacular,' I say at the 20 or so fat turkeys making gobbling sounds and standing in a group. '*Salaam, Salaam*,' I giggle.

'*Salaam, Salaam*,' the group of turkeys sound off, which makes us both laugh out loud.

The sight of the community leader and his turkeys is a proud moment indeed. I clap my hands in sheer delight and happily chat to him in a language he doesn't understand. Maybe he thinks I'm a silly foreigner. I don't care. I am just happy to see those turkeys and not Taliban. Then the rest of our group catches up, and when I introduce him to the turkeys, Dr Katiby is amused. 'They speak Dari,' I laugh.

When I turn around, the little boy with the white dog (named Jake) is right beside me. His eyes never stop staring at me, except when I make direct eye contact with him. Shyly he looks at the ground until I look away, then his curious brown eyes watch me again. The small boy is quite handsome. Who is he? I overhear Dr Katiby explaining to Judy that the community leader's brother was killed by insurgents and this is his brother's son. Since there is no mention of his mother, I assume she must have died too.

I slowly watch as a woman and four young girls approach. She is wearing a green and cream floral wrap that covers her from head to toe. She is slightly surprised when I say 'hello' in Dari and giggles when I give her the customary three kisses. She is a kindly looking woman with a lovely smile and dimples in each cheek. I guess her age is somewhere in her mid-40s. I assume the four lovely girls are her daughters.

An older boy then steps up. He has startling blue eyes and doesn't look at all like the community leader. He looks more Soviet than anything else, I estimate his age at around 23 years. I want to pry into their private lives. I want to know everything about them, which is hardly polite. Ours is a whirlwind tour and there never seems to be enough time to get to know people beyond '*As-Salaam Alaykum*'. I want to know what they know of the world. Have they met foreigners before? Have they ever met people who are genuinely concerned for them? Apparently only a few foreigners have ever ventured this far from the city. It's way too dangerous. I wonder what it would be like to stay overnight. I so wish I could. Everything about this strange world fascinates me. It makes me want to take chances and that, of course, is the very thing I have to guard against.

After spending a few moments with his family and taking some snapshots with our cameras to show people back home how rural Afghans live, we follow the community leader back into the tunnel to another section of the compound through another mud corridor.

We enter a narrow doorway and this time we find ourselves standing in a small one-room girls' school. The teacher is giving lessons to 10 to 20 young girls. One is standing at the front, writing on a very old blackboard nailed into the mud wall. Dr Katiby explains that the teacher has travelled a great distance to teach these girls and it has been a long time since she has been paid a salary. I ask what a few dollars might achieve. The answer is: five dollars will cover the cost of glass for the classroom window, Sadly they don't have AUD\$5, which means the children get cold. I imagine what AUD\$100 might do for them. Then I stop imagining and discreetly slip a one hundred US dollar bill to Dr Katiby and ask him to give it to her, at his discretion. 'Perhaps she can use it for books and other things,' I whisper.

Dr Katiby passes her the note. She accepts my donation, thanks me and kisses me several times on both cheeks. 'I honestly wish I could give more,' I reply, feeling completely overwhelmed. Diana silently stands by my side; she knows how I feel. Diana knows the ropes.

I imagine my children living in such desolation with no opportunities to be educated beyond primary school; it is too incredible to comprehend! The young girls in this classroom want to learn and the community leader wants them to have an education. How brave he is to embrace the future and how fortunate the girls are that they are being allowed to learn. Perhaps one of them might become a teacher, or a doctor like Dr Katiby.

As I stand with my back to the far wall in that dark room, I smile for the camera as Dr Katiby takes our photograph. I find myself wanting so much more for these sweet young girls. Sweet smiles shine back at me and make my heart glow. What I wouldn't give to help these girls! I want to take them home with me and give them that same opportunity that someone once gave Dr Katiby. I want to change their lives forever.

Imagine if we all cared just a little. Imagine how much good we could do, helping others restore their lives.

In an adjoining room we find a women's sewing cooperative. The dozen women in the room are making clothes from scraps of material. The hunchback lady with her cheeky smile mutters something to Dr Katiby. He laughs then looks directly at me.

'What is it?' I ask.

'She said she was far more beautiful than you when she was your age!'

'What the …?' I look from Dr Katiby to the wrinkly old woman. Her toothy grin smiles back at me in obvious delight. 'Oh, you funny woman,' I laugh. Then just as suddenly, I take her by surprise with a very genuine hug.

It causes quite a commotion, and by the end of the conversation Dr Katiby says the women have invited me to remain with them in their village.

'It's very tempting but I must get back to my poor children in Australia,' I sweetly reply.

The old hunchback woman speaks quickly to an attentive Dr Katiby, who then turns to me and translates. 'She says in that case, you can take her with you to Australia!' Er…? Help!

We all laugh. They are such a delightful group of ladies.

Dr Katiby tells us that the community leader is concerned for our safety. Although he has authority within this village, there are outside elements that can still harm us. The Taliban are not far from here. He advises us to continue our tour and then be on our way. I could happily remain chatting with the women for hours, but I want to stay alive.

As we make our way from the village compound we see a tube well. Dr Katiby explains that this one is working but in summer it sometimes runs dry. The second well is located next to a vacant school building, across the road from the village. When we get there Dr Katiby explains that the well is dry and the school hasn't been accessed in a very long time. The two most deadly health risks in Afghanistan are unsafe water and inadequate sanitation. The people here can't just slip down to the local store and buy a bottle of water. For a moment I think back to when I was in the Laos jail when the only water to drink was that which came from the kitchen.

'Is it clean?' I ask.

'Best not to ask too many questions,' says the Thai prisoner. And soon, like everyone else, I developed a terrible skin rash and dark brown stains on my teeth. I shuddered to think what it was doing to my liver and kidneys. I wondered why everyone got so sick so quickly but that's what happens when you drink contaminated water. You can get all sorts of chronic health disorders. Disorders of the nervous system, damage to the immune system etc ...

I quietly collect my thoughts and put them back in the box marked 'Lao memories'.

'We need to help here,' says Diana, pulling out her list and pen. 'I'm sure our fellow Rotarians will want to help when we tell them.'

I am standing a short distance away from Diana and Judy with the two boys and Jake, the little white dog. They are such sweet boys with beguiling smiles. I wish that I could speak their language; there is so much I want to ask. Have they ever kicked a football? Do they even know what a football game is? What are their dreams of the future? Do they ever long to leave the remote village? What will become of them in five years from now? Will they still be tending goats?

'Come along, Kay,' calls Dr Katiby. 'Before we go, the community leader wants to show us one more thing.'

'Okay,' I start catching up and waving at the boys to follow. They just laugh. The community leader observes all this with mild curiosity. Perhaps I am not supposed to play with them, but it feels so natural — as if they are friends of my son, Nathan, who have come out with us for the day. I catch up.

We walk for a few minutes until we arrive back to the place where our mini-van is parked. I notice the driver has used his time to change the rear tyre. Driving here, it sounded like there was something wrong with it. Chris said he hoped it wouldn't blow out on the way back. We go inside another compound where we are surprised to find a grape vineyard. This is the last thing I expected to see. The community leader says that Herat grows 82 varieties of grapes and that Afghanistan is well recognised for its grape produce, mainly grown for consumption, not for commercial resale or wine. At least that answers my previous question. I joke with Judy that a bottle of chilled chardonnay would certainly put a sparkle into this meeting. We nod in agreement as we picture the community leader sneaking into the vineyard at night with the other elders and all of them getting plastered.

Our discussion takes us to the rooftop of the vineyard compound from which we are able to see for kilometres across the desolate landscape. A couple of hundred metres away I spot a white pickup truck near a clump of trees. Is it dangerous? Has it been dumped? No, there's a small group of people gathered around it. Cautiously I eye the group through the viewfinder of my DVD camera but they are oblivious to us, or I hope they are.

Then Dr Katiby asks if I have met any Taliban during our trip. He laughs when I reply, 'Yeah, I met some in Jalalabad — so I think that's enough for me.'

As I pan my camera towards the north I see a mysterious man dressed in a black robe and black turban standing near the edge of the road filming me. I almost drop my camera. How did I not see him when we crossed the road? Who is he? What does he want? I ask Dr Katiby.

'Taliban,' he says. 'They are watching us to see what we are up to.'

His face turns serious for a moment before he turns away to go talk with the community leader.

Maybe coming here wasn't such a good idea. What was I thinking? As discreetly as I can, I tuck my camera back into the knapsack I've slung casually over my shoulder. My hand automatically checks my headscarf even though I know it's respectfully in place. I dare not look at the mysterious man in the black robe and turban. I *will* him to disappear. What would Muslim say if he were here? God I wish he was here!

Seconds turn to minutes. Stay calm, Kay! Maybe he'll mistake me for a local like everyone else, although the camera is a dead giveaway, and my clothes are a little fancier than those of the women in the village. Damn it!

'It's okay.' Dr Katiby moves silently to my side. 'The community leader says they don't mind if we come here and help the villagers so long as they get a piece of whatever we leave behind.'

'Great,' I reply, silently hoping they're not going to change their mind and hold us hostage.

'Look ... he's gone now,' says Dr Katiby. 'It's fine.'

I sigh with relief.

Judy and Chris are marvelling at the countryside oblivious to the mysterious man in black. Diana is making adjustments to her list. The healthcare services are obviously quite limited in this place and the villagers are most interested in developing a small medical clinic in one or two classrooms in the boys vacant school building. Diana adds this request to her list, along with assistance for the development of the sewing cooperative, classroom equipment, supplies, and two computer rooms (one for boys and one for girls). Her list is now quite long: textbooks, paper, pens, pencils, learning materials, desks, chairs, blackboards, art supplies, computer supplies, as well as farming equipment, seeds and fertilisers, wheelchairs and other urgently needed items. A new well is desperately needed too, and a generator, if possible.

'Perhaps we can get the US Embassy out here,' Judy chips in. 'I'm sure Brad Hanson would love to help these people.'

'Good idea,' Diana responds. 'We'll talk to him when we get back.'

'Yes, I think it will be very good to seek their involvement,' says Dr Katiby.

I try to forget about the mysterious man in black as we drink tea with the community leader in a carpeted room below. It's surprisingly clean and comfortable. I wonder who lives here or perhaps it is best not to know.

After we are seated the young boy brings tea and eyes the sweets placed before us.

'*Tashakor*,' I thank him.

Shyly he lowers his eyes and backs away. He sits quietly against the mud wall a few feet away. I offer him a sweet but he shakes his head and so I insist. Dr Katiby laughs.

Following our meeting we ask if the community leader would like to accompany us to the neighbouring town to purchase some supplies. The answer is yes. The community midwife begs to go with him, which makes things interesting. I don't think he will allow her but the conversation turns in her favour. She smiles and runs out the door, obviously to off load her crying baby to the other women. Minutes later, her policeman husband drives her back in a beat-up car which they park next to our mini-van. Does this car belong to the mysterious man in the black robe and turban? I decide not to think about that.

The community midwife wraps herself in a pale blue burqa and before she totally vanishes underneath, she flashes me a victorious grin. I wonder when she last ventured beyond the village.

'Goodbye, handsome boy,' I say to the young man with the lovely brown eyes. 'Grow up to be an honourable man.' I give him and his older brother a key ring each in the shape of Australia, then point on the map to where I live. I don't know what they think of it. Judging by their shy smiles, I think they like my funny little gifts. Perhaps this will remind them of our visit.

Off we go, the mini-van followed by their car. We drive for almost a quarter of an hour, back towards Herat, along the desolate sands. We pass very few people: a man doubling on a motorcycle, a small boy riding a donkey. We come to a little village that has all the food supplies we need. Dr Katiby takes us inside a shop while the community leader's driver goes in search of a new tyre to replace the one punctured en route. The community midwife remains in the backseat of the car. I feel her watching me. I think I know what she wants. I smile at the community leader and use my hands and body language to ask him to allow her to come into the store. He understands me and goes over to the car, leans through the window and chats with her husband. Then an amazing thing happens, she throws off her burqa and walks briskly towards me, doing her very best to hide her smile. I hug her and for a moment it is like we are old friends who haven't seen each other in a long time. We giggle very discreetly and I take her hand and lead her deeper into the shop.

'I think you would like some of these.' I point to the delicious cookies in their brightly coloured tins. 'These too.' I sniff the perfumed soap. 'Yes, definitely some of these.' I add them to our pile of shopping.

'Oh yes indeedy,' says Judy, adding a few more bars.

Diana instructs the storekeeper that we need lots of baby formula, powdered milk, and rice or oat cereal for the very young children. We also buy a few boxes of toothpaste and several toothbrushes. The women in the village have virtually no dental care available, no immunisation, no sanitary items, no disinfectant and so many more things that we take for granted in our society back home. It is such a terrible shame that we haven't more money, but then again, we hadn't planned for this particular visit.

Diana reassures the community leader that we will bring more aid on our next trip. For less than AUD$20,000 they could build a complete water irrigation system that would supply clean drinking water for the entire village. But where will we get our hands on that sort of money? At the same time, we need to be careful not to create an economic benefit that might expose the village to nearby political power structures that may then take a renewed interest in them. Although it seems they may have already done that. There are so many things to consider before thrusting money at projects. Diana knows this better than any of us. She knows that while we might have feelings on these subjects, we have to trust the community leader to see how these recommendations should be handled in advance, so that the outcomes are positive and successful for all concerned.

Having loaded their car with supplies, we wave goodbye to the community leader, his driver and the community midwife. I hope they make it safely back to their village. I hope they don't have too difficult a time with the mysterious man in the black robe and turban. I also hope that we will return without mishap to the Marco Polo Hotel. We have been lucky to avoid trouble with the insurgents. But how long can our luck last?

Back at the Marco Polo, we drop our bags in our rooms and all head for John's room. Diana enters first and then calls the rest of us to follow. The last thing I want to find is him sitting there in his underwear. He's not. He's in bed and looks a bit better than he did this morning. Thankfully he is still taking fluids although he said that most of what he drank didn't stay in his stomach for long. At least he hasn't lost his sense of humour.

'Hello, little Egypt,' he says. It is a nickname he's given me.

'Hey, Papa John, feeling any better?' I reply sitting on his bed.

'A little.'

Diana assures him Dr Katiby is on his way, 'He's just getting some medicine for you.'

Meanwhile, instead of us telling him about our day, he tells us about his. John had a dream — wild hallucinations that were a mish-mash of things that have happened in his life, woven together with things we've experienced in Afghanistan. Pretty good medicine, I reckon. Dr Katiby enters the room, which is our cue to leave.

'You take care, Papa John.' I bend down to kiss him on the cheek.

'I'll be fine,' he croaks.

Dr Katiby prescribes antibiotics and plenty of rest.

Back downstairs I thank Dr Katiby for taking us out today. I don't mention the mysterious man in black but judging by the smirk on Dr Katiby's face, he knows that I am thinking about him. I smile. 'I am sure I will remember this day for as long as I live.'

'Then I hope you shall live a very long time,' he laughs.

Next stop, check emails. I wonder how Kerry is getting on without me. If he's not missing me, I'll be very upset. I wonder how Jessica, Sahra and Nathan are doing.

And I wonder where Mum thinks I am.

Chapter 18
Extremes

The home of Haji Mohammad Rafiq Mujaddadi, the Mayor of Herat Province, is palatial. It makes our own Government House in Canberra, Yarralumla, seem modest by comparison.

At the invitation of Mayor Mujaddadi, Diana, John, Judy, Chris and I are invited into a long parlour room surrounded by treasures that remind me of a set from the movie *Aladdin*. Everything is magnificent. There's a row of marble vases of varying heights and colours, each intricately crafted with battle scenes from the nation's turbulent past. Gilt-framed paintings hang on the walls. We are ushered past a nest of armchairs — pale green velvet, gold-leaf finish, saddle arms. The cushions are also exquisite. And then, to cap it all, carved Louis XVI-style oak settees (one each) positioned between beautifully adorned coffee tables — Corinthian base with hand-decorated gilt edges. I feel as if I've stepped into a museum. Mayor Mujaddadi invites us to sit on the Louis XVI-style oak settees and to enjoy the various refreshments, served on the coffee table with the Corinthian base. I want to photograph this lavish spread of nuts, dates, exotic savouries and gourmet chocolates. I sip at the tea and nibble a date, hoping it is as delicious as those I'd tasted in Dubai. It sure is. And there are plenty more.

Brad Hanson, US Department of State Representative, Provincial Reconstruction Team, Herat Province, joins us and sits opposite Mayor Mujaddadi. To his left is Mr Nazir, from the Herat Rotary Club. On his right is Dr Katiby, then Diana, Judy and John. I'm next to Chris who is beside the Head of the National Reconciliation Commission (NRC). Mayor Mujaddadi sits at the head of the table, beside his eldest son, who will translate. To his right is one of his younger sons and some Afghan dignitaries.

Naturally we are eager to hear what the Head of the NRC has to say about the Taliban.

'Many Taliban fighters are eager to lay down their arms and join the government of Afghanistan,' he says through the language assistant. 'About 1600 armed Taliban have been reconciled in the last month. It is a very big undertaking but we are committed to this task.'

He says there are obviously hardcore extremists who will never reconcile and who can only be dealt with by force. But some are being won over with money, promises of jobs, education, offers of land, and with it, hope.

Then it's their turn to ask questions. They want to know about projects that are being supported through the Childlight Foundation, which Diana explains. She also relates our visit to the remote communities with Dr Katiby. Mayor Mujaddadi is impressed with our efforts and offers us every support. Talk of support leads to the Rotary connection. Mr Nazir from the Herat University handles that. He explains Rotary's role in Herat and says that they hope to establish a sister group with Rotary in either Australia or the United States to tap into the many opportunities that will assist them to further develop their existing programs. For example, Rotary's programs for students and youth can change the lives of those who participate. Young people can earn scholarships, travel on cultural exchanges, or help a community through a service project. Sounds good.

Then Judy is bursting to speak, so am I. We tell them about the disability centre and all the amazing people we have met and how hospitable they have been. We're full of enthusiasm for the task of engaging further support to these types of projects. And I guess that's when I get the idea to write down these experiences in Afghanistan. No-one back home knows anything about the positive things happening here. Could I change that? After all, from everything I've seen so far in this dusty land, surely nothing is impossible.

Sipping tea in this room full of so many luxurious items is so extreme after a stint in the grey-dust outposts where the dogs look hungry and the children look hungrier. Speaking of food ... Mayor Mujaddadi must like what he's heard because he upgrades his afternoon tea invitation and invites us to join him in the dining room. Before us is a table spread with an even more lavish meal. Given that men and women don't usually eat together in this country, I half-expect Judy, Diana and me to be banished to the Women's Room. Mayor Mujaddadi laughs at this. Everything is different around here. Not only are we joining the men, but Mayor Mujaddadi invites me to sit beside him, right in the heart of it all. He relaxes and reveals his less serious side as an official government representative. I feel most honoured.

It is a wonderful evening. We gather that the people of Herat are pioneers in their country. They are first to participate in the free elections, and have elected the very first mayor to administer the affairs of the city. Zealous and respectable, under Mayor Mujaddadi, Herat is a notable symbol of reconstruction. His office encourages the development of important infrastructure through the building of roads, airways and trains. In his master plan, Mayor Mujaddadi envisages all Herat roads being sealed. With the support of many people in Herat, he has created a number of green zones within the city.

Tourism is an odd subject in wartime, but it gets discussed. There's a touch of 'what might have been' in some conversations, and 'what could still be' in others. And while tourism hasn't exactly taken off in Herat, nor anywhere else in Afghanistan, there are certainly some wonderful places that tourists might want to visit.

After dinner, Mayor Mujaddadi takes us on a late-night cruise through the city. We follow his four-wheel drive vehicle. *Oh look, there's the Herat Provincial Military Museum, built to highlight the military victories of the Heratis in their numerous campaigns for freedom!*

On our way up a mountain, we stop at the Governor Anwari's VIP Guesthouse, which overlooks the city. Wow. It is a two-storey octagon. We are welcomed at the door by a servant who leads us upstairs. We walk past antiques, crystal chandeliers, Persian rugs, tall marble vases and other magnificent furnishings. Even the plaster on the ceilings is patterned, like icing on a wedding cake. Recessed lighting and heavy drapes shade the wall-to-ceiling windows and here we are in the tearoom.

'Be seated, please,' says the servant.

Two matching golden 'King and Queen' chairs take the most prominent position in the room. Between them is the Afghan flag. The heavy red royal drapes create an amazing image, and I invite Mayor Mujaddadi to sit with me, so we can pretend to be a Royal couple. I'm getting cheeky now. He laughs at my childishness.

Tea is served in fine china cups rimmed with more gold.

Gold? 'I feel like a queen,' I say. I'm hamming it up now.

Everyone laughs. Mayor Mujaddadi looks me up and down, strokes his chin and says something to Dr Katiby who conveys, 'The Mayor would like to know if you would like to live here permanently.'

'Oh, I certainly could,' I reply, without thinking.

'Steady, my girl ...' Judy cautions, 'be careful.'

Mayor Mujaddadi and Dr Katiby confer once again, and with Judy's 'be careful' ringing in my ear, Dr Katiby says, 'If you would like to, then Mayor Mujaddadi says he would be happy to arrange it.'

'Arrange what?'

'Arrange for you to remain here permanently.'

Had I not seen Dr Katiby chuckle out the corner of my eye, I might have thought they were serious.

'Oh, you boys are so naughty!' I scold.

When it is almost time to leave, Mayor Mujaddadi takes Dr Katiby aside and talks. When the doctor comes back he says, 'The Mayor has one more thing to show you; it requires driving.' Diana, Judy and John get into Mayor Mujaddadi's car and Chris and I scramble into the mini-van with Dr Katiby and his driver. 'You guys go ahead,' I call out, 'We'll follow.'

People in power inevitably attract the attention of others with a political or revolutionary agenda. Some are simply concerned with financial gain and eliminating the competition, or in a worst case scenario, exacting revenge. Strategically, I feel more comfortable in the mini-van because it doesn't look nearly as flash as the four-wheel drive and should someone take a pot shot at the mayor, I wouldn't be in that vehicle. The drive through the night is unsettling. There is no street lighting. Giant granite boulders, thick shrubbery and tall trees line the roadside so there are plenty of ambush points. I am relieved when we eventually stop. Dr Katiby indicates to join him outside.

It is a magnificent vantage point. Diana and the others can't wait to get to the edge of the cliff, which overlooks the entire city. So that's Herat spread before us, a city that wants freedom, tourism and a financial place in the commercial world. After gasping at the view, we begin to notice our immediate environment, the car park. It reminds me of my courting days.

'Hey, Judy, is this the mayor's version of 'going parking' with us?' I laugh out loud, not thinking anyone will understand the term. None of their English is that good. Or is it?

Dr Katiby looks up and laughs. He moves closer to Judy and me. 'You remember I told you in the mini-van that I once knew a French girl?'

'Er, ye...s,' I reply, wondering what's coming next.

'Well, she was a little bit naughty too ...'

'Dr Katiby!' I waggle my finger at him and pretend to be shocked. 'So you DO know what 'parking' is?'

'Yes, I do,' he confesses. 'That French girl told me many things.'

'Told? Or taught?'

'Oh my!' laughs Judy, before I can squeeze out his answer. 'Come on, kids, settle down!'

To Diana, Mayor Mujaddadi proudly points out the captured Soviet gunships and the tanks below. We gather around and listen too. By the time the Soviets were driven from Afghanistan the tally of casualties was high. Death and carnage followed them. Scattered all over the land are graveyards filled with the charred remains of Soviet battle vehicles. The Afghan people suffered a great deal during that bloody war and despite the Afghan victory, there was no real peace. Time after time this country has been invaded. Faced with no other choice, the resilience of the Afghan people is impressive. 'Endurance' is a word they know well.

Dr Katiby points out the Herat Cinema, destroyed by the Taliban. The mayor says it reopened on 2 June 2008.

'How big is it?'

'It holds around 800 and the first film to be screened was the life of the Prophet Muhammad,' Dr Katiby replies. 'Now, the director of the cinema would like to feature the works of Afghan filmmakers as a cultural place for families to enjoy.' I guess it will be quite some time before they get round to screening *Harry Potter*! Regardless of what they screen, a cinema in Afghanistan is remarkable. Then Mayor Mujaddadi announces that we should be on our way.

Heading back to the Marco Polo Hotel, I chat with Dr Katiby about things in general in his country. He is a walking encyclopaedia on local customs, the state of the nation, internal politics and the type of things tourists like us want to know. For example, the menfolk: I've never been so exposed to Afghan men before this part of the trip. What do they think about me travelling so far from home? What do they think about me working in their country? I had so many misconceptions based on news reports and security briefs. Now I am pleasantly surprised to learn that many of the habits of the Afghan typical male are similar to what our men do back home. Of course, Afghan men are more religious, but there are plenty of religious men back home too. They don't think ill of me. To the contrary, they hope that I can help make a difference to the poverty that devastates them. They hope that more foreigners will take the time to understand them and their ways and not stereotype them by what the fundamentalists may do. I believe the Afghan people are kinder than anyone gives them credit for.

The morning of the next day brings another glorious blue sky and we are now heading towards the city's first congregational mosque, Masjid-I-Jami, the Friday Mosque. I much prefer its generic name, the Blue Mosque. Dr Katiby says it is stunning but he has understated its beauty. We park the mini-van nearby; I glimpse its magnificence. Built in 1200 on the site of a 10th century mosque, it is breathtaking. My spirits lift a little. This is the beauty Ali spoke of when we sat in the sunlit room at the disabled rehabilitation centre.

'There is much to live for and so much beauty in this country,' he said.

We remove our shoes and enter the courtyard by one of the five secondary entrances along the east wall. All exterior and courtyard walls are richly decorated with pink bricks covered with plaster and predominantly blue tile work with vegetal and floral motifs. The exterior is entirely and heavily restored.

'They restored it in around 1970,' says Dr Katiby. 'Soon we shall speak to some people who are responsible for its continued restoration.'

Bi-level arched niches, minarets, and long walls with blind arches surround me. To the left of the entrance is the original completion plaque announcing the date of construction. At the southernmost edge of this façade, behind a screen wall, is the portal from the Ghurid Mosque, the original mosque from which the Blue Mosque was built. It has been lightly restored but is nowhere near as wondrous as the main structure. The doorway flanks two engaged columns. Their surfaces and archways are covered with geometric carvings. The colours are exquisite. On either side of the doorway are stone panels of Arabic inscriptions, highlighted in blue tiles. We stand in the middle of the mosque courtyard, an expansive paved surface, measuring

121 x 174 metres. It is lined with single-storey arcades and features four vaulted halls. Several men sit on the outskirts of the courtyard praying. Dr Katiby says they don't mind our intrusion, although a little man, whom I imagine is a Mullah, (a religiously-educated man), starts barking at us when we have our picture taken. Dr Katiby laughs it off and waves him away.

We meet the head of the International Project for Preservation of Historical Monuments, who shows us how they restore the mosque in their workshop. He allows me to take his picture and says he is honoured by our visit. I slip him a US$20 bill as my humble donation to the restoration project. Diana, Judy and Chris also make contributions. He accepts with deep humility.

'*Tashakor* (thank you).'

We wander through the gardens, into the narrow alleys and through the maze of shops lining the streets beyond. We stop to admire the work of a glass blower. Sultan Hamidy (or Ahmad) and his family have been making famous Herati blue glass for generations. He has a hunched back and sits in a cave-like shop, putting the final touches on his latest traditional Herati blue glass design. It is striking. For such a poor country they certainly have amazing resources that could proudly support a booming tourist trade.

Dr Katiby receives a phone call and tells us to return quickly to the vehicle. We have just been invited to attend afternoon tea at the residence of Governor Anwari. We hasten back to Government House. Upon our arrival we are pleasantly surprised to see Mayor Mujaddadi present too. What an afternoon! To be spent amidst the fragrance of beautiful rose gardens dotted with tantalising scents of rosemary and thyme and bordered with hundreds of low-lying jasmine hedges.

When we are seated, Governor Anwari looks around at his guests as if something is amiss. He turns to Diana and asks her to ring Brad Hanson to invite him to join us. To everyone's astonishment Brad arrives within 15 minutes. Taking the seat between me and the Governor, I am amazed how quickly he got here.

'You must have broken the land speed record!'

'Indeed,' he nods. 'I also had quite a bit of explaining to do …' He reckons he was in the middle of some important meeting, but nothing, of course, is more important in Herat than attending afternoon tea with the Governor.

Tall conifers and massive oaks screen the border of the vast property. Everywhere I look, there is breathtaking scenery.

'So … you have seen my guesthouse?'

'Yes.'

'And did you like it?' Governor Anwari asks me directly.

'It is magnificent,' I smile. 'I felt rather like a queen there.' I playfully nudge the mayor sitting beside me. A flurry of Afghan language breaks out and Dr Katiby starts laughing. He is seated directly across from me and failing miserably at translating. Governor Anwari has a terrific sense of humour and is indeed a wonderful and gracious host. There is a pause; Governor Anwari speaks to me, as Dr Katiby translates.

'The Governor says that he would like to offer you the guesthouse as a gift,' Dr Katiby laughs. Then Mayor Mujaddadi puts up his hand politely and says something to the doctor, who points to the mayor and adds, 'He too also would like to offer you a house.'

'Oh my goodness!' I nervously laugh.

'So, do you think you will decide?' Dr Katiby asks a little too wickedly. All the occupants at the table are keen to know how I will respond. Anxious to protect my virtue, Diana then reminds everyone that I am married.

'This will be interesting …' mutters Brad Hanson under his breath.

'Well,' I pause, having captured everyone's attention. 'I do have a man in Jalalabad who's offered me a house … with a camel too. I really should consider his offer before giving you both my final word!'

Dr Katiby translates and everyone at the table laughs heartily, even the gardeners and waiters.

When the laughter eventually subsides, Governor Anwari reassures Diana that it is all just good fun.

'Please understand we are joking,' he explains. 'We just want to make you all feel comfortable.'

On our final day in Herat, John is feeling more like his usual self and back in action. We can't leave without seeing the hospital, so Judy and I ask Dr Katiby to give us a tour. Judy really wants to see it, and I want to see everything. Prior to arriving, Dr Katiby says the 400-bed non-military hospital is the only one for an entire province similar in size to the entire Fiji Islands, or nearly twice the size of Wales. We meet a female doctor, who along with Dr Katiby shows us, very quickly, through the hospital. She says, 'The ward is awaiting a major overhaul.' And it certainly needs one, it's paint is chipped and peeling. It is not a pleasant place to be.

Over 70 per cent of children at this hospital are diagnosed with infectious diseases, such as acute gastroenteritis, acute respiratory infection, septicaemia, meningitis and typhoid. Additional causes of death include close to 200 cases of anaemia, almost as many cases of dysentery, renal and urinary tract infections and over 150 cases of drug poisoning. Malaria, cholera and tuberculosis are also common and many of the neonatal admissions are virtually all due to birth asphyxia or sepsis.

We pass several rooms and I look for an empty one so we can snap a photo. We see two iron beds, one broken, with both sheets pushed up beside a cracked wall. We glimpse a dirty mattress made of the thinnest foam. In this room there are no pillows, no blankets and no curtains to shield patients for privacy. In this one there are no bedside tables or lockable cabinets, no mirrors, no drapes to cover the broken windows. It is depressing. When we arrive at the labour ward, things are hardly better. Dark blue curtains shield those in labour from view but the doorway to the labour room is open. Anyone can look in. Several beds are crammed into each small room. Ancient red, white and grey linoleum covers the floor. Dirt-stained white tiles cover the bottom half of the walls. The windows are rusty. Two plastic aprons are hooked onto a window latch. They look like those used to kill pigs at a slaughterhouse. They are blood-stained.

Behind the blue curtains, we hear the distinct moans of a woman in early labour. She sounds terrible. Since I can't see any feet standing beside her bed, I have to assume that she is alone but I am told that there are others inside the room waiting, just like her, to give birth.

'Oh, my God.' I bite my lip as she moans again. And then I hear the faint moan of another woman, and another. Those first early throes of childbirth are something no mother can forget or the memory of the pain that follows. Yet in this room there is no nitrous oxide to take the edge off it. There is no hot shower to numb the contractions. A cry is suddenly torn from the lips of one woman behind the blue curtain.

'Oh, dear,' Judy whispers.

There is no comforting husband to hold her hand. He must wait outside with the other men. The woman, whoever she is, perhaps even a young girl, does not want to be alone. She's very afraid. Judy wants to rush to her side just as much as I do, but that would be 'intruding' wouldn't it? And we're not allowed to do that. We are told that some of the women need to have caesarean deliveries but they lack knowledge of the operation and so they refuse. Many of their families do not give permission either because they believe that afterwards the women will become infertile. It's a tragic story and one that is so common here.

Another tortured moan escapes from behind the blue curtain. Silently I pray that the time ahead for the unknown woman goes quickly and will not be too unpleasant. We walk to the end of the hall to the Newborn Intensive Care Unit. There Judy and I are invited to see the tiniest little bundle sleeping in an incubator. It's a girl. We are pleasantly surprised that she is healthy and that the hospital has this kind of technology. I am invited to take pictures so I take a couple of the baby wrapped in pink and a couple of the nurses attending. It takes a little prodding to get them to smile.

As we are leaving the ward, a senior female doctor explains to us that we must not despair too much because there is a new hospital being built by NATO's provincial reconstruction team, civilian efforts and the Italian Government. Her face radiates like the sun as she describes its new lovely white beds and coloured doors, the baby and toddler play area, the Radiology Department, the pharmacy, the Surgical Department and several incubators.

'Soon things will be a little better than they are now,' she says. 'There have been many positive changes for women in Afghanistan. They can easily enter medical school now. Even in some provinces there are limited numbers of girls at school but because of the need for female doctors, the Government has enabled them to enter medical school without any entering exam.'

'That's amazing,' says Judy turning to me in surprise.

I am relieved to hear this and begin to feel the shadow of hopelessness lift. So even in the darkest moments of despair, there can be hope. I would love to return someday to see the new hospital.

I smile and kiss the doctor's cheeks. She smiles.

'*Insha'Allah*, I hope you will return too,' she says.

Another emergency beckons.

'I am sorry but I must go.' The doctor turns and makes her way quickly back down the hall.

Inside the mini-van everyone is quiet. Obviously we are all affected by the hospital tour despite the promise of improved conditions. Dr Katiby explains that the problem is widespread and in some regions things are far worse. In some regions women and children just die because they cannot get to any medical care, and those who do may still die because there is no medicine at the hospitals to treat them.

'Like the Mirwais Hospital in Kandahar,' says Dr Katiby. 'The doctors themselves have no formal training. They just graduate from school and go there to work. They earn very little, some AUD\$50 a month if they are lucky … and the little they earn, they often use to buy food for those in their care.'

I can feel my heartbreaking all over again as I listen to Dr Katiby describe the hardships faced by Afghan people. Anyone who believes that they are better off left to their own devices needs to come here. They need to see firsthand the despair. The plight of these victims hits the headlines one day and then the next day is forgotten. But how can I forget everything I have seen?

Diana senses, rightly, that we are all a little overwhelmed. This confrontation with reality is not easily shaken off and she soon becomes concerned for all of us.

'Let's go to the Minarets and Mausoleum of Queen Goharshãd,' she suggests to Dr Katiby.

He too seems relieved by the suggestion.

'Yes, this is a very good idea, Diana,' he smiles and then turns to instruct the driver.

Chris distracts us by telling us what he knows of the Minarets.

'They're in a pretty desolate state now but they used to be quite magnificent, or so I've read,' he says.

'Yes, you are correct,' Dr Katiby agrees. 'They just look like old mud-brick towers now, but once they were many colours of sparkling blue, green, white, and black mosaic tiles. Now the traffic is the problem for them.'

And so we soon discover as we join the throng of traffic that drives close by to the remaining minarets.

'Can't the government just close off the road?' I ask.

'They tried to explain to the people that the traffic is sending tremors through their foundations but the people objected to the road closure and the government did not make a diversion route … so this problem is unresolved.'

We pull up near the sole minaret that is held up by dozens of wires and looks as if it is going to crumble at any time. It's held up by two spans of cable, bracing it against seemingly imminent collapse onto the road. It's a temporary measure but Dr Katiby says it's been that way for ages.

'Do you see that gaping hole about halfway up the tower?' he asks.

'Hey, yeah ... there's a stairwell inside,' I reply and shield my eyes from the sun to get a better look.

'That hole is made by a rocket or artillery attack in the 1980s, when the Soviets were fighting Mujahedeen in this area,' he explains.

'Well, I sure wouldn't want to park my car beside that thing,' I joke, thankful that the mini-van does not belong to me.

Judy laughs and snaps another photo. We are lucky that an old man is living at the mausoleum as a caretaker and he agrees to allow us inside to view the tomb of Queen Goharshãd and her family.

'Imagine if you could bring busloads of tourists to this place,' I tell Judy. 'It would be right up there with China's Great Wall or even Cambodia's Angkor Wat.'

'It's incredible,' she agrees.

Soon it's time to go to the 'Old City,' to the original citadel 'Qala-e Ikhtiyaruddin' — otherwise known as the 'Old Fort'. This is what Chris has been dying to see. Not that you can really miss it as it virtually towers over Herat.

According to Dr Katiby, the giant piece of ancient land is currently undergoing renovations and is one of the favourite attractions in Herat. Built by Alexander the Great, the citadel withstood many battles. It was planned to be demolished in the 1950s but was saved through the intervention of King Zahir Shah. There are 18 towers and it features huge battlements. An impressive site now occupied by the Afghan Army. We try to get inside but after about half an hour of arguing, the Army tell us to leave.

'Maybe next time,' says Dr Katiby as we drive back to the Marco Polo Hotel.

What an amazing day it's been. Truly unforgettable.

'Thank you for giving us a remarkable day, Dr Katiby,' I say as we arrive back at the hotel and walk through the lobby door to the reception area.

'I am glad that you were able to see so much,' he replies.

'Yes, thank you indeed,' chimes in Diana.

'The hospital was something else,' says Judy.

Dr Katiby shakes his head and waves his hand like it's no trouble at all.

I'm still curious to know certain things when we make our way to the computer area, to the left of reception but I'm not exactly sure if it's appropriate for me to ask. He is a doctor after all. How more different can he be from any of the doctors back home? Will he be offended?

'Dr Katiby, are male doctors allowed to treat women?' I begin rather tentatively.

At that moment the young Tom Cruise look-a-like suddenly enters the room with a tray of piping hot tea.

'Sure ... there is no restriction in the law or in Islam that prevents us from treating and operating on women,' he explains as he receives the first cup.

'But are you allowed to examine the woman ... the patient I mean ... to check her private area ...' I struggle a little with how best to pose my question.

Dr Katiby immediately realises my difficulty and smiles reassuringly. He adopts a tone that I instantly recognise. He's all medical, purely professional. Just like the doctors back home.

'Some families are very culturally traditional and have restrictions for not allowing male doctors from performing more personal examinations or delivering the baby.'

'So how do you get around that?' Judy asks.

'In such cases we call the midwife if she is available to give the exam and then she can report in terms of diagnosis. If she is unable to diagnose then she must talk with the husband and he must agree.'

'And does he?' I ask.

'Mostly yes. Day by day the ideas are changing but it all takes time,' he replies. 'Some people are very conservative. I think it is the same in your country too.'

'Yes, I think so. I know I prefer to visit a female doctor over a male doctor.'

'There you see … our cultures are similar in more ways than we think,' he concludes wisely.

In the early morning of 2 November it is time to leave Herat. We settle our hotel account and say farewell to the manager, his staff and Tom Cruise, the tea boy. We hand over our suitcases to Dr Katiby's driver then board the mini-van for our final leg of this journey, Herat Airport.

I sure will miss Dr Katiby and his infectious sense of humour, his smile and cheeky eyes. I have learnt a great deal from him and even though our time together has been short, I feel as if I have known him forever. I've loved listening to his stories and I've loved the way he just views life as something to be enjoyed and not agonised over. Certainly in Afghanistan there is much to cry for, but Dr Katiby has reminded me that we should just help where we can, and not worry too much about what we cannot do, or where we cannot help. We are, after all, only human.

I do hope he continues to stay safe in this unsafe paradise. He assures me he will, if it is the will of Allah.

'Oh, I think Allah will continue to watch over you, Dr Katiby. You are such a good man!' I proudly shake his hand.

'Thank you again for your hospitality and thank you for showing us so much,' says Judy. 'We promise to keep in touch.'

She has Dr Katiby's email address.

'Yes, please email me when you are settled from your journey,' he says then motions us towards the departure area.

It isn't, as we discover, anywhere near the arrivals area. Instead, we are taken to a completely different part of the airport and asked to wait in a dirt clearing, surrounded by mud walls. There is no place to sit, no place to get a drink and there are no toilets. Most of the travellers are curious but my eyes are fixed on Dr Katiby, who is saying his final goodbyes to Diana.

'We'll be fine,' she says.

With a final farewell he retreats back the way we came as the dust kicks up around him. The crowd begins to move and we fall into line behind the sea of turbans and pakols (Afghan hats). It's a little cramped but no-one seems to be in a hurry. I link my arm through Judy's as we edge closer to the security checkpoint. Diana goes through, then Chris and finally John. A small group of people squeeze in ahead of us and all of a sudden our group is separated.

'Oh, dear,' says Judy.

We get to the security checkpoint but the guards signal us to go back to where we were standing and to wait. Naturally, we become anxious, since neither of us can speak the language and we can't get a message to the others. They're gone!

'Now this is the part where they sell us to the Middle-Eastern sex trade,' I joke.

'I'm far too old to be worried about that, whereas … you on the other hand, Kay …'

'Oh thanks!' I laugh.

Dr Katiby's long gone. Dozens of stranger's eyes stare back at us. What a sight we must look standing there in the middle of a dirt clearing, in a war zone, surrounded by Muslim men.

'At least we are covered from head to toe,' says Judy.

'I'm actually getting to appreciate this get-up,' I say, pulling the scarf a little firmer around my head.

'Yes, it does have its advantages,' Judy eyes the crowd.

Thankfully, John realises that we haven't followed. He tries coming back for us, but is stopped at the security checkpoint. Judy and I see him and quickly rush forward.

'Papa! Papa!' I call out.

He exchanges words with the guards and we edge closer. The guards aren't sure then I put my hand on his arm.

'Papa!' I call.

The guards smile and seem apologetic; I think the body language finally registers. We walk to the other side of the compound and vow to stay much closer to John after that.

'What happened?' says Diana rushing forward to hug us both.

'We were right behind you and then suddenly we weren't,' says Judy.

Huddled together on the dirt clearing we wait. And we wait. The plane eventually arrives and we finally board.

As the heavy aircraft drags itself into the sky, the pilot forces it to bank sharply. This is the moment I fear the plane will rebel and hit the ground with a giant explosion. The cabin is silent. It's eerie. We are all thinking the same thing. The wings eventually level and we begin to climb over the mountains.

Phew!

'Goodbye, Herat.'

Chapter 19

Farewell

At Kabul Airport we make another uneventful landing, navigate through the security checkpoints and then join the throng heading to baggage claim where we are greeted by a sea of dirty little baggage boys. We then hail our pre-booked cab that takes us to our accommodation. Diana has checked us in at the Kabul Inn, a modest guesthouse secured behind high walls on Qala-e Fatullah Road. She really wanted the Gandamack Lodge but it was completely booked out, so the Kabul Inn will have to do. Actually it's quite nice and is considerably cheaper, conveniently located and has internet facilities. *Hi Kerry, Jessica, Sahra, Nathan and Mum, see you real soon ...*

We haul our suitcases up three flights of stairs and are forced to stop mid-stair to give way to the maid coming down. She drags cleaning buckets, mops and cloths behind her, *bump, bump, bump*.

'*Salaam*,' I gasp, breathing in as she draws level and we manoeuvre buckets, mops, my suitcase and two people around one small stair. I squash myself against the walls.

'*Salaam*,' she replies with a smile.

We've booked a girls' room and a boys' room. Diana, Judy and I rent a room that is really only big enough for two. It's really noisy. At least it has its own bathroom and, upon further inspection, hot water and a two-bar electric heater. The floor is carpeted in soft mauve and blue. Two large persian rugs are thrown on them. Nothing matches in the room. There's a small colour television in the corner near Diana's bed. None of us really watch TV so it really doesn't matter if it works or not, but to our surprise it does work, and is equipped with cable TV.

'Here we are then,' says Diana taking the closest bed to the door. 'We're lucky to have beds; some people don't.'

The other beds are through an archway that divides the two small rooms. Two single beds sit side by side, separated by a glass-topped coffee table. It will do. I don't care where I sleep so long as I can wash the dust off my body each night.

'I'm sorry the room's so small,' Diana apologises.

'Its fine,' Judy replies.

'I've slept in worse,' I laugh, ah *Laotian jail cell furnishings!*

'I bet you have!' says Diana.

I peer out the window to the street below. It is practically deserted. I don't know if that is a good thing. I watch two men ride bicycles. They are in no hurry. I check out the buildings around us. The plot outside my window is vacant and there's a partly built three-storey red brick building on the adjoining plot. It is completely abandoned. I can't tell if the building is half-finished, half-started or if the workers have no intention of doing anything more. I shut the window, draw the curtains, take a step back and sit on my bed. It's fine.

There is a light rap on the door and Diana opens up to John and Chris.

'It's pretty much the same set-up as what we have,' says Chris, checking out our room. 'Except that we got bigger beds.'

'I bet you don't have the noisy neighbour.' I point to the connecting door from which the television is blaring.

At around 7 pm we pile into a black four-wheel drive Toyota Landcruiser with its black-tinted windows, which belongs to the Secretary of the local Rotary Club, Mr Rafi. He tells us he has made all the appropriate security arrangements in lieu of our 'night excursion'. None of us has any idea what he means by that. We are on our way to dinner at his home.

Ten minutes later we find ourselves stuck in an alleyway and surrounded by a dozen men with guns. Of all the places to be stopped, I can think of none worse than Sherpur, the 'suburb' of the super-rich drug lords. Their palatial mansions loom to our left and to our right. The traffic is chaos as gunmen shout orders, 'Turn around! Turn around!'

Mr Rafi assures us everything is okay and drives forward a few metres until we find a spot to do a U-turn then back we go, the way we came. Mr Rafi is a quiet man and not easily ruffled. He doesn't discuss the drug lords or what just happened. He says traffic congestion is typical here. I'll bet it is. Business must be booming.

We all breathe a sigh of relief when we are safely beyond Sherpur, though we can't help but wonder about how high drama to us is an ordinary occurrence for others. The contrast between the drug lord palatial mansions and the squatter-type slum housing of ordinary Afghans is extraordinary. Their streets are paved, their driveways secured with impressively ornate steel security gates, and their homes are bathed in brightly burning flood lights. But driving beyond the palatial mansions we are suddenly plunged onto rough dirt roads. The shanty shacks are shrouded in darkness. It seems most residents can't afford generators let alone the fuel to power them. There is virtually no street lighting apart from the occasional glow in one in ten of the houses that we drive past. Weaving our way through dark streets is not a comfortable feeling, nor are my thoughts when we pass the Ghazi Stadium, once a place of bloody retribution for crimes against the Taliban.

The image flashes in my mind of a young woman dressed in a blue burqa, kneeling on the ground. Her name is Zarmina. The gunman stands behind her with the barrel pointed at her head and within minutes she is dead.

Many women like Zarmina were executed for so-called moral crimes. They perished in Ghazi stadium, which we are now passing.

'Do you like football (soccer)?' I ask politely.

Mr Rafi smiles, 'Yes, my son plays.'

I am tempted to ask if practice sessions are held at Ghazi stadium, but think better of it.

Mr Rafi's apartment is welcoming and we enjoy a wonderful night filled with good conversation and delicious traditional Afghan food prepared by his wife, with the help of a lovely man named Nimat.

'He is a chef,' says Mr Rafi. Then his wife scolds him for letting on that she is not solely responsible for the fine feast laid out before us. He laughs about that.

After dinner we retire to the lounge where Mr Rafi's son performs a traditional Afghan dance. He moves gracefully around the room as John claps in time with the music. It is delightful to see his young face so alight with happiness. Following his performance, his mother sings a song as she beats gently on a daf, an Afghan drum that resembles a large tambourine. She blushes when I tell her she is easily as good as any professional singer.

At the instigation of their father, all three children stand and proudly sing Afghanistan's national anthem.

So long as there is the earth and the heavens;
So long as the world endures;
So long as there is life in the world;
So long as a single Afghan breathes;
There will be this Afghanistan.
Long live the Afghan nation.
Long live the Republic.
Forever there be our national unity;
Forever there be the Afghan nation and the Republic.
Forever the Afghan nation, the Republic and National Unity-National Unity

How proudly they sing and even though we cannot understand a single word, other than Afghanistan, it is joyous to see their faces filled with national pride. Our applause follows their performance and the smiles that over take their fresh faces are a delight.

Up I get, at their invitation, and follow with an enthusiastic 'Advance Australia Fair'. Next it's the turn of the Americans, who decline because theirs is in the wrong key. So I prompt them with the opening lines of, 'The stars at night, are big and bright, deep in the heart of Texas ...' which will do for now as their national song.

Around 9 pm Mr Rafi advises that we should return to the Kabul Inn so we don't break curfew. He leaves the room and phones the security checkpoints that we're coming through and we start saying our goodbyes.

'Thank you so much for having us, we hope to see you again ...'

'You come again to my country,' Mrs. Rafi smiles.

'We hope that we may in the future,' says Judy.

'Please we must go now,' says Mr Rafi.

He has been the perfect host and his family are generous in their hospitality. All of us agree, as we farewell him and his son from the gates of the Kabul Inn, that the night has been marvellously entertaining. It has been our most enjoyable night for our entire trip.

Back at the inn the television is still blaring in the next room and dashes our hopes of a good night's sleep. From about 1 a.m to 3 am the room occupant receives about a dozen phone calls, all of which we hear. I want Judy to bang on the wall and tell him there is no need to shout. Instead I stare at the ceiling and wonder whether he knows that there are three Western women next room door? Diana sleeps, but of course she's exhausted. Judy has her earplugs in. I pull the pillow over my head and turn on my side.

'Oh what a night!' I exclaim when morning breaks through the frosted windows of our room.

Judy stretches, Diana heads for the shower and I think of home. Judy and I sort through our clothes, figuring out what to wear today.

After breakfast we meet our guide, Ester, a young Swedish woman who has spent most of her childhood youth in Pakistan with her missionary parents. She plans to take us to the Turquoise Mountain School of Ceramics in Istalif, and to the famous Garden of Babur Shah on Sarak-e-Chilsitun Road. The 11-hectare terraced garden is located on the western slopes of the Sher-e-Darwaza Mountain, south of Kabul. They are reportedly the most beautiful gardens in Kabul, laid out by the founder of the Mogul Dynasty, Muhammad Zahir al-Din Babur (r. 1526–1530), a descendant of the great Genghis Khan. The tradition of Mogul princes at that time was to develop sites for recreation and pleasure, and then choose one as their final resting place. The magnificent gardens of Babur Shah have endured more than two decades of war, rocket fire and near complete destruction but for the dedication of 20 or so gardeners, who toil, plant new shrubs, and masses and masses of rose beds, tall trees and flowers. Ester says it is a 'must-see'.

'The final terrace at the top of the gardens is the tomb of the former king himself, Babur Shah,' Ester explains. 'His wife is buried separately, but her tombstone is possibly even more beautifully carved than her husband's. We'll go there after we visit Istalif.' Unfortunately, we never made it to Istalif despite it being only 40 kilometres north of Kabul, in the foothills of the Hindu Kush. We were stopped by Afghan police just before leaving Kabul and forced to abandon our adventure following the kidnapping of the French aid worker, Dany Egreteau. He was eventually freed on 3 December 2008.

Istalif will have to wait for another time and although we were all considerably disappointed, we were relieved that the men escorting us back to Ester's compound were in fact police and not Taliban. We do, however, get to spend a few hours at the Turquoise Mountain School of Ceramics in Kabul and afterwards, we stop by a little gallery to purchase a few handmade items. Inside the little gallery we come across two Canadian soldiers.

'Last minute shopping, hey?' I ask.

'Yes, ma'am,' the giant soldier replies. 'More dangerous going home without gifts you know.'

I laugh. That is something Kerry would say!

'Well you boys travel safe,' I turn to the young sales attendant and complete my purchases.

Among the souvenirs I place on the counter, I buy several pieces of Afghan beaded jewellery for my two daughters, a T-shirt for my son and a few trinkets for friends and family. But the most valuable things I cannot buy are all the treasured memories of our journey and the people we met along the way, and especially all those radiant smiles.

On our final evening in Kabul we dine at the Kabul Inn. Diana has organised a special surprise for us. We will meet Haji Nasrullah 'Baryalai' Arsalai, the man who first introduced Diana to Afghanistan.

'You really must meet him, Kay,' says Diana as we change for dinner. 'He is quite impressive.'

As I gently rub moisturiser into my face, I listen as Diana tells Judy and me all about Baryalai, born 3 March 1958 into a distinguished Afghan family with a long record of service. His forefather was a Foreign Minister of Afghanistan under the famous King Amir Sher Ali and a leader of the resistance against the British in the second Anglo-Afghan War. His most famous brother was a legendary Afghan resistance commander who fought courageously against the Soviets and Afghan Communists during the Soviet-Afghan War. He mobilised tens of thousands of Afghans to fight for the freedom of Afghanistan and was a devout Muslim and a proud Pashtun. He despised the then Taliban for starving and oppressing the people. When the September 11 attacks occurred, Baryalai's brother warned the US against retaliation and urged them to leave matters in the hands of the Afghans.

'It will only be a few months [before the Taliban are toppled],' he said.

In the days leading up to the US air strikes over Afghanistan, the resistance commander again warned that civilian casualties would only serve to build a resistance force in support for the Taliban. It is a great pity the US did not listen to him. Perhaps Afghanistan would be a different place today or at least this is the popular belief among Afghans.

Resistance Commander Abdul Haq was an honourable man who stood for freedom and democracy but he was never going to be anyone's puppet. He was executed on 26 October 2001 after the Taliban hunted him down. His older brother, the former Afghan Vice President and Governor of Nangarhar, was also executed one year later on 6 July 2002.

In the days of the Soviet occupation, Baryalai helped organise the underground resistance before he was forced to migrate to Germany as a refugee. In his new homeland he continued to run the administration of the resistance front against the Soviets. He published a weekly review of political and military developments. It wasn't until 2006 that Baryalai was able to return to his beloved homeland, and upon his return he helped organise the People's Advisory Shura, a mass movement of people in Nangarhar and eastern Afghanistan aimed to mobilise popular participation in bringing democracy to Afghanistan.

'He sounds fascinating,' I say and fasten the thick brown belt around my waist. 'Who wouldn't want to dine with him?'

Judy nods.

Minutes later, the three of us meet John and Chris in the lobby downstairs to await his arrival.

At 7 pm Baryalai arrives promptly and the thing that catches my eye when I first meet him is his amazing silk turban. I have seen many Afghan men wearing turbans. The fabric, colour and styles vary from region to region but the soft gold folds of Baryalai's turban are exquisite and quite mesmerising. My eyes follow the folds of the material as it billows down to the carpeted floor. His voice gently carries across the table as he invites us to be seated. Diana invites him to sit at the head of the table with me on his left and her on his immediate right. I am a little overwhelmed at first. Baryalai is the stuff Hollywood films are made of; a living, breathing Mujahedeen legend. I have a dozen questions to ask but I'm fearful of monopolising the conversation. So I remain quiet for most of the night just listening, hoping to learn the true fate of Afghanistan and where he thinks it will end up. To be honest, I'm a little in awe of him. Baryalai is a very powerful and well revered figure in Afghanistan. I can't believe I'm actually dining with someone of his great importance. *Do I pinch myself for the third time?*

Baryalai is a fascinating man and like so many Afghans I've met, he longs for his country to be at peace. He believes all Afghans should defeat those who take up arms against Afghanistan, but his focus is similar to that of the Herat Mayor, Haji Mohammad Rafiq Mujaddadi, which also centres on peace and reconciliation. Baryalai explains why many Afghans have joined the current insurgency, mostly because they have been harassed and dishonoured. And like Mayor Mujaddadi, he also supports the pursuit of private sector development to create an atmosphere where commerce can replace long-term aid. Baryalai talks of national unity, good neighbourly relations and his view on international partnerships,;that no-one should be able to use Afghanistan to conduct terrorism elsewhere.

It is an informative evening and I find myself 'all ears'. Baryalai too is inquisitive to learn what each of us think of his country. We take turns telling him about our travels and the people we've met and the places we've been. The journey through Sorubi, the disabled centre in Herat, and, of course, the marriage proposals that I almost became entangled in. Baryalai laughs at that.

'She's very much like Anne Mickey,' Diana informs him.

Running his hand thoughtfully over his bearded chin, Baryalai's eyes probed mine. 'Yes, I think she is,' he responded.

'Well, I'll take that as a compliment as everyone I've met loves Anne Mickey!'

'Ha!' he laughs aloud. 'Indeed she is!'

Anne Mickey was on Diana's 2004 and 2005 humanitarian mission and a delight to everyone who met her.

As the evening draws out, we are joined by a German woman, who we met at breakfast, and two of her male colleagues. They are working for a NGO and have been in-country for quite some time.

'Germany gives a lot of aid to Afghanistan,' I announce as one of the German males sits down next to me. 'We've been told this by everyone we've met on our journey.'

He glows with pride. 'Yes, we help a lot.'

And so the evening is filled with conversation about all things German, Australian, Afghanistan and American. Who will win the 2008 US presidential election? That's a question, plus all the stories we share from our incredible encounters in Afghanistan.

Baryalai asks me if I want to go out to a nightclub. I take it he's only joking. He laughs.

'I think we'll turn in,' says Diana. 'We have an early start in the morning.'

And so we say goodnight and as I float upstairs to my room, I think to myself that it would have been intriguing to have seen the nightclub. An image of Baryalai on the dance floor doing an impersonation of John Travolta's 'Saturday Night Fever' suddenly makes me smile.

Hours later, in the quiet of our bedroom we sort through our suitcases and leave what we don't need for the Afghan maid.

'Just put whatever you don't need in the top shelf of that cupboard,' I tell Diana. 'Our maid already knows we are stockpiling things in there for her.'

'She came by just before,' said Judy. 'Kay threw in her old pair of shoes.'

'You did?' Diana asks.

'Well, yeah. I'm not likely to wear them back home, so I thought it would be better to leave them here ...'

We leave the Afghan maid a stash of soaps, powder, shoes, jumpers and loose rupiahs that aren't worth changing at the money exchange. We shower, get into bed and settle for what we hope will be an uneventful night without the TV blaring from the room next door.

When morning comes there is no time for breakfast or at least that's what we think. None of us expect our driver to be late. Diana gets on the phone to him. There must be some explanation. Perhaps there has been a car bombing or an insurgent attack on the town? Or maybe he is simply stuck in traffic? We just hope he arrives safely and soon. We sit outside in the garden courtyard, soaking up the sunshine, waiting patiently. 'Do you know if the planes run on time?' I ask Diana.

'They usually do,' she responds. 'They know that most people have connecting flights in Dubai.'

We only have a three-hour window to make our flight once we land in Dubai.

'Don't worry, I'm sure you'll make your flight,' Diana reassures.

Leaving Kabul signifies the end of an incredible journey for all of us. John, Judy, Chris, Diana and I formed a strong bond of friendship over the last few weeks that we know will stay with us all our lives. Soon we will not only be saying goodbye to Afghanistan, but to each other.

It is a sobering thought as we sit and wait for the driver.

'You really are a very special young woman,' says Papa John to me. 'Your husband is very lucky.'

'Oh, Papa John,' I smile naughtily 'I'd be chasing you if we both weren't so happily attached!'

I will miss Papa John a great deal. He is the sweetest type of father any girl would dream of having. I hope fate brings us back together sometime soon.

'I'm gonna miss ya, girl,' says Texas Judy as we inspect the concrete duck statues strewn across the square patch of garden.

'I'm gonna miss you too, Ms Judy.' I hug her knowing we'll be friends for life. 'It's been great.'

'It sure has,' she smiles.

'Come on, guys, the driver's here!' calls Diana.

Judy and I quickly make our way to where our suitcases are stacked neatly in a row. The driver greets us with an apology and a '*salaam*'. He says our drive to the airport will not take long and he pulls away from the curb and heads down the main street. It seems symbolic that our journey will end on a beautiful sunny day. On the sidewalk, an Afghan policeman, dressed in a grey uniform with a ballistics vest, lays his rifle and kneels on his red prayer mat in front of a tall green cyprus pine and prays. It is odd seeing a soldier praying in a public space, but they do in Afghanistan. It's certainly not something you'd ever see back home. Such images are imprinted in my mind like the war, carnage and despair, mixed with the beauty, wonder, courage and resilience of the Afghan people. I will miss this place. I will miss all the people I have met like, Tim Lynch, Dr Dave Warner, Todd Huffman, Dr Katiby, Faye Spencer and Richard Boyed, all of whom have a tremendous will to make this country a better place for future generations. Despite the dangers, I will, I expect, hope to return.

I will think kindly of Mr Saddaquat, the headmaster of the Jalalabad girls' school. I see him now, his tall thin frame squeezed into that dilapidated wheelchair. I also will remember the day when I was called '*teacher*' and the faces of those lovely little girls who lit the room with their ever so-sweet smiles. I will laugh whenever I think of the community leader in the remote village outside Herat with his '*salaam salaam*' turkeys and the old hunchback lady who boldly said that she was more beautiful than I. And I will surely smile thinking of that day in the garden with

Governor Anwari, US Envoy Brad Hanson and Mayor Mujaddadi, and my promise to get back to them on the matter involving the man who offered me a house *and* a camel in Jalalabad.

Most of all, I will miss my dear friend Muslim, who opened my mind to so many incredible experiences and discussions about life and family. It will be difficult going home knowing that he remains trapped in this war. How easy it is to be unaffected by war until you experience it. How easy it is to sit home beneath the blue skies and palm trees and to feel so disconnected. I doubt I will ever feel that way again. It is horrible to think that the people you have come to know are living under the constant threat of death. And though some of the areas where some of them live may not be directly affected by terrorism, they still live every day in the knowledge that anything could happen and usually does.

No-one ever feels safe in any part of the country. Not in the towns, in the villages, on the roads or in an open field. All are exposed to extreme risk of losing lives at any moment, anywhere in the country. Whenever there's an attack or explosion in town, the first thing they do is to trace their relatives, to find out if they are safe. I shudder to think of Muslim searching for his family through the carnage of a bomb blast. I think this is the saddest thought I will carry with me, but I pray it never comes to that. *Insha'Allah.*

Our journey is almost over; we are looking forward to seeing our husbands, wives and children again. Diana is missing her husband Bob. Judy is longing to see her husband John and not a day went by that I didn't think of Kerry waiting at home for me. Of course, the army is waiting for him, counting down his leave days. Let them wait. After all, I've waited more times than I can remember for Kerry to come home from some mission. I can't wait to see my kids and tell my mum of my adventures. I'm sure she'll be surprised.

We arrive at Kabul International Airport and to that surreal feeling of déjà vu. Our driver drops us off at the security checkpoint and points to the building to our right. This is where we must have our bags X-rayed before entering airport grounds. We will then walk 100 metres, dragging our suitcases behind us, to another baggage check, a body search and into a crowded line of people, and then to yet another screening area. Beyond that we will finally enter the automatic doors to the airport itself. Inside the room we lift our bags onto the X-ray machine and then queue again, for the official check-in and ticketing.

'Thank you for coming to Afghanistan,' says the short, stout-bearded man behind the counter.

I smile and moved to the next security checkpoint.

'Go to women search,' says the policeman, politely pointing to Judy, Diana and myself.

Minutes later we are standing before a female police officer who inspects the contents of our carry-on bags. I giggle as she pats me down; she giggles too. In fact, there is a lot of laughter coming from our cubicle over the next few minutes. By the time we come out, there is also a great deal of interest from the male policemen. A rally of conversation follows as I step into view and one of them pats his head and points to mine. Yes, I have exchanged my headscarf for a sparkly new one previously worn by the female Afghan police officer patting me down.

Ten minutes later, I find myself seated in the middle of a busy internet cafe, the only female in a room full of men, tapping away my very last email to Kerry. 'Hi, Babe, We're about to board the flight from Kabul, I'll email you when we get to Dubai. I had the most amazing time here. I can't wait to tell you all about it! See you soon! Love always, Kay.'

With the dust of Afghanistan in my veins I say goodbye to this tragic but glorious country, but not forever, I hope.

I will return.

Insha'Allah

Kay's Favourite Charities

Soldier On

Soldier On is about Australians coming together to show their support for our physically and psychologically wounded. We want to show the men and women of our Defence forces that we will always have their backs.

Founded in 2012, the organisation was inspired by the death of a friend. Lieutenant Michael Fussell was killed in an IED blast in Afghanistan in 2008 and his friend John Bale looked for a way to support those who survived the blast. John quickly realised there was no easy or accessible way for members of the Defence forces, or the public, to show their support for those wounded in battle.

With his wife Danielle, they reached out to his fellow soldiers and enlisted the help of Cavin Wilson, who had been posted in Afghanistan, involved in returning soldiers killed or wounded in action. Together they decided it was time to start an organisation that connected these men and women to the wider public, ensuring these brave sailors, soldiers, airmen and airwomen could be cared for and lead fulfilling and successful lives. Website: https://www.soldieron.org.au

The Australian Aid Organisation, MAHBOBA'S PROMISE

The Australian Aid Organisation, MAHBOBA'S PROMISE, delivers desperately needed food, shelter, medical attention, education and HOPE to hundreds of children and women in Afghanistan.

Mahboba Rawi came to Australia as a refugee from Afghanistan and is now an Australian citizen. After facing many hardships in her own life, she founded Mahboba's Promise in 1998 to raise funds and awareness among the Australian community as a way to create a sustainable, self-sufficient future for Afghani women and children. Since Mahboba's Promise was established, Mahboba's determination to work has seen a number of schools started for young girls, primary health care services set up in rural areas and clean drinking water provisions introduced to various areas of Afghanistan. Website: http://mahbobaspromise.org

About the Author

Kay Danes has become one of Australia's leading advocates for human rights and social justice. She has worked in some of the most challenging environments across the Middle-east, Africa and Asia as a researcher and humanitarian. Her contributions to bridging impoverished communities are recognised by Australian and Foreign officials. Her humanitarian aid work in Afghanistan was an integral part of a national debate on Australia's commitment in Afghanistan. In 2014, Kay was awarded the prestigious Medal of the Order of Australia for her social justice and human rights work world-wide. The honour of the award is the principal and most prestigious means of recognizing outstanding *citizens* in Australia. Her Majesty Elizabeth II, Queen of the United Kingdom, established the OAM.

Kay is completing a Masters degree in Human Rights (2015) through Curtin University and uses her profile and academic qualifications to advance awareness of human rights and social justice. Kay moved to the Kingdom of Saudi Arabia for three years, accompanying her husband on a diplomatic posting. Her proximity to the middle-east enabled Kay to continue her humanitarian service in supporting the creation of educational opportunities for displaced children devastated by war. Kay has achieved a great deal through persistence and unwavering commitment to improve the lives of others and has only been limited by the limitations of her personal funds. Even so, Kay continues to support a number of campaigns that improve literacy among children devastated by war and at home, indigenous women and children living in poverty. Kay also supports a number of Australian defence welfare organisations that directly sustain the welfare of Australian Defence members and their families.

Kay is a highly sought after speaker on the International circuit, having addressed several US Congressional forums on Democracy, the US National Press Club and the Conference on World Affairs. She was the key note speaker to the Australian Women and Leadership Symposium (2014), Australia's most prestigious women's leadership event, drawing together Australian women from aspiring leaders to the highest office holders. She has also provided consultation to the Joint Standing Committee on Treaties and the Secretary to the UN Special Rapporteur on Torture. As a former political prisoner and torture survivor, Kay uses her insights to raise awareness for the victims of extra-judicial abduction, forced disappearance and torture. Her campaigning over decades resulted in her being appointed (9 July 2014) as an Envoy Extraordinary to Australia of the Association of Envoys Extraordinary of the Royal Lao Government in Exile Worldwide. (http://www.aeerlge.org)

In 2013, Kay was named a finalist for the Pride of Australia Medal, recognising extraordinary and inspiring Australians. In 2012, Kay was named by the Australia Day Council as a finalist in the Australian of the Year Awards for outstanding service to community. In 2011, Kay was inducted by Rotary International as a Rotary Paul Harris Fellow for providing tangible and significant assistance for the furtherance of better understanding and friendly relations among people's of the world. Kay is also the bestselling author of these highly acclaimed books: Families Behind Bars — Stories of Injustice, Endurance and Hope' (2008 & second edition 2011), Standing Ground — an Imprisoned Couple's Struggle for Justice Against a Communist Regime (2009).

Contact

http://www.kaydanes.com

https://www.linkedin.com/in/kaydanes1

https://www.facebook.com/kay.danes

PO Box 391, Capalaba Qld 4157 Australia

Email: kay.danes@gmail.com

f